Caribbean for Lovers

Caribbean
for Lovers

Paris Permenter and John Bigley

PRIMA PUBLISHING

PRIMA PUBLISHING and colophon are registered trademarks of Prima Communications, Inc.

Library of Congress Cataloging-in-Publication Data

Permenter, Paris.
    Caribbean for lovers / Paris Permenter and John Bigley.
       p.   cm.
    Includes index.
    ISBN 0-7615-0627-6
    1. West Indies—Guidebooks.   2. Caribbean Area—Guidebooks.
  I. Bigley, John. II. Title.
  F1609.P47 1996
  917.2904'52—dc20   96-33171
                                                 CIP

96 97 98 99 00 01 HH 10 9 8 7 6 5 4 3 2 1
Printed in the United States of America

How to Order
Single copies may be ordered from Prima Publishing, P.O. Box 1260BK, Rocklin, CA 95677; telephone (916) 632-4400. Quantity discounts are also available. On your letterhead, include information concerning the intended use of the books and the number of books you wish to purchase.

Visit us online at http://www.primapublishing.com

To the people of the Caribbean,
for sharing their slice of paradise

$\mathcal{C}$ontents

APPENDICES

Introduction

Picture the two of you on a tropical isle. Palm trees sway in the gentle breeze. Beyond a garden of blossoming bougainvillea and hibiscus, a fringe of powdery sand gives way to a sea as clear as white rum. Your time is spent together—Adam and Eve in tropical splendor. Days roll into nights as you are lulled to sleep by the song of whistling tree frogs or the rhythmic roll of waves.

If this is your idea of paradise, as it is ours, then you are ready for the Caribbean. Whether you are headed to the tropics for a honeymoon, to get married, or just to enjoy a romantic retreat, this guide is written for you. We'll take you to special places where lovers feel not just welcomed but worshipped. Places where you can get away from the crowds on deserted beaches and in secluded inns, or be part of the action in flashy casinos and red-hot nightspots. Destinations where you can spend your days scuba diving, exploring historic ruins, shopping for duty-free goods from around the world, or hanging out in a hammock built for two. We'll show you places where the two of you can be a couple, away from everyday worries and distractions, with no excuse not to concentrate on romance.

Whether you are seeking a fiesta, siesta, or something in between, it's available in the Caribbean. A wide array of vacation experiences await you in the islands. Take your pick. Luxurious resorts where you can enjoy spa treatments during the day and casino gambling at night, or small inns where you are two of only a handful of guests. Fine gourmet meals enjoyed by candlelight or side-of-the-road discoveries that serve island specialties. Large islands that promise a peek at more history and culture around the next bend or small islands where you will start seeing familiar faces within a few days. Add to this diversity a jigsaw of cultures, ranging from French to Dutch to English, and you have a lifetime of vacation opportunities to celebrate events from your honeymoon to your 50th anniversary.

That smorgasbord of islands makes a guide like this one a necessity. Selecting an island, then narrowing down your choice of resorts and activities, is the first step in planning your romantic getaway. Once the choices are made, we'll help you decide what to pack, how to get there, how to fit in, and how to get around. And we'll look at how to have fun, whether that means viewing marine life from 100 feet below the surface in a high-tech submarine or cruising down a Jamaica river on a bamboo raft for two. To bring back memories of your vacation, we'll direct you to the best shops for island specialties and duty-free treasures.

For those with marriage in mind, we'll tell you what it takes to make your walk down the aisle a walk down the isle. Residency requirements, fees, and paperwork vary from island to island, and is all covered in a separate section in each chapter. We look at beautiful sites for your tropical ceremony and examine the wedding packages offered by island resorts, designed to make your special day carefree and extraordinary.

The islands and resorts in these pages represent our personal picks. No doubt, some hidden jewels are left out of this guide. We haven't included some islands popular mostly with foreign travelers, or others that require multiple transfers to reach. Unquestionably, there are stretches of sand and hedonistic hideaways we have not yet discovered. That's part of the fun for us. No Caribophile likes to think that he or she has already seen the best of the best. It's better to dream that the pinnacle of palm tree–lined beaches and the ultimate in thatched roof beach bars still lies beyond the next cove.

We offer here our favorites, places where we know you'll enjoy walking hand-in-hand and find yourself smiling for no reason at all.

Grab your partner, a bottle of sunscreen, and go on a journey to sample different cultures, taste new foods, enjoy beautiful resorts, and dance under a starry sky. Travel to places where the nightlife is as hot as the daytime sun, to resorts where the boundaries between indoors and outdoors blur, and, most of all, to a part of the world where love is more than a word.

Caribbean for Lovers

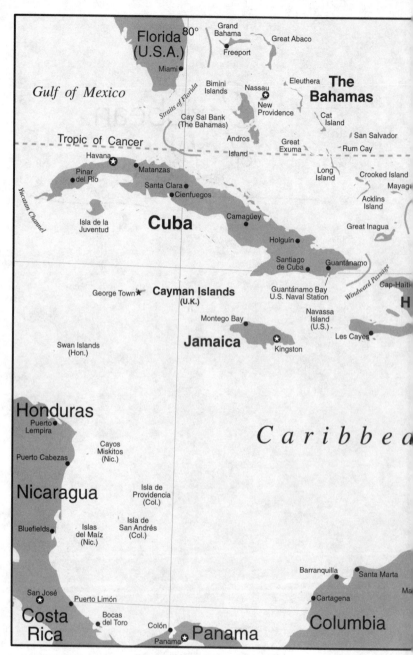

©1992 Magellan Geographix^{SM}Santa Barbara, CA (800) 929-4627

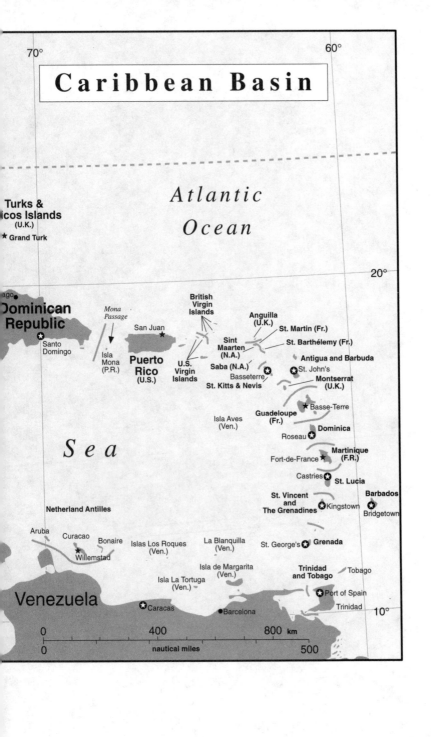

Caribbean Basin

70°   60°

Atlantic

Ocean

Turks &
icos Islands
(U.K.)
★ Grand Turk

20°

ago

Dominican
Republic
✪ Santo
  Domingo

Mona Passage

Isla
Mona
(P.R.)

San Juan
★

Puerto
Rico
(U.S.)

British
Virgin
Islands

U.S.
Virgin
Islands

Anguilla
(U.K.)   St. Martin (Fr.)

Sint
Maarten
(N.A.)   St. Barthélemy (Fr.)

Saba (N.A.)   Antigua and Barbuda
Basseterre   ✪St. John's
St. Kitts & Nevis   Montserrat
(U.K.)

Isla Aves
(Ven.)

Guadeloupe
(Fr.)   ★ Basse-Terre

Roseau ✪   Dominica

Sea

Martinique
Fort-de-France ★   (F.R.)

Castries ✪   St. Lucia

St. Vincent
and   ✪Kingstown   Barbados
The Grenadines   ✪
Bridgetown

Netherland Antilles

Aruba   Curacao   Bonaire   Islas Los Roques   La Blanquilla
(Ven.)   (Ven.)   St. George's ✪ Grenada
★
Willemstad

Isla de Margarita
(Ven.)   Trinidad
and Tobago   Tobago

Isla La Tortuga
(Ven.)

Venezuela   ✪Caracas   ●Barcelona   Port of Spain
✪
Trinidad   10°

0   400   800 km

0   nautical miles   500

PART I

Before You Leave Home

CHAPTER I

$\mathcal{T}$he Caribbean

Before examining individual differences, look at the region as a whole. The Caribbean spans an area that stretches over 2,000 miles east to west and 1,000 miles north to south, starting off the coast of Florida and arching to the coast of South America.

This part of the world is blessed with year-round sunshine, water warmed by Caribbean currents, and shores cooled by gentle trade winds. Winter and summer temperatures differ by only about five degrees.

If you look at a map of the Caribbean, you will see that the islands arch out like a cracking whip, with the largest islands to the west and the small islands to the east, curving down to South America and ending with a "snap" with the ABC islands: Aruba, Bonaire, and Curaçao back to the west.

The whole formation of islands is referred to as the Antilles, usually divided into the Greater Antilles and the Lesser Antilles. The Greater Antilles, as the name suggests, are the Caribbean's largest islands: Cuba, Hispaniola (an island shared by the Dominican Republic and Haiti), Jamaica, and Puerto Rico. The term Lesser Antilles encompasses the other islands.

Often, the area is divided up into the Eastern and Western Caribbean. The Eastern islands are the same as the Lesser Antilles; the Western Caribbean is the Greater Antilles and the Cayman Islands.

The multiple names given to this region is a hint at the diversity the Caribbean boasts. In researching and writing this book, we traveled to the Caribbean every few weeks and many friends asked us, "Are you getting bored of visiting the same area again and again?" Besides the fact that it would be pretty tough to tire of perfect weather, postcard-pretty scenes, and a sea as clear as glass, the Caribbean holds endless fascination for us, as it will hopefully for you, because it offers so many different types of experiences.

Every one of these countries is an island surrounded by the Caribbean Sea, and they differ in many ways. The political structures range from crown colonies to independent nations. Some islands span hundreds of square miles; others can be covered by bicycle in a single afternoon. Languages vary as well: English, Spanish, French, Dutch, and a beautiful mélange of languages called Papiamento greet visitors. English is spoken in just about every resort area.

Technically not part of the Caribbean, the Bahamas, beyond reach of the Caribbean borders, share its azure waters and perpetual summer.

Time Zones

The Caribbean straddles two time zones. The western islands—Jamaica and Cayman—fall in the Eastern time zone, the same as the east coast of the United States.

The eastern islands fall in the Atlantic time zone, one hour ahead of Eastern time.

To confuse matters, the Caribbean islands do not observe Daylight Savings Time. During the summer months, the western islands are the same as the Central time zone; the eastern islands the same as the Eastern time zone.

But why worry about the time? Forget the time zones and enjoy island time. When the sun is up, roll out of bed. When it sets, head off for the beach and clean up for dinner. When you are hungry, eat, and when you feel tired, go to bed.

CHAPTER 2

$\mathcal{M}$aking the Decisions

Get the hard choices out of the way first so you are free to concentrate on the more enjoyable aspects of romantic travel. This chapter will help you decide which island is best for you, based on your budget and interests.

Where to Go

Here's the toughest of your Caribbean vacation decisions: where should you go?

It is a question that only the two of you can answer, based on your personal tastes. Do you want high-rise luxury or Robinson Crusoe-type seclusion? Glitzy dinner shows or evening serenades from tiny tree frogs? Days spent shopping, snorkeling, scuba diving, or sunning on a sandy beach?

When friends ask us to help select a destination, we advise them to identify their expectations first. In our many trips to the Caribbean, we have found that sometimes we like the bustling atmosphere of busy islands like Jamaica, St. Thomas, or Puerto Rico; other times we long for the serenity of St. Kitts, Nevis, or Virgin Gorda.

To help make this decision, begin by asking yourself these questions:

• Is budget a major factor?
• Will this be a quick three- or four-day getaway, a relatively leisurely week-long vacation, or more?
• Do we enjoy casino gambling and shows?

- Are we looking for luxurious accommodations?
- Would we prefer the convenience of an all-inclusive resort?
- Do we want to rent a car and explore on our own?
- What activities are most important to us? Snorkeling? Scuba? Golf? Tennis? Windsurfing? Sailing? Hiking? Shopping?
- Are we expecting a lush, tropical environment?
- Do we want white sand beaches? Nude beaches?
- Do we want the familiarity of remaining on U.S. turf or would we rather experience a different culture?

Consider Your Options

Sit down together and study your answers. Then take a look at your options:

Budget Getaways   There is no soft way to put this: a trip to the Caribbean is not cheap. Even if you select a budget hotel, transportation to the islands is a big expense that cannot be avoided.

Some islands are less expensive to reach than others because certain destinations are high volume, bringing in commercial and charter flights on a daily basis. This may mean more crowds, but look at the positive side: your airfare will probably be lower than traveling on to more secluded islands. Some destinations offer deals that include air, hotel, and ground transportation in one affordable package. Jamaica, Puerto Rico, U.S. Virgin Islands, Bahamas, and the Dominican Republic offer such deals.

Charter airline companies serve most of these islands. For more information on low-cost carriers, see "Getting There, Getting Around."

Quick Getaways   If you are planning a three- or four-day retreat, make the most of your visit by minimizing travel time. Choose the islands that are easy jumps from the United States: Bahamas, Turks and Caicos, Cayman Islands, U.S. Virgin Islands (either St. Croix or St. Thomas), British Virgin Islands (Tortola), Puerto Rico, and Jamaica (if you stay in the Montego Bay area; Negril and Ocho Rios are nearly two hours from the airport, Port Antonio is farther.)

Casinos   The click of the roulette wheel and the ring of slot machines are being heard on more and more Caribbean islands. The top gaming destinations are Puerto Rico, Aruba, Nassau, and Dutch Sint

Maarten. More limited gaming is also found in the Turks and Caicos, the Dominican Republic, Curaçao, St. Kitts, Bonaire, and Antigua.

Mega Resorts   Twenty-four-hour room service, full treatment spas, and satellite television are not commonplace throughout the Caribbean. However, the two of you can be pampered at full service properties in Puerto Rico, Aruba, the Bahamas, Jamaica, and St. Lucia in hotels that offer more than the comforts of home.

Bed & Breakfasts   B & B aficionados should look to St. Kitts and Nevis for the greatest concentration of plantation inns. For more on small inns, see "Where to Stay."

All-Inclusive Hotels   In the early days of Caribbean tourism, travelers from the United States were usually well-to-do. Today's all-inclusives make all their guests feel wealthy by offering all-you-can-do opportunities at high-volume prices. Jamaica is the king of the all-inclusive but you will also find these resorts in Aruba, Barbados, St. Lucia, Antigua, the Bahamas, and the Turks and Caicos. For more on all-inclusives, see "Where to Stay."

Scuba and Snorkeling   The clearest water for these activities is generally found around those islands without rivers or steep hills to create runoff. Add underwater features such as coral reefs and walls or submerged shipwrecks and you have a diver's paradise. Among the best dive destinations in the Caribbean are the Turks and Caicos, the Cayman Islands, Tobago, and Bonaire.

Golf   Golf courses are popping up like hibiscus blossoms throughout the region. The top choices are Puerto Rico and Jamaica; each offers championship courses designed to keep even the most dedicated golfer happy. You will also find courses on St. Croix, St. Thomas, Nevis, St. Kitts, Aruba, Tobago, and Barbados.

Tennis   Resorts with top tennis facilities are available in Puerto Rico, Jamaica, Antigua, and St. Croix.

Windsurfing   Aruba is the top windsurfing destination in the Caribbean due to ever-present trade winds. Puerto Rico offers windsurfing (taught by a former member of the U.S. Olympic Team) and so do the British Virgin Islands, home of an annual international tournament.

Sailing   The Caribbean Sea around the British Virgin Islands is a sailor's paradise. Opportunities abound for voyages of all durations, and beginners are reassured by the fact that one is seldom far from land. The Moorings and other services catering to the sailor are numerous here. Other top sailing destinations are Antigua, St. Lucia, and St. Martin/Sint Maarten.

Shopping   Those who are ready to shop 'til they drop should head to the U.S. Virgin Islands for the Caribbean's highest duty-free allowance. Shoppers in St. Thomas, St. Croix, and St. John can bring back more goodies (twice as much as some Caribbean islands) without paying duty.

Other shopper's delights are Nassau (Bahamas), St. Martin/Sint Maarten, and Grand Cayman.

White Sand Beaches   Believe it or not, all beach sand is not created equal. Variations in texture and color (ranging literally from black to white) can effect your vacation. The sand on most Caribbean beaches is made from crushed coral and is somewhat coarse. On windy days it tends to stay put more than will finer, siltier sands so it stays out of your camera and your picnic lunch. Underwater visibility is affected by sand color: the lighter colors reflect more light. If your vision of paradise includes chalky-white beaches, head to the Turks and Caicos, Bahamas, St. Thomas, St. John, or Antigua.

Nude Beaches   Clothing-optional beaches tend to be of two types. There are the resort beaches where nudity is encouraged (and, in a couple of cases, even dictated) on a separate, specified area of the shore. These locations tend to be safe, somewhat crowded, and close to amenities such as food, drink, and rest rooms. Look to the French islands and to Jamaica (especially Negril) for resorts featuring nude beaches. The other type of nude beach can be found on many islands where access to undeveloped, isolated beaches means that nudity is more-or-less tolerated. This may seem more romantic, but bear in mind that these beaches may not always be safe. On some islands such as St. Lucia nudity is illegal.

Tropical Lushness   It is rather surprising that within the Caribbean, landscapes can range from desert to jungle. Some islands include both desert and rain forest climates. If your Caribbean adventure must be back-dropped by tropical splendor, head to Jamaica or St. Lucia for lush scenery punctuated by brilliant hibiscus and bougainvillea and every imaginable tropical fruit and vegetable.

Cultural Atmosphere   All islands boast a rollicking Caribbean spirit but their separate cultures borrow heavily from their founding fathers. Visitors who would rather remain in the United States and skip the hassles of passports, immigration cards, and currency exchange can choose Puerto Rico or the U.S. Virgin Islands: St. Thomas, St. John, and St. Croix.

Dutch architecture creates picturesque waterfront communities in Aruba, Bonaire, Curaçao, and Sint Maarten. A rich Spanish heritage pervades the islands of the Dominican Republic and Puerto Rico. The British Virgin Islands, Montserrat, the Cayman Islands, and the Turks and Caicos still operate as British dependencies. In the former British colonies that include the Bahamas, Antigua and Barbuda, Barbados, St. Kitts and Nevis, Trinidad and Tobago, and Jamaica, British influence is still strong. Driving is on the left side of the road and the royal family is seen smiling on postage stamps.

How Long to Stay

Package vacations usually come in three-, four-, and seven-night lengths, with the option of adding additional nights if you like. If you are setting up your own vacation, then the sky (or your budget) is the limit. All but the smallest islands have daily air service, so you can usually schedule arrival and departure whenever you like.

We have found that three-night trips are a little too short, even for a quick getaway. Three nights sounds like it should also include four days, but be realistic. Your arrival day will be lost; departing from Texas, we arrive in the Caribbean no earlier than mid-afternoon and sometimes much later than that. If you are arriving from the West Coast, expect a full travel day. You will probably miss dinner and the evening shows so just be ready to roll into bed after you check in.

The departure day is also lost. With a two-hour international check-in, you are likely to be off to the airport just after breakfast.

On a three-night, four-day package, expect two full days of vacation: the days between your arrival and your departure. We've done it but it's not relaxing. If you have never been to the island before, it can also be very frustrating. If you must consider a three-night package, re-read the "Quick Getaway" section for the easiest destinations to reach from the United States.

If your budget is a major factor or if you need to be back home with the kids, we suggest a four-night trip. You will have more time to start to feel at home and in the island groove and state of mind.

On a week-long trip you will start to feel really relaxed and you will have time for exploring around the island on day trips.

Two-week trips are the epitome of luxury, usually enjoyed more by Europeans than Americans who generally have shorter vacations than their trans-Atlantic neighbors. If you are lucky enough to afford the time and money for a long getaway, think about island hopping. See "Getting There, Getting Around" for tips on inter-island flights.

ꞨRAVEL TIP

If you are arriving very late, consider spending the first night at an inexpensive hotel close to the airport. An inexpensive business hotel without the amenities of a resort will look fine if you are coming in just in time to hit the sack anyway. The next morning, take a taxi to your resort hotel. You will be there early and have all day to enjoy the resort and get your money's worth. If you arrive early enough, you may have to store luggage until your room is ready but most resorts have changing facilities so you can go ahead and hit the beach.

When to Go

The time of year you visit the Caribbean may have more to do with your budget than with the weather. Prices can vary as much as 40 percent between high and low season.

High season generally extends from December 15 through April 15. During this time, prices are at peak and rooms can be difficult to reserve (especially during the holiday season). Prices soar during Christmas week. After the holidays, package prices (although sometimes not room rates) drop during January. They rise again by February and remain high until mid-April.

Low season covers the summer and early fall months, for two reasons. First, these are the warmest months in the Northeast, the area of the country that most often flees to the sunny Caribbean during the chilly winter months, so demand is down. Second, this is hurricane season.

Mention the Caribbean and weather in the same sentence, and one concern quickly arises: hurricanes. These deadly storms are officially a threat from June through November, and the greatest danger is during the later months, August through October. (September is the worst.)

Keep in mind that the Caribbean is a large region. We have been in the Western Caribbean when storms were picking up force in the eastern reaches and never felt a gust of wind or saw a wave over ankle high.

To minimize the chances of a hurricane ruining or postponing your trip, plan a vacation outside the hurricane season or outside the hurricane zone. In the far southern reaches, the islands of Aruba, Bonaire, and Curaçao (also known as the ABC islands), and Trinidad and Tobago are below the hurricane zone and should be safer bets during the summer and fall months.

Except for the hurricane season, weather in the Caribbean is a wonderfully monotonous topic. (In Papiamento, the language of the Dutch islands, there is no word for weather. It's almost always perfect, so why waste a word?)

In the summer, days peak at about 95, with lows in the 70s. In the winter, temperatures run about 5 to 10 degrees cooler. The sea remains warm enough for comfortable swimming year-round. (The Bahamas are technically not part of the Caribbean, and you will find temperatures there are slightly cooler.)

If budget is not your prime consideration, then when's the best time to go to the Caribbean? Anytime!

$\mathcal{W}$here to Stay

Whatever you are looking for in the way of accommodations—high-rise hotel, seaside bungalow, bed & breakfast inn, small traditional hotel, or private villa—you will find it in the Caribbean.

Just as varied as the type of accommodations is the range of prices for these properties. Everything from budget motels with Spartan furnishings to private islands that attract royalty and Hollywood types is available.

This guidebook covers things in between, places where the everyday vacationing couple can enjoy safety and comfort in surroundings where romance can flourish. The resorts, hotels, and villas featured on these pages cover all levels of activity. Some offer around-the-clock fun and evening theme parties for their guests; others point the way for guests to find their own entertainment. Some are located on the beach; others up the mountains with grandiose views. Some are full-service properties with everything from beauty salons to jewelry shops to a half dozen bars and restaurants located on the property; others are simple accommodations where the guests enjoy dinner in former greathouses built over 200 years ago.

Choosing a Caribbean accommodation is even more important than selecting a hotel at other destinations. You will find that a Caribbean hotel, unlike a hotel stay in a downtown American city, for example, becomes your home away from home. This is not just where you spend your nights, but also a good portion of your days, languishing on its beach, lying beneath towering palms, and luxuriating in a warm sea.

What form will your paradise take? White sandy beaches? Rugged limestone cliffs that fall into baby blue water? Mountainside vistas?

A resort with daily activities and a pulsating nightlife? A historic inn furnished with Caribbean antiques? Or a quiet getaway where the only footprints are your own?

The choice is yours.

All-Inclusive Resorts

As the name suggests, all-inclusive means that all activities, meals, drinks, transfers, and tips are included in the price.

This all-inclusive policy means that you are free to try anything you like without worrying about spending your vacation budget for the next five years. Ever been curious about windsurfing? Take a lesson. Want to know how to reggae dance? Throw off your shoes and jump in line. Wonder how those brightly colored drinks with the funny umbrellas taste? Belly up to the bar. You are free to try it all.

Some folks don't like all-inclusive because of the concern (not unfounded) that once you have paid for the whole package you are less likely to leave the property to sample local restaurants and explore the island.

The all-inclusive confinement is up to the individual couple. Perhaps your goal for this trip is to languish away the mornings in bed (this is, after all, a guide for lovers), roll out to the beach, grab a rum punch in one hand and your partner's hand in the other, and sit there until the sun slowly sinks into the sea. An all-inclusive is just right for you. You won't have to worry about taxis or rental cars or reservations.

Or maybe the two of you want to try it all: scuba diving, sailing, windsurfing, golf, or tennis. An all-inclusive is just the ticket for you as well. The one-price-pays-all policy will be a better deal than paying for individual lessons.

Who else should check out an all-inclusive? Those who are:

- On a tight budget: You know how much to put aside for the entire vacation before you ever buy your ticket. Once you arrive, feel free to live like a king and never have to count how much money is left or how high the tally is going on your credit card. All-inclusives, like other hotels, come in a varied price range.
- Traveling with the kids: You can still have a romantic trip thanks to all-inclusive resorts with children's programs. The kids have fun

doing age-appropriate activities, making new friends, and learning about a new culture, while the two of you enjoy a romantic respite.
- Receiving the trip as a gift: All-inclusive resort vacations are increasingly popular as wedding gifts. They permit parents to pay for the trip up front and for honeymooners to enjoy themselves without feeling like they are running up a huge tab for parents or in-laws.
- Getting married on your honeymoon: Several all-inclusives offer free weddings; all offer various wedding packages. You will find experienced wedding planners at these resorts who can simplify paperwork and make your wedding a special, hassle-free day.

We love all-inclusive resorts, but we are careful to balance a stay there with island tours or visits to off-property restaurants. Even with these extra expenditures, we have found most of these resorts to be economical choices.

Some all-inclusive chains in the Caribbean that are especially popular with couples are Sandals, SuperClubs, and Jack Tar.

The Sandals resorts are for couples only. On islands with more than one location (St. Lucia and Jamaica), vacationers can hop from resort to resort and enjoy facilities and dining privileges at each.

SuperClubs originated in Jamaica and offers a variety of properties for varying interests and varying price ranges. On the lower end, the Breezes properties (one in Nassau, Bahamas, and two in Jamaica) offer all-inclusive luxury at affordable rates. For couples traveling with children, Boscobel Beach offers supervised fun so the two of you can enjoy some private time. Fun seekers will find plenty of action at Hedonism II, and luxury lovers can be pampered at either Grand Lido or Sans Souci Lido. SuperClubs also offers the best lovers' bargain in the Caribbean: free weddings.

Jack Tar properties, with locations in St. Kitts, Dominican Republic, and Jamaica, offer budget all-inclusive fun. Some of the bells and whistles of other properties are missing, but the price helps make up for any loss. These properties are included in many package offerings with one price for air and land.

The *Club Med* chain also offers several locations in the Caribbean, however, we were warned by company personnel that many of these properties cater to singles. Also, the Club Med chain offers less of an all-inclusive package than others in this book; drinks are served in exchange for Club Med beads which are purchased by guests.

Bed & Breakfasts and Small Inns

If you are looking for peace and quiet, B & Bs and small inns offer good getaways and a chance to immerse yourself in more of the local atmosphere.

These small inns, many built around historic greathouses on former plantations, are intimate properties that only host a handful of guests at a time. Here the two of you will be part of a small group of guests, and you will get to know each other as you would aboard a small cruise. Often the owners of the inn reside right on property, so you will receive personal attention.

Our favorite inns make us feel like guests of the family returning for another stay. We enjoy chatting with other guests, usually experienced travelers, and with the owners, who give us insights into island life. Over the years, we have shared dinner conversations with hoteliers about hurricanes, gardening, local specialties, local sports, and island life in general. It gives a perspective on these destinations that we wou' never have gained at a larger property.

Just as you would if booking a B & B in the United States, ask plenty of questions before booking a stay in a small inn. These properties may offer limited services and may be restrictive. If applicable, be sure to ask:

> Is smoking permitted indoors?
> Are children allowed as guests?
> Is breakfast served at one time or as guests wander in?
> Are intimate tables available or are meals served family style?
> Are special dietary considerations met?
> Is there a minimum stay?
> Does a remote location necessitate a rental car?

Villas

For some couples, the idea of real romance is a private villa, without other guests. Just the two of you—alone, except for the occasional visit by a cook or maid who is there to meet your special requests, to introduce you to island cuisine, and to make you feel pampered in what really is your home away from home. St. John, St. Thomas, Jamaica, and Barbados are especially popular islands for villa rentals.

Villas vary in price, services, and level of luxury. Before you make a commitment, check:

- Maid service: Many villas offer maid service before your arrival and after your departure; additional cleaning can be arranged for a surcharge. At other properties, you may have daily maid service. Check with your villa management company.
- Groceries: Can you send a deposit for groceries and have a cook stock up before your arrival? Finding a refrigerator and cabinets ready with your favorites can be a big boost after a long flight.
- Cook service: Many villas can arrange for cook service as you choose: three meals a day, dinner only, or just one special meal. In Jamaica, villas typically include cook service. Check your options.
- Air conditioning: Do not assume your villa is air conditioned; ever-present trade winds make this an optional feature. If it is more of a necessity than an option to you, inquire.
- Car rental: Many villas are located away from the resort areas. See if you should rent a car to avoid pricey taxi rides for long hauls.
- Minimum stay: Unlike hotel minimums of three nights, villas often require a minimum seven-night rental.

Many resorts also offer villa rentals. These homes are located on the resort property and guests enjoy the security and services of the resort while at the same time having the space and facilities of a villa home. Some resorts that include villa homes are the BVI's Peter Island, Four Seasons Nevis, Antigua's Jumby Bay, and Bitter End Yacht Club in the British Virgin Islands.

ℋONEYMOONS AND ANNIVERSARIES

A tip for those celebrating a wedding or anniversary: let your hotel know when you make the reservation that you will be celebrating a special occasion. Most have honeymoon/anniversary packages that you can purchase for extra amenities such as breakfast in bed or champagne on arrival, and many hotels like to recognize honeymooners and couples on an anniversary. Some hotels offer a special gift or even a room upgrade if available.

Remember, you want to have a good time, and the hotel also wants to make this an extra-special trip for the two of you. What better way to bring back return guests than to help create an idyllic honeymoon?

CHAPTER 4

What to Pack

When we first began to travel in the Caribbean, we envisioned an elegant destination where visitors wore the most stylish sportswear and fine evening wear. It was an image created by stories of Caribbean travel earlier this century, when wealthy travelers made the long journey with steamer trunks and remained in the islands for weeks at a time. Today's jet travel has shortened the length of stay—and diminished the necessary amount of luggage.

We quickly learned that in the Caribbean, the key wardrobe words are comfort and cool, not necessarily chic. Even if you will be staying at the most posh resort and dining in the toniest restaurants, comfort comes first. A few restaurants require jackets for men (especially during high season), and those are identified throughout this guidebook. Neckties are seen as rarely as conquistadors' armor.

We keep a permanent packing list for our Caribbean trips. For a four-night trip, we bring:

His	Hers
1 pair casual slacks	1 pair casual slacks (for the plane)
1 pair nice slacks or khakis	1 casual skirt, 1 dress
2 T-shirts	1 T-shirt
2 polo or short-sleeve shirts	2 short-sleeve/sleeveless blouses
2 pairs shorts	2 pairs shorts
2 swimsuits	2 swimsuits
	1 swimsuit cover-up
1 pair walking shoes	1 pair walking sandals
1 pair sandals or tennis shoes	1 pair evening sandals

We carry all necessary accessories (which on some islands can be expensive or difficult to buy):

film and camera, extra camera battery
sunscreen (usually two bottles of different strengths)
snorkel gear (certified divers must bring a "C" card)
aqua shoes
insect repellent
all prescriptions (in prescription bottles)
2 pairs sunglasses each
paperback book or two
antiseptic for bug bites
aloe vera lotion for sunburn
first aid kit with aspirin, stomach medicine, bandages, and so on
passports
airline tickets
mini-address book for postcard writing

This may seem sparse, but we always carry-on our luggage if possible (sometimes we have had to surrender bags on small propeller planes). Toting bags may seem like more trouble, but it minimizes the chance of lost luggage. When we debark from the plane, we are first in line for customs and immigration, so we breeze through and add a little precious time to our island vacation.

CHAPTER 5

$\mathscr{O}$Island Weddings

More and more couples are choosing to tie the knot in the sunny Caribbean. Recognizing this trend, islands are relaxing their marriage requirements. You will find that island weddings are increasingly easy to arrange, with shorter (or no) residency periods, simplified paperwork, and usually no required blood tests. Many resorts offer wedding packages and have full-time staff members to simplify paperwork.

Island weddings have caught on for several reasons. After talking with various tourist bureaus in the islands, we have learned they are especially popular with:

- couples on a budget who don't want the expense of an elaborate wedding
- couples who don't want the fuss of a wedding and all that goes with it at home
- couples on their second marriage looking for something a little different
- those on their second marriage who will be bringing along children. The children's programs at many resorts offers the couple privacy with a chance to enjoy a vacation with their new family
- couples who are bringing a small wedding party. Often the bride and groom stay at one resort and the wedding party at a neighboring resort, giving everyone privacy. This works especially well with resorts such as Sandals, whose guests can dine at any of the Sandals resorts, or resorts like Puerto Rico's neighboring Hyatt Cerromar and Hyatt Dorado or Barbados' Almond Beach Village and Almond Beach Club, where guests enjoy reciprocal privileges at two resorts.

• couples who are bringing a sizable wedding party and would like to take over a resort. Many small inns (under 30 rooms) offer groups the option of taking over an entire resort, usually with a minimum stay of one week. This type of stay must be arranged far in advance and is usually done in low season. The wedding party has run of the resort for their stay, with plenty of room to party and play. (Why don't we ever get invited to this kind of wedding?)

This book describes each island's specific restrictions, such as residency periods, paperwork, and fees. Each has a minimum period for filing papers, and remember that—as with income taxes—it's better to file early. The islands observe holidays that are not celebrated in the United States, and court offices close during those days. Give yourself plenty of leeway for getting papers to the courts. Send documents by courier rather than mail service. Mail delivery on many islands is painfully slow.

Getting married on the honeymoon can relieve the stress and expense often associated with this special day. More and more couples are finding that it is an opportunity to enjoy this occasion in just the way they want it. Island weddings also engender other joyous celebrations: island anniversaries. Couples who wed in the Caribbean are finding how much fun it is to revisit the very spot where they married and share the memory of that occasion.

The simplest way to plan an island wedding is to work through your resort's wedding coordinator. This staff member counsels guests before their stay to bring all necessary papers. After arrival, the coordinator helps couples complete paperwork, explains where to go if the country requires an in-person visit to obtain a marriage license, arranges for a minister or other officiating party, and helps with wedding extras such as photography and music.

Once you decide on a resort, call the local number and ask to speak with the wedding coordinator for information on how the resort assists in the process. Also, inquire about special wedding packages to make your special day that much more extraordinary.

Typically, most countries require you to send documents and complete paperwork before your stay. If this is the case, *do not* send documents by surface mail. Mail service throughout most of the Caribbean is extremely slow (we once arrived back home a month before our postcard). Rely on fax transmissions and courier services such as Federal Express for delivery of papers.

Two resort chains are especially popular with marrying couples. SuperClubs and Sandals have each planned and performed many thousands of weddings.

SUPERCLUBS (800-859-SUPER)

What a deal. This chain, with locations in Jamaica and the Bahamas, offers couples free weddings and vow renewals. As part of their all-inclusive offerings, SuperClubs offers ceremonies that include marriage license, minister, witnesses, tropical flower bouquet and boutonniere, champagne, and a wedding cake. Individual properties in the chain offer additional free services such as a facial for the bride at Grand Lido, a sunset horse and buggy ride at Breezes Runaway Bay at Jamaica-Jamaica, and live music at Sans Souci Lido.

Additional packages are available for a fee including video and still photography.

SANDALS (800-SANDALS)

This chain has resorts in Antigua, Jamaica, Bahamas, and St. Lucia. Sandals offers wedding packages for their guests. The "Wedding Moon" package includes preparation of documents, legal fees, minister or other officiating party, witnesses, wedding announcement cards, champagne reception with three bottles of bubbly, bouquet and boutonniere, Caribbean two-tier wedding cake, video of your ceremony, a 5×7 photo, candlelight dinner for two, "Just Married" T-shirts, continental breakfast in bed the morning after the wedding, and taped musical accompaniment.

Wedding packages are priced at US $750.

Other services are available for an additional fee, including massages, photo packages, rehearsal dinner, calypso band, classical violinist or harpist, and a guest fee so visitors who are not registered at Sandals can attend the ceremony.

OTHER RESORT PACKAGES

In Jamaica, check out the complimentary weddings at Swept Away, one of Negril's most beautiful properties; Couples, a luxurious Ocho Rios getaway; and Jamaica's Friends Hotels: Negril Gardens, SeaCastles, Plantation Inn, and Point Village. These packages include everything you need to make your wedding pure pleasure.

PART 2

Getting There, Getting Around

$\mathcal{C}$aribbean Flights

Once the two of you have decided where you want to go, here is your second hurdle: getting there. You have several options because most islands are served by several air carriers.

Just as you did with resorts, shop around for an airline. Start early, be patient, and do some research. Check with several carriers, even those that are not the primary airlines in your region. Chances are, unless you are starting from an East Coast hub, that you will be making connections along the way, so sometimes it pays to do some creative routing—even if you pay for it in travel time.

Travel to Caribbean destinations is easier than ever, with ample airlift to even the smallest islands. Most connections from major mainland American cities are made through either Miami or San Juan, Puerto Rico's Luis Muñoz Marin Airport, the American Airlines hub for Caribbean flights. From San Juan, American Eagle serves many neighboring islands.

The following carriers offer flights to at least one Caribbean destination. The flight schedule varies by season (the most flights, and for some airlines the only flights, are offered during peak season from mid-December to mid-April).

- Air Aruba (800) 88-ARUBA
- Air Canada (800) 776-3000
- Air Jamaica (800) 523-5585
- ALM (800) 327-7230
- American Airlines (800) 433-7300
- Bahamasair (800) 222-4262
- BWIA (800) 538-2942

- Carnival (800) 824-7386
- Cayman Airways (800) 422-9626
- Continental (800) 231-0856
- Delta (800) 221-1212
- Guyana Airways (800) 242-4210
- Kiwi (800) 538-5494
- Northwest (800) 447-4747
- Prestige Airways (800) 299-8784
- TWA (800) 892-4141
- United (800) 538-2929
- USAir (800) 428-4322

Air/Land Packages

Several airlines offer package deals that provide a complete vacation: room, transfers, air, and, if you choose all-inclusives, meals, drinks, and tips. Is this cheaper than putting a package together on your own? Usually. Check it out for yourself by calling hotel reservation numbers, asking for their room rate, and adding it to the cost of an airline ticket. You will usually see a substantial savings since the airlines are buying rooms in bulk and have more purchasing power than an ordinary consumer.

Some travelers worry about the term *package*, imagining a trip where they are herded on a tour bus with a plane full of tourists. Have no fear. Some packages include the services of a greeter at the airport who will welcome you and show you the way to the transfer bus to your hotel, but beyond that you are on your own. If you want to rent a car and explore, go for it.

Packages are also offered by charter airlines, carriers who offer service at lower cost, usually with few frills. (Often only one class of service is available, seat assignments are given only at check-in, and carry-on allowances may be only one bag per passenger due to an increased number of seats on board.) Some charter companies offering Caribbean service include Adventure Tours, FunJet, Apple Vacations, GoGo, and others. See your travel agent for information on charters available from your area.

If you don't want the package vacation, some charters sell "air-only"—the airline tickets alone.

Frequent Flyer Programs

When you purchase your airline ticket, sign up for the frequent flyer program. Also, check to see if your resort is part of the frequent flyer program. Sandals offers American Airlines frequent flyer miles for every night's stay.

Today you can earn mileage in many ways other than flying. Long distance companies, credit card companies, dining programs, and others offer miles, sometimes as many as five for every dollar spent.

What's in it for you? With enough miles, you will soon be earning a frequent flyer pass for a free ticket. What better way to head back to the Caribbean!

Between Islands

Want to island-hop? It's fun and, if you are visiting small islands, a necessary part of a Caribbean vacation.

Two carriers offer special passes designed for island hopping. LIAT (268-462-0700) and BWIA (800-538-2942) each offers a special pass that permits you to hop from island to island—with certain restrictions. We took LIAT's Explorer's Pass, a US $199 bargain, and made three island stops within a 21-day limit. The catch is that you must make all your travel in one direction, except for the return flight back to the island from which you started. These passes must be purchased and ticketed (a very important detail) within the continental United States. They cannot be purchased in the Caribbean.

When traveling on small carriers, be prepared to carry on only one small bag. You will be able to check in other luggage at the ticket counter or right at the airplane door as you board (our choice, so we can be sure the bags board the same plane as we do).

Service may be limited on some flights. A few times we have flown on prop planes when the only staff members were the pilot and co-pilot, seated just a few seats ahead of us. The flights are generally short, and show a bird's eye view of the islands that can't be beat.

Check-in requirements are unwavering with the small carriers. Some flights have been known to leave early, so make sure that you check in well ahead of schedule. Call the night before and reconfirm your seats, then arrive at the airport at the stated check-in time.

Travel Agents

Travel agents offer a free service, making hotel and air reservations and issuing airline tickets. They can shop around for the lowest rate for you and often know about sales not known to the general public.

They cannot, however, read your mind. We have seen couples go to a travel agent and say, "We'd like to go somewhere warm." That—as you will see in this book alone—covers a lot of territory!

Every vacation is a once-in-a-lifetime opportunity. The two of you may return to the islands, but no other trip will be exactly like this one. Each is unique and offers wonderful opportunities to explore the world together.

Part of the fun of travel is the anticipation. Go over this book together. Go by the travel agent's office and pick up brochures. Rent travel videos. Talk about your options.

When you have your minds made up—or at least narrowed down—contact a travel agent. If it's a large office, ask for the agent who specializes in the Caribbean.

Entry Requirements

Specifics vary from country to country but plan to bring along either a current passport or a certified birth certificate (or voter registration card on some islands), and a photo ID. Passports are the easiest form of entry (plus you gain the neat immigration stamps as a free souvenir).

To obtain a passport, call your post office and ask which post office in your area handles passports. When you turn in the completed form, you will need to hand over a certified copy of your birth certificate (one with the raised seal) and passport photos, which can be taken at the post office for an extra fee or at one of the quick-copy stores in your city. The birth certificate, photos, and form are sent to the passport office for your district and will be mailed back to you, a period that can range from one to two months, depending on the time of year (spring is especially busy because of upcoming summer travel).

If you are headed to the Caribbean on your honeymoon (or if you will be getting married while in the tropics), do not have your airline tickets issued under your new name. Your tickets must match the name on the passport that you will be using for entry. If you are presenting your certified birth certificate and you have changed your name since birth, bring along a copy of your marriage license.

Currency

You will find that US currency is accepted on many Caribbean islands, and you will often receive change back in the local currency.

We recommend using a credit card for everything but tips and street purchases. Besides avoiding the hassle of currency conversion (and back again when you leave), you usually receive the best possible exchange rate on a credit card. The credit card company shops for the best exchange rate for you—saving you some extra pennies and time along the way.

Customs Requirements

When you leave the United States then return home, you will pass through U.S. Customs at your point of entry. (A few islands have Customs Pre-Clearance so you can go through the declaration before returning home, usually a faster process.)

You will complete a customs declaration form, one per household, identifying the total amount of your expenditures while out of the country. Each person has an exemption of either $400, $600 or $1,200 (depending on the island you visited). Families can pool their exemptions so a family of four can bring back $1,600, $2,400, or $4,800 worth of merchandise without paying duty.

Some items cannot be brought back to the United States. These include:

- books or cassettes made without authorized copyright ("pirated" copies)
- any type of drug paraphernalia
- firearms
- fruits and vegetables
- meats and their by-products (such as paté)
- plants, cuttings
- tortoise shell jewelry or other turtle products (sold in the Cayman Islands, among others)

CUSTOMS TIPS

Here are some tips to make passage through Customs a little easier:

- Keep your sales slips.
- Pack so your purchases can be reached easily.
- Get a copy of the "Know Before You Go" brochure (Publication 512) from the U.S. Customs Service at your airport or by writing the U.S. Customs Service, P.O. Box 7407, Washington, DC 20044.

CHAPTER 7

Feeling Good and Fitting In

The Caribbean is the land of "no problem" and, for the most part, it's just that. Travel here is easy and carefree, and residents are generally as warm as the weather.

You are, however, entering a different culture, one with its own traditions and expectations. And, as with travel to any part of the world these days, there are precautions to take to ensure that yours is a safe and healthy vacation.

Dress

The citizens of the West Indies are modest, conservative people who generally frown upon displays of skin. Although nudity or topless bathing is permitted on some beaches, it is typically not practiced by locals. Most islanders follow a more conservative style of dress than is seen in United States beach communities, perhaps echoing back to the European influences felt on many isles.

Bathing suits are appropriate only for swimming; off the beach grab a cover-up. Bare chests are frowned upon outside the beach. Leisure wear—T-shirts, shorts, sundresses, and sandals—are readily accepted in any Caribbean community.

Good Morning

Throughout the West Indies, it is customary to greet folks before blurting out a question or request. A polite "good morning" or "good afternoon" will help you fit in and get your interaction off to a good start.

Patois

English is the primary language of most Caribbean islands, but you will quickly find that you may not understand everything, especially if locals are talking to one another. English is spoken with a distinct Caribbean lilt, a delightful sing-song rhythm. Each island has its own patois, local words that are often a mixture of African languages dating back to the island's slave days. Jamaica's patois is perhaps the most distinctive and also most difficult to understand. (Some travel writers claim that after a few days you will understand the patois. Forget it.) Here are a few Jamaican patois terms:

Me diyah	I'm here
Nyam	eat
Irie	great, wonderful. If someone asks you how your vacation is going, just say "irie" (pronounced *eye-ree*).
Rass	This all-purpose word can mean a person's posterior, or it can be a term of endearment, surprise, or even a negative description of someone's character. Use this one with care.

Taxis

Modes of transportation vary from island to island, but for the most part taxis are the best means of travel. Even the smallest islands like tiny Salt Cay in the Turks and Caicos have taxi service, and you will find that they are generally operated by professionals who are happy to talk about their island. We have had some of our most interesting conversations about island life with taxi drivers, who are well informed about history and tourist attractions. Often drivers will present their business card at the end of the journey in case you have further need for transportation.

Crime

Crime in the Caribbean, as in any other part of the world, presents a potential problem, albeit an infrequent one. Along with their everyday cares, unfortunately some vacationers also leave behind everyday precautions. On vacation, use the same common sense you would exhibit at home, especially at night. Don't bring expensive jewelry;

locally produced shell necklaces can give you an island look without tempting thieves. Use safes and safety deposit boxes provided by hotels. Also, don't leave valuables on the beach while you are in the water—one of the most common scenarios for theft.

Drugs

Depending on the island (Jamaica is the most notable example), your age, and your style of dress, you may be offered illegal drugs from a smooth-talking local salesman. These ingenious entrepreneurs offer their goods both on and off land. We have had more than one swim interrupted by salesmen in canoes, boats, and, once, on horseback in the shallow water. A polite "no, thank you" usually ends the transaction without further problems.

Marijuana, or *ganja* as it is known locally, is illegal throughout the Caribbean. Drug penalties are becoming stiffer, and drug prevention measures more stringent in many countries.

We caution vacationers not to carry any packages that they have not personally packed. We have been approached by locals asking us to mail packages for them once we arrive in the United States. The requests may be legitimate, but the risk is too great.

Food and Drink

Stomach problems from food and water are at a minimum in the Caribbean. Most stomach distress is caused not by the food itself, but by larger-than-usual amounts of food (combined, for many vacationers, with large amounts of rum).

Water is potable on nearly every island, and some resorts offer bottled water because the tap water produced by desalinization is slightly unusual to the taste. In the Dominican Republic, we recommend drinking bottled water. Most islands offer excellent water supplies (and some, like St. Kitts, are so above average that cooks swear it accounts in part for their delicious cuisine).

Sunburn

Nothing will destroy romance on a vacation any faster than a sunburn, your biggest danger in the Caribbean. You will be surprised, even if you

don't burn easily or if you already have a good base tan, how easily
the sun will sneak up on you. At this southern latitude, good sunscreen,
applied liberally and often, is a must. (And for those of you frequenting
nude beaches, let's just say you need to be extra generous with the sunscreen for the sake of your romance.)

Insects

Oh those pesky bugs! While the number of mosquitoes are generally
fewer than in the American South (the omnipresent sea breeze keeps
them at bay), the worst insects in the Caribbean are sand fleas. Popu-
larly known as no-see-'ums, these pesky critters raise itchy welts where
they bite, usually along the ankles. Use an insect repellent if you
will be on the beach near sunset, the worst time of the day for these
unwelcome beach bums.

Manchineel Trees

Manchineel (*Hippomane mancinella*) trees present an unusual danger.
These plants, members of the Spurge plant family, have highly acidic
leaves and fruit. During a rain, water dropping off the leaves can leave
painful burns on your skin and the tree's tiny apples will also burn when
stepped on. In most resorts, manchineel trees have been removed or
are clearly marked, often with signs and with trunks painted red.

Marine Dangers

For the two of us, a trip to the Caribbean isn't complete without snorkeling in the warm waters that circle every island.

Some inhabitants of these waters look scary, but most pose little
danger. Exceptions are scorpionfish (a mottled pinkish fish that hangs
out on coral and is so ugly it actually looks dangerous), sea urchins
(painful if you step on their brittle spines), jellyfish (which cause painful
stings with their tentacles), and stingrays (which are dangerous if
stepped on; can be avoided by dragging your feet when wading). Fire
coral, of which there are many varieties but all edged in white, will burn
you to defend itself if you brush against it.

The best precaution is to follow your mother's advice: Look but
don't touch.

PART 3

The Islands

$\mathcal{U}$sing This Guide

Hotel prices vary drastically between high and low season and also by view. Garden view rooms are generally the least expensive, followed by ocean view then ocean front. Suites are the priciest accommodations, with rates that can be more than double that of a standard room.

Rather than specific prices, which come and go as quickly as a hibiscus blossom, here are price ranges for Caribbean accommodations. These rates reflect high winter season (expect prices to be as much as 40 percent lower during the off season), for a standard room for two adults for one night; prices are in U.S. dollars.

$\mathcal{R}$ATINGS FOR ACCOMMODATIONS

$	under $150
$$	$151 to $300
$$$	$301 to $450
$$$$	over $450

Restaurant prices are for dinner per person, including an appetizer or salad, entree, and drink.

$\mathcal{R}$ATINGS FOR RESTAURANTS

$	under $15
$$	$16 to $30
$$$	$31 to $45
$$$$	over $45

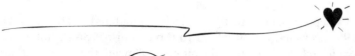

$\mathcal{A}$ntigua

Language	English
Currency	Eastern Caribbean (EC) dollar (fixed at US $1 = EC $2.70); U.S. dollar accepted
Population	66,000
Driving	left
Best romantic feature	beaches, sailing

Antigua (*an-TEE-ga*) doesn't have the quaint shopping zones of islands like St. Thomas or St. Croix. It lacks the friendly attitude of destinations such as St. Kitts or Curaçao. Nor will you find the lush tropical beauty of islands such as Jamaica or St. Lucia.

What Antigua has are beaches: 365 of them, the tourism folks claim. Stretches of white sand that border turquoise waters teeming with marine life. Beaches where the two of you can walk hand-in-hand and hardly see another soul. Beaches where you can shop for local crafts and buy a burger at a beachside grill. And beaches where you can curl up under a tall coconut palm and sit until the sun sinks into the sea and marks the end of another Caribbean day.

We have to be honest about Antigua: we noticed a distinct attitude problem here. Tourists are not welcomed with warm smiles and friendly service just everywhere, so be prepared for a more aloof attitude than you will enjoy on most islands. We are not saying that we found impersonal service everywhere—we had an impromptu island tour from a friendly taxi driver who didn't mind spending a few extra minutes proudly pointing out highlights along the way. We did encounter less than friendly attitudes in towns, restaurants, and resorts.

On a positive note, Antigua, which was battered by Hurricane Luis in 1995, is well on its way back to top condition. Some hotels were closed for refurbishments in the months following the storm, but most properties are up and running at full speed these days, sporting fresh facades and few indications that the island ever suffered such a terrible storm.

A Little History

Pre-Colonial Antigua was originally inhabited by the Siboney Indians. In 1493 Christopher Columbus named the island in honor of Santa Maria de La Antigua of Seville, a saint at whose namesake church Columbus had prayed before his journey to the Americas.

Antigua has had close ties to England, ever since an English patrol from St. Kitts landed on the island in 1632 and claimed it for the mother country. Since 1981, the twin island nation of Antigua and Barbuda has held the status of an independent country.

Compass Points

This 108-square-mile limestone and coral island is somewhat scrubby with rolling hills, especially on the southern reaches. The capital city is St. John's, home of most of the tourist shopping and the cruise port.

The south shore of the island is favored by "yachties," who call into Nelson's Dockyard at English Harbour.

Just the Facts

Getting There

Air travelers will arrive at V.C. Bird International Airport, located near the capital city of St. John's. Served by American Airlines, Continental, and BWIA from the United States, as well as Air Canada and BWIA from Canada, the airport is a bustling hub for airlines such as LIAT for many inter-island flights.

Antigua is a popular destination for cruise ships. The terminal is located in downtown St. John's and is within walking distance of the main shopping areas.

Departure tax is US $12 per person.

Getting Around

Taxi travel is the most common means of transportation, especially for couples not comfortable with driving on the left side of the road. Taxi fares from the St. John's area to Nelson's Dockyard on the far side of the island run about US $50 round trip.

Rental cars are available; a temporary Antiguan driver's license is required. The license can be obtained at the V.C. Bird International Airport or at any Antiguan police station. We found that some roads are a little bumpy, and that a full tank of gas (as well as a spare tire) was recommended for visitors who would be traveling out on the island away from the major destinations.

Entry Requirements

U.S. and Canadian visitors must show a passport or a birth certificate and photo ID as well as an onward or return ticket.

For More Information

Contact the Antigua and Barbuda Department of Tourism, 610 Fifth Avenue, Suite 311, New York, NY 10020 or call (212) 541-4117. In Canada, contact the Antigua and Barbuda Department of Tourism and Trade, 60 St. Clair Avenue East, Suite 304, Toronto, Ontario MT4 1N5 or call (416) 961-3085.

For the Marriage-Minded

Antigua is one of the simplest Caribbean islands on which to tie the knot. There is no waiting time, so you could fly in and get married that same afternoon.

On weekdays, bring your paperwork (proof of citizenship and, if applicable, a certified divorce decree or death certificate of previous spouse) to the Ministry of Justice in St. John's, sign a declaration before the Marriage Coordinator, and pay the US $150 license fee. The Coordinator makes arrangements for a Marriage Officer to perform the civil ceremony. The Marriage Officer is paid US $50.

Romantic Resorts

The Admiral's Inn, (268) 460-1027; fax (268) 460-1534. $

- restaurant
- transportation to beaches

Located right in Nelson's Dockyard, this 17th century building now offers 14 guest rooms (each with twin beds). Each is decorated with antiques, wrought-iron chandeliers, and hand-hewn beams; some rooms feature air conditioning. The inn hosts the awards ceremonies for April's Sailing Week, so book very early during that peak time.

Curtain Bluff Hotel, (800) 672-5833, (268) 462-8400; fax (268) 462-8409. $$$$

- beachfront
- casual and fine dining
- watersports, dive shop
- tennis
- golf, squash, croquet

This exclusive hotel, home of one of the Caribbean's best wine cellars, is located on a private peninsula with two beaches. The all-inclusive property includes all meals, drinks, afternoon tea, watersports, tennis, golf, and even mail service so you can send those postcards home.

Hawksbill Resort, (800) 223-6510, (268) 462-0301; fax (268) 462-1515. $$$

- beachfront
- fine and casual dining
- watersports
- freshwater pool
- nude beach

Located a few minutes from St. John's, this resort is our favorite kind: quiet, restful, and located on, not one, but four superb beaches. With a primarily British contingency, the resort is somewhat reserved but just a few minutes from the action of St. John's. Nudists can wander over to the fourth beach to seek the total tan at the only nude beach in Antigua.

Jumby Bay, (800) 421-9016, (268) 462-6000;
fax (268) 462-6020. $$$$

- beachfront
- all-inclusive
- casual and fine dining
- pools
- children's program in summer months
- watersports
- tennis

One of the Caribbean's most exclusive resorts, Jumby Bay is located, not just on a private beach, but on a 300-acre private island. This luxurious retreat has 38 guest rooms and 12 two- and three-bedroom villas, some with private plunge pools. Guests enjoy all-inclusive everything: gourmet meals, fine wines, sports, airport transfers, and even postage. One warning: this all-inclusive luxury comes at a price. If you have to ask how much, perhaps you had better look elsewhere.

Sandals Antigua, (800) SANDALS, (268) 462-0267;
fax (268) 462-4135. $$

- beachfront
- all-inclusive
- couples only
- watersports
- fine and casual dining
- freshwater pools, hot tubs
- tennis

Like other couples-only resorts in this popular chain, Sandals Antigua offers an array of activities that can keep even the most restless vacationer happy. Activity coordinators, or Playmakers, keep things going for those who want to stay busy. For couples preferring inactivity, two-person hammocks and "love baskets," swinging wicker baskets, offer quiet afternoons beneath shady palapas.

Unlike other Sandals, about half of the clientele at this resort is European. Most visitors are young couples, and, especially during the spring and summer months, many are honeymooners or couples getting married on their honeymoon. During our late-May visit, we counted three weddings on one afternoon alone.

We liked this Sandals for its low-slung buildings spread along a wide swath of white beach. We stayed in a rondoval room, an octagon-shaped cabin with a tall conical ceiling, louvered windows, and a true Caribbean atmosphere.

At this resort, guests in the upper category rooms enjoy Suite Concierge Service for booking restaurant reservations or assistance with island tours, a fully-stocked, complimentary in-room bar, daily *New York Times* by fax, and terry robes.

Like other properties in this chain, the resort has many restaurants from which to choose: an open-air main dining room that offers international fare in the evenings served a la carte, an Italian restaurant (with an excellent sunset view—get there early for a beachside table), and a Japanese restaurant where active chefs will prepare your meal right at the table amid a flurry of flying knives and implements.

Shopping

The primary shopping area on the island is in St. John's, near the cruise ship terminal. This area does not have the charm of many Caribbean shopping districts, and is somewhat littered, smelly, and dirty. Still, it's worth a two- or three-hour excursion to have a look at the goods offered in the small boutiques.

Along the waterfront you will find the most tourist-oriented shopping, with duty-free wares such as fine jewelry, perfumes, and liquor. Look for Gucci, Colombian Emeralds, Little Switzerland, and other fine shops at Heritage Quay. Besides these pricey gift items, you will also find a good selection of tropical prints and batik fabric sportswear (made on the island). Caribelle Batik has an excellent selection of shirts, skirts, and shorts in tropical colors.

Nearby, Redcliffe Quay is a more scenic place to shop and have a drink or some lunch. You won't see the duty-free shops of Heritage Quay here, but you will find plenty of cool shade, brick courtyards, and restored buildings where you can shop for Caribbean items or enjoy a cold beer in a charming atmosphere.

If you want to get away from the tourist center, take a walk up to Market Street for shops aimed at the local residents, including many fabric stores offering beautiful tropical prints.

Outside of St. John's, head to Harmony Hall in Brown's Bay Mill. This art gallery originated in Jamaica and features work by many

Caribbean artists. Original works as well as prints and posters are for sale, accompanied by crafts, books, and seasonings that capture the spice of the island.

Dining

At the resort restaurants, you will find familiar dishes on the menu as well as a few island specialties such as christophine, a type of squash; pepperpot, a spicy stew; *afungi,* a pudding of cornmeal and okra; and *ducana,* a pudding made from grated sweet potato and coconut, sugar, and spices, and boiled in a banana leaf. Save a little room to finish off your meal with a taste of the sweet Antigua black pineapple. The most popular beer on the island is Wadadli, made locally.

Admiral's Inn, Nelson's Dockyard. $–$$

This inn is also home to a very popular eatery with outdoor dining near the yachts that come to this dockyard from around the Caribbean. Along with great people-watching, the restaurant also offers breakfast, lunch, and dinner. Save time before dinner for a stop by the lounge area filled with yacht club flags.

Hemingways Veranda Bar and Restaurant, St. John's. $$

Located near Heritage Quay, this informal, second-story restaurant is located in a West Indian-styled building constructed in the early 1800s. Start with a Hemingways fruit punch or pineapple daiquiri then move on to an entree of Caribbean seafood or steak.

Redcliffe Tavern, Redcliffe Quay, St. John's. $–$$

Just steps from the shopping district of St. John's, this restaurant is housed in a former red brick warehouse that dates back to the 19th century. Enjoy quiche, sirloin steak, smoked salmon, or seafood in a casual atmosphere.

Vienna Inn, Hodges Bay. $–$$

Austrian food in Antigua? Why not? When you are ready for a break from island fare, stop by this eatery for Swiss schnitzel, veal filled with ham and cheese and topped with egg, Wiener schnitzel, or veal schnitzel.

Festivals

The hottest event of the year is Antigua Sailing Week, held in April. During this time, Antigua hotel rooms can be hard to come by (in fact, many hotels continue their high season beyond the weeks designated as such by other islands just to include this busy week). On this week, Nelson's Dockyard at English Harbour comes to life with the color and pageantry of the largest regatta in the Caribbean. Parties, barbecues, races, Lord Nelson's Ball, and more highlight this annual event, now in its third decade.

Other special events include the Culinary Exposition in May and Independence Day on November 1st. Carnival is the hottest summer activity, with musical entertainment, parades, and Antiguan cuisine.

Romantic Activities

Antigua's most romantic activity is a trip to its splendid beaches. Some of the most popular spots are Dickenson Bay, where you will find beach bars and watersports action, Hawksbill beaches on Five Island peninsula, home of a clothing-optional beach, and Runaway Beach, lively with watersports activities.

If it's beach seclusion you're after, consider a day to Antigua's sister island, **Barbuda**. Day trips to this uncommercialized island, popular with bird watchers because of its population of frigate birds, are available from several operators. Barbuda lies about 30 miles north of Antigua.

Nature lovers will find plenty of activity on Antigua. **Scuba diving** and **snorkeling** is a popular activity. Certified divers can enjoy a variety of dives, from walls to wrecks.

Antigua is rich in historic attractions. The most visited is **Nelson's Dockyard National Park**. Built in 1784, this dockyard was the headquarters for Admiral Horatio Nelson. Today you can retrace the history of this site at the Dow's Hill Interpretation Centre or at the complex's two museums: Admiral's House and Clarence House, former home of Prince William Henry, later known as King William IV.

Another historic site is **Betty's Hope Estate**, the island's first sugar plantation.

Nightlife

Casino gambling is a popular nightlife activity, with several casinos from which to choose. The most popular is the King's Casino in St. John's.

OUR IMPRESSIONS OF ANTIGUA

- excellent beaches
- wonderful destinations for sailing
- less friendly atmosphere than on other Caribbean islands

ROMANCE ON ANTIGUA

- stroll Nelson's Dockyard and see yachts from around the Americas
- see how many of those 365 beaches you can sink your toes into
- feed each other cool chunks of Antigua pineapple

$\mathscr{A}$ruba

Language	Dutch and Papiamento, English widely spoken
Currency	Aruban florin (US $1 = A.Fl 1.78 approx.); rate fluctuates; US $ accepted
Population	71,000
Driving	right
Best romantic features	duty-free shopping, casinos, beaches

Aruba has its own special beauty. Don't look for mountains covered with tall palms. Or walkways lined with flowering bougainvillea. Or roads shaded by willowy casuarina trees.

Instead, you will have to search a little deeper for the beauty of Aruba. You will have to venture to the rugged Atlantic shore and watch the tumultuous waves carving the natural bridge, continually changing the demarcation line where the land meets the sea. Or you can hike to some of Aruba's highest hills, curious bumps on the landscape, and look out at the *cunucu* or countryside for traditional Dutch-style houses with their sun-baked orange tile roofs.

But perhaps the best way to see the beauty of Aruba is to look into the faces of the Aruban people, the island's greatest asset. This tiny island, a mere 70 square miles, truly is a melting pot of cultures. Over 43 nationalities are represented here, and with them a mélange of languages. Arubans learn from an early age the benefits and necessity of working with other nations and learning different languages is a skill that most young Arubans master. The language of the Aruban home is Papiamento, a mixture of Spanish, Portuguese, French, Dutch, Indian, English, and even some African dialects. When youngsters head to school, they receive instruction in Dutch, because of Aruba's continuing ties to the Kingdom of Holland. Once they reach third or fourth grade, instruction in English begins. Spanish is introduced during the junior high years, and in high school students select from French or German.

That familiarity with many languages translates into a welcoming atmosphere for visitors of any nationality. There is no hostility to tourists on this island; no language barrier to overcome. There is just a spirit of "Bon Bini" or "Welcome" which greets visitors from the moment they arrive in the airport and continues throughout their visit.

Papiamento is the language of the streets. To the ear, it resembles Spanish. Here are some common Papiamento phrases:

bon dia	good day
dushi	sweetheart, wonderful
sushi	trash
sunchi	kiss
kubi bon	how are you
my stim abo	I love you

A Little History

Aruba was discovered by the Spaniards a little later than most of the Caribbean islands, and to say that they were not impressed would be an understatement. After claiming the island in 1499, the explorers labeled it and neighboring Bonaire and Curaçao as "isla inutil" or "useless island." One resource the Spaniards did exploit were the resident Arawak Indians, who were sent to work the gold mines of Santo Domingo.

A decade later, some of those native peoples were returned to Aruba to work the cattle ranches the Spanish established here. Things continued at that pace until the Dutch took possession of the desert isle in 1636. The Dutch West India Company prohibited settlement in those early years, but by the late 1700s immigrants began arriving from Europe.

Through the years, Aruba has revealed various treasures to its residents and fortune seekers. Gold was discovered in 1824, and today the remains of those early mines can be spotted. Aloe became the next moneymaker, topped by petroleum refining in the 1920s. The oil industry flourished until the refinery activity greatly diminished in the mid 1980s.

The next year, Aruba experienced another major change—independence. The island seceded from the Netherlands Antilles, a group of islands that includes Bonaire, Curaçao, Sint Maarten, Saba, and Saint Eustatius, and became a separate entity in the Kingdom of the Netherlands. Today, Aruba has its own currency and postal system, and is led by a governor appointed by the Queen.

Compass Points

Located 12½ degrees from the equator, Aruba's climate is drier than that found on most Caribbean islands. Less than 24 inches of rain fall normally, resulting in a desert landscape of tall cacti, aloe, and wind-blown divi-divi or watapana trees, bent permanently at a 45 degree angle by the ever-present trade winds.

That rugged countryside is known as the *cunucu,* and it spans the length of the 20 by 6 mile island. The island is dotted by communities, especially San Nicholas, and the capital, Oranjestad (literally "orange city"). Here Dutch-style buildings punctuate the landscape with cool pastel hues, red roofs baked a pumpkin color by the sun. Today's streets are bathed in restful tones of ochre, pink, baby blue, and sea green—everything but white. Supposedly an early leader of Aruba, plagued by migraine headaches, ordered that all buildings be painted a more soothing shade to stop the glare.

Just the Facts

Getting There

Aruba is a 2½-hour flight from Miami or four hours from New York. Service into Queen Beatrix International Airport is available from American (from New York, Miami, and San Juan) and Aeropostal (from Orlando and Atlanta). Air Aruba, (800) 677-7888, is the national carrier, and offers non-stop flights from Newark, Miami, and Houston. Nonstop service from Houston is also available twice weekly aboard Viasa, (800) GO-VIASA.

Departure tax is US $12.50.

Entry Requirements

American citizens need to present a current passport or either an official birth certificate or voter registration card and a photo ID.

Getting Around

Taxis are available in resort areas or you can have one dispatched by calling 22116 or 21604 on island. Rates are fixed (no meters), so check with your driver before the ride.

Rental cars are widely available. The minimum age for driving a rental car is 21.

For More Information

Call the Aruba Tourism Authority at (800) TO-ARUBA.

For the Marriage-Minded

Aruba makes a great honeymoon destination, but for a marriage ceremony, look elsewhere. Civil ceremonies are not legal unless one member of the couple is either a Dutch citizen or was born on Aruba.

However, many couples, after a civil ceremony in the States, come to the island to exchange vows in a beautiful tropical setting. The hotels can arrange a ceremony for couples, without the hassle of paperwork.

Romantic Resorts

Oranjestad

Aruba Sonesta Resort and Casino, (800) SONESTA, (011) 297-8-36000; fax (011) 297-8-34389. $$

- downtown
- casual and fine dining
- casino
- shopping mall
- private island
- children's program

- watersports
- freshwater pool

After a day of connecting flights, we arrived in Aruba late, very late. But in Aruba, and especially at the Aruba Sonesta Resort and Casino, the lateness of the hour was no problem.

Aruba and this fun-loving hotel come alive in the late night hours, a time to enjoy life with a roll of the dice, a walk through the open-air lobby in a glittery dress, or a stroll down the waterfront to enjoy the sound of live bands, the smell of fresh Italian food, and the gentle lap of waves. Crime is as rare here as anywhere in the world, and the atmosphere is perfect for a couple in love.

The hotel is ideal for lovers, who will find comfortable rooms with views of the waterfront, an array of restaurants (including L'Escale, one of our romantic favorites), and a shopping center that features everything from the latest European fashions to Blue Delft china.

But the Sonesta Resort's most romantic feature is Sonesta Island, located less than ten minutes away by private launch. This is not just any boat ride. Venturing up into the hotel via a canal that slices into the shopping mall, guests are transported to a private world where they can primp and parade on a crowded adult (often topless) beach, play volleyball on the family beach, dine at the open-air restaurant, or, for the ultimate in togetherness, enjoy a day alone on a private honeymoon beach, served by a waiter.

Aruba Sonesta Suites and Casino, (800) SONESTA, (011) 297-8-36000; fax (011) 297-8-34389. $$$

- beachfront
- casual and fine dining
- shopping mall
- watersports
- children's program
- freshwater pool

Ah, what a delightful dilemma: to choose the Sonesta Suites or the Resort? The choice is up to individual taste. The Sonesta Suites is located just a block from the Resort, but it is a beachfront (albeit a small beach) property. This hotel includes suites with all the comforts of home: a full-furnished kitchen, dining area, and bedroom. As you might expect, it's a popular property for those traveling with children.

The free-form swimming pool is the focal point for the property, which includes a slightly less elegant casino than its nearby cousin.

If you are traveling with the children, the Sonesta Suites (like its sister property, Sonesta Resorts) offers the "Just Us Kids" program with daily, year-round activities for children ages 5 through 12.

Palm Beach and Eagle Beach

Americana Aruba Beach Resort and Casino, (800) 447-7462, (011) 297-8-23500; fax (011) 297-8-23191. $$$

- beachfront
- casino
- casual and fine dining
- tennis
- watersports
- freshwater pool
- children's program

The swimming pool is the centerpiece of this 419-room resort. The pool has its own current, so you can float along the stream or swim against it to work off that Aruban food and drink. The pool also features "Spa Island," which has two whirlpools and a rock waterfall.

Enjoy romantic time together while the kids have fun at the Americana Aruba Adventure Club for ages 4 to 13. Activities range from arts and crafts to merengue dance lessons and pool olympics.

This hotel offers either a European (no meals) or all-inclusive plan.

Aruba Marriott Resort and Stellaris Casino, (800) 223-6388, (011) 297-8- 69000; fax (011) 297-8-60649. $$$

- beachfront
- casual and fine dining
- freshwater pool
- casino
- watersports, diving
- tennis

This 413-room hotel is one of the newest on Palm Beach, a flashy property with a free-form pool, oversized guest rooms, and just about any activity a couple could want. A special honeymoon package includes welcome gift and champagne, breakfast-for-two on your private balcony, a candlelight dinner along with a tableside serenade at the resort's Northern Italian restaurant, and more.

Hyatt Regency Aruba Resort and Casino, (800) 233-1234, (011) 297-8-31234; fax (011) 297-8-21682. $$$

- beachfront
- casual and fine dining
- freshwater pool
- casino
- tennis
- watersports
- children's program

One of Aruba's most luxurious properties, the 365-room Hyatt is located on the northern end of Palm Beach. Like other Hyatts, this property is for anyone looking for a body holiday: be pampered in the health and fitness facility, slice across the clear Caribbean on a sailboat at the watersports facility, or luxuriate in the warmth of the sun at the three-level pool complex.

La Cabana All-Suite Beach Resort and Casino, (800) 835-7193, (011) 297-8-37208; fax (011) 297-8-77208. $$

- across from beach
- freshwater pool
- watersports
- racquetball, squash
- casino
- casual and fine dining
- children's program

Located across the street from Eagle Beach, this orange sherbet–tinted property has plenty of action, including a huge casino, one of the island's top showrooms (see "Nightlife"), a host of restaurants, and more. With 803 suites, the property is large but bountiful services keep things moving smoothly. All guest rooms are suites—from studios for couples to three-bedroom suites for families, and all include a fully equipped kitchenette.

Radisson Aruba Caribbean Resort and Casino, (800) 333-3333, (011) 297-8-66555; fax (011) 297-8-63260. $$

- beachfront
- watersports, diving
- freshwater pool
- shopping arcade
- fine and casual dining
- casino

This 372-room hotel has plenty to keep couples busy on the beach with water skiing, wave runners, catamarans, scuba instruction; the list goes on and on. The hotel offers a romantic adventure package with welcome drinks, souvenir T-shirts, champagne, breakfast in bed, candlelight dinner, and more.

Dining

As you would expect on an island that is home to 40 nationalities, Aruba offers cuisine from around the globe. Chinese, Indonesian, French, Japanese, Argentinean, Italian, Russian, Spanish, Mediterranean, Dutch, and American food are found around the island. Fast food outlets are plentiful, especially along the Oranjestad waterfront. (Don't laugh—they can offer an interesting slice of Aruban life. We popped into McDonald's for an inexpensive breakfast one morning, and, as in a small town diner, eavesdropped on conversations over the Papiamento newspaper.)

But don't miss the Aruban dishes. Fried fish with *funchi* (cornmeal), stewed lamb with *pan bati* (pancake), and *keshi yena* (a hollowed wheel of Edam cheese filled with meat and baked to combine flavors) are popular local dishes.

Charlie's Bar, San Nicholas. $$

Located about a 15-minute ride from downtown Oranjestad in San Nicholas lies Aruba's best-known and loved bar. Charlie's is an institution known to generations of Caribbean travelers looking for a watering hole. Many of those visitors have left memorabilia—from yacht flags to pieces of clothing—on every available surface in the structure. After a drink, settle in for a meal of garlic shrimp.

L'Escale Restaurant, Aruba Sonesta Resort and Casino. $$$–$$$$

We think this is one of the most romantic restaurants in the Caribbean, thanks not only to its beautiful decor, harbor view, attentive staff, and excellent dishes, but also to its musical entertainment. Every night, from 8 to 10 P.M., a Hungarian string quartet strolls through the eatery, taking requests from diners. We heard everything from Beatles to Brahms, all performed tableside under low romantic lighting by these outstanding musicians.

If that's not enough for lovers, the menu presents plenty of additional reasons to visit L'Escale. Baked Caribbean grouper, calypso chicken stuffed with king crab, chateaubriand, and pasta with shellfish are presented along with an extensive wine list, including many Chilean vintages. Reservations are recommended; call 36000 on island.

Le Petit Cafe, Oranjestad. $$

Located on a busy corner off Oranjestad's main street, this indoor-outdoor eatery specializes in meat prepared on hot stones. Waiters bring the sizzling dish to your table.

The Old Cunucu House Restaurant, near Palm Beach. $$$–$$$$

Housed in a restored 80-year-old Aruban homestead, this well-known restaurant features local cuisine. Entrees include specialties such as an appetizer of Aruban mezze, a fish cake, cheese pastiche, octopus and meatballs, or Aruban fish soup. Follow up with keshi yena, fresh conch, or seafood Palm Beach, a dish of lobster, fish, scallops, and squid with a cream sauce with wine and flamed with pernod. Other dishes such as Cornish hen, New York sirloin, and coconut fried shrimp are also available. Open for dinner Monday through Saturday. Reservations are recommended; call 61666.

Pavarotti, Palm Beach. $$$

Operated by the same management as the Old Cunucu House, this Italian restaurant and American grill tempts diners with an extensive menu. Choose from Italian favorites such as pasta with clams, penne pasta with vodka pink sauce with shrimp and crab, or angel hair pasta with clams, scallops, calamari, shrimp, and octopus in marinara sauce. Grilled items include lamb chops, filet mignon, and T-bone. Open for dinner only, Monday through Saturday. Reservations are recommended; call 60644 on island.

Festivals

Aruba's biggest blowout is Carnival, a colorful celebration that rocks the streets with dancing, parades, steel bands, and a general party atmosphere similar to Mardi Gras. The culmination of the festival is the Grand Parade, always scheduled for the Sunday preceding Ash Wednesday.

Other special events include National Anthem and Flag Day on March 18, when the island shows its patriotic spirit. In June, the island jams to the Aruba Jazz and Latin Music Festival.

The Bonbini Festival is your best chance to join in the party spirit of the island; it happens every Tuesday night in Oranjestad's Fort Zoutman.

Shopping

Aruba definitely ranks as a top Caribbean shopping destination. International goods—perfumes, china, crystal, jewelry, cameras, and clothing—are best buys. Unlike the practice of many islands, bargaining is not customary in Aruba.

Stores are open 8 A.M. to 6:30 P.M., Monday through Saturday, and usually close during the lunch hour. If a cruise ship is in port, you may find some shops open on Sunday.

The primary shopping district stretches along Oranjestad's waterfront. Malls as colorful as sherbet line this route, tempting shoppers with goods that range from T-shirts and Delft Blue salt and pepper shakers to European très chic designer outfits and fine jewelry.

Seaport Mall and Seaport Marketplace have the lion's share of the mall business. The Mall is located adjacent to Sonesta Resort and includes high-priced shops on its lowest level. Upstairs, boutiques offer moderately priced resort wear, jewelry, china, and more for a total of over 65 shops. At Sonesta Suites, the Seaport Marketplace is an outdoor gallery of nearly 60 shops specially targeted for vacationers.

Nearby, the Holland Aruba and Harbourtown Malls also offer a good selection of gift items.

Crafts are few, and most are imported from South America. There is a small market with crafts and picturesque displays of tropical fruit near the cruise dock. Here you can also find a true souvenir of the island: an Aruba license plate for US $4.

If you forget someone special on your list, you will also find shops at the Queen Beatrix International Airport. Fendi, Hummel, Gucci, Mont Blanc, and other top names are represented, along with many liquors.

Romantic Activities

As home to both the cruise port and the airport, your first look at Aruba will probably be the city of **Oranjestad**. This beautiful city, where nearly every building sports a fresh coat of paint and a distinct Dutch style, is home to several historic sites. **Fort Zoutman** is the city's oldest building, constructed in 1796. Today it is home to a small museum, but better known as the site of an open party (see "Festivals").

You will want to schedule at least half a day in Oranjestad for some shopping, but have a look at the rest of the island first. The biggest tour operator is DePalm Tours, with desks in every major hotel. This firm offers an excellent half-day tour aboard air-conditioned motor coaches with hotel pick-up. At the conclusion of the tour, you can return to your hotel or get off in downtown Oranjestad for an afternoon of shopping.

Island tours reveal terrain with windswept romantic beauty that couples learn to love for its contrast of ochre colors against the turquoise sea and for its rugged beauty. You will have an excellent view of the *cunucu*, or countryside, atop **Casibari Rock Formation**. It is a fairly easy climb (you may find yourself bent over and squeezing between rocks a few times), but wear good shoes for this trek.

Couples should visit the **natural bridge**; like the divi-divi tree, a symbol of Aruba. This bridge was carved by the tumultuous sea waves that continue to crash on the rocks and spray visitors. You will always find a crowd at the natural bridge, which is somewhat touristy with a bar and souvenir shop, but still worth a visit, especially if you are doing photography along the way.

Golfers are in luck; Aruba now has a championship course. **Tierra del Sol**, designed by Robert Trent Jones II, combines sand dunes, cacti, rock formations, and views of the sea. Tennis buffs can also enjoy a new facility: the $1.4 million **Aruba Racquet Club**. With eight courts, an exhibition center court, pro show, swimming pool, fitness center, and even a shopping center, the club attracts world-class events.

Guided horseback rides at **Rancho del Campo** are popular with many couples. On tours, you can ride through Aruba's only national park: **Arikok National Wildlife Park**, home of Indian rock markings, gold digging ruins, and a restored *cunucu* home. Don't forget to bring long pants for the horseback ride!

Of course, much of Aruba's allure is the sea: its **beaches** and the action in the water. On the southwest end of the island, Palm and Eagle beaches are some of the most popular because of their proximity to major hotels, but for the calmest waters head to Baby Beach. Located on the far southern tip of the island near the town of San Nicolas, it is well-known for its lake-calm waters. Swimmers should avoid the waters of the island's north shore, which are rough and often plagued by undertow.

Below the surface, divers will find numerous sites in the 40- to 60-foot depth range, including the *Antilla*, a German freighter that is the largest wreck in the Caribbean, and the wreck of the *California*, the ship that didn't respond to the distress signals of the *Titanic*.

Above the waves, Aruba offers some of the Caribbean's top **windsurfing**. Fisherman's Hut is an ideal beginner's site because of its calm, shallow waters, while experts head to Boca Grandi's rough waves. Every year, the island hosts the Aruba Hi-Winds Pro Am World Cup in June with the best competitors from the world of windsurfing.

For more romantic **sailing**, the Seaport Fantasy, a 73-foot yacht, can be rented for a sunrise brunch, lunch cruise, barbecue at sea, sunset cruise, or even a gourmet dinner. Popular for parties, the yacht accommodates groups up to 35 people, perfect if you've brought down a wedding party. For rental information, call (305) 442-2266 or fax (305) 442-2227.

Nightlife

Nightlife is a hot topic on Aruba. The island sizzles when the sun sets and really heats up in the wee hours. Casino gambling is a favorite pastime, with nearly a dozen casinos from which to choose. Crystal Casino, located downtown at the Sonesta Resort, is one of the most elegant, with Italian marble, Austrian crystal chandeliers, English carpet, and Spanish gold-leaf mirrors.

Look for Las Vegas-type revues at the Tropicana Showroom, located at La Cabana's Royal Cabana Casino. The Tropicana features headliner acts as well as a female impersonator revue. The Americana Showroom at the Americana Aruba Resort and Music Hall at the Wyndham Aruba Beach Resort also offer lavish revues.

You can kick up your heels at the Aladdin Theater at Alhambra Casino, styled like a Moorish palace. If you get tired of dancing or run out of luck at the tables, you can always enjoy some late-night shopping at the arcade.

OUR IMPRESSIONS OF ARUBA

- pulsating nightlife ranging from dance clubs to casinos
- excellent shopping for European clothing and Dutch imports
- windswept beauty
- many high-rise hotels
- friendly atmosphere
- good island for independent travelers who want to take off on their own

ROMANCE ON ARUBA

- kiss in the salt spray at the natural bridge
- try your luck in an elegant casino
- have a photo taken of the two of you in front of Dutch-style buildings

$\mathcal{B}$ahamas

Language	English
Currency	Bahamian dollar, equivalent to US dollar; US dollar accepted
Population	278,000
Driving	left
Best romantic features	duty-free shopping, casinos, nightlife, beaches

Technically, the Bahamas lie outside the boundaries of the Caribbean. Except for a few days when the islands are cooled by winter's chill, you will have a hard time telling the difference. These 700 islands, sprinkled like seashells across shallow water, share the same sun, sand, and festive atmosphere as their southern neighbors.

A trip to the Bahamas can be as quiet or as active as the two of you choose. For privacy and a real island atmosphere, select one of the Family Islands like Eleuthera, tiny Harbour Island (where motorized transportation means a golf cart), or San Salvador (site of Columbus's first landfall in the New World). For a more active vacation, Grand Bahama offers golf, casino gambling, and even the chance to swim with dolphins.

For most vacationers, a Bahama vacation includes a trip to Nassau, the capital city located on the island of New Providence. Nassau tempts travelers with glitzy shows, top duty-free shopping, and water that is as beautiful as any found in the Caribbean.

Located a half-hour flight from Miami, this island may be just a stone's (or a conch shell's) throw from the United States mainland, but

Nassau gives visitors a wonderful taste of Caribbean life. The atmosphere is a delightful combination of the British and the Caribbean.

Both locals and vacationers tend to use the word Nassau to identify the island of New Providence, but the city proper is located on the north side of the island. Nassau is a compact city filled with activity, especially along Bay Street where locals and visitors shop for duty-free items. Just blocks away, the seat of the Bahamian government operates in buildings the color of a conch shell. Downtown Nassau offers several inexpensive hotels that utilize nearby public beaches.

Prince George Dock always bustles with cruise ship passengers enjoying the city for the day. From the cruise port you will also see a tall, curving bridge which leads to Paradise Island. Nicknamed "Monaco of the Bahamas," this is the most luxurious area. It is an $8 taxi ride between Paradise Island and the city (plus a $2 bridge toll when entering Paradise Island). Once named Hog Island, this area was revitalized by the investments of Donald Trump and Merv Griffin and now by South African businessman Sol Kerzner, who recently renovated the Atlantis hotel at the cost of $1 million a day for a six-month renovation and building spree.

Tourists also flock to Cable Beach, 10 minutes west of downtown Nassau. This stretch of sand is lined with high-rise hotels and some of the island's hottest nightspots. Shuttles run between these resorts and Nassau several times daily.

Beyond these two resort areas, the island moves at a quieter pace. If you crave tranquility, head to the south shore, about a 30-minute ride from downtown. Here, beneath willowy casuarina trees, couples can enjoy privacy and beautiful beaches that give way to a shallow sea.

You may want to book your visit in spring, summer, or fall to be assured of a warm-weather vacation. Winter temperatures are usually balmy, but occasionally a cold front reaches its chilly fingers into these waters and drops temperatures to spring-like levels. On an early March visit, we dug into our luggage for sweatshirts and enjoyed the temperatures, which were perfect for island touring but chilly for comfortable swimming.

Be careful of March and April bookings for another reason: spring break. The low-cost downtown properties (and some Paradise Island and Cable Beach resorts) swell with students during breaks from school. Because of charter packages Nassau is the Caribbean for the masses and, during certain weeks, that means raucous students.

For a quiet, romantic getaway, consider an alternate month or a different destination.

Another warning: Service is often slow and requests are sometimes met with indifference in Nassau. Be prepared for a cool reception at some businesses.

A Little History

Historians still debate exactly where Columbus first made landfall, but one long-held theory is that his introduction to the New World was at the Bahamian island of San Salvador. From that day on, the Caribbean would never again be the same.

The Spanish held the islands until 1718 when the British laid claim to this area following a quarter century of upheaval. The Union Jack flew over these islands until July 10, 1973 when the Bahamas became an independent nation.

Compass Points

The islands of the Bahamas are scattered in the relatively shallow waters just east of Florida's shore. In all, over 700 islands and cays make up the Bahamas; only 20 of these landforms are populated.

The Bahamas enjoy a Caribbean climate due to the nearby Gulf Stream, a current of warm water that was discovered by Ponce de Leon while searching for the Fountain of Youth. The Gulf Stream certainly bestows a youthful feeling on those lucky enough to take a dip in the warm Bahamian waters. Look for slightly cooler temperatures during winter months, but equally wonderful water.

Just the Facts

Getting There

Most visitors arrive via Nassau International Airport. Delta, American Eagle, USAir, Bahamasair, Carnival, Comair, and Air Canada provide service to this airport. Paradise Island also has a small airport with flights from Miami, Ft. Lauderdale, and West Palm Beach aboard Paradise Island Airways.

Departure tax from the Bahamas is US $15 per person.

Cruise ship passengers arrive right in town at the Prince George Dock. Located just off Bay Street between Nassau and Paradise Island, cruise passengers find they're in the heart of the action.

Getting Around

You will find plenty of taxis throughout Nassau. Public mini-buses, called jitneys, are widely available and run during business hours. They are slower and more crowded than a taxi ride, but an inexpensive option if you are not in a hurry. Catch jitneys on Bay Street next to the Best Western British Colonial. Be sure to check the destination with the driver before you board, and have correct change (drivers do not give change).

For real luxury, limousine service is available (a novelty throughout most of the Caribbean). We recommend Lil Murphy Limousine Service, (242) 323-4555 or 325-3725.

Car rental desks are available at the airport and major hotels. Plan on plenty of traffic within Nassau, however, and don't forget that you will be driving on the left.

Entry Requirements

U.S. citizens must carry proof of citizenship (passport or certified birth certificate and photo identification). Voter registration cards are not accepted as a proof of citizenship. Visas are not required for stays shorter than eight months.

You will be issued an immigration card when entering the Bahamas. Hold onto it; you will need to present the card upon departure. When departing, you will clear U.S. Customs and Immigration in Nassau, a real time-saver.

For More Information

Call (800) 4-BAHAMAS or (800) 8-BAHAMAS.

For the Marriage-Minded

Getting married in the Bahamas is a simple task. Couples must reside on the island for three days with a signed waiver from the Registrar General. The Bahamian wedding license costs US $40. Couples must present certified birth certificates, and, if applicable, divorce papers and parental consent if under 18.

The Ministry of Tourism operates the People-to-People program, designed to bring together tourists and local residents. This program also offers "Weddings in Paradise," a complimentary service for planning weddings and vow renewals.

Contact the People-to-People program to get permission for a marriage ceremony at one of the Bahamas' most romantic wedding sites: The Cloisters. Located on Paradise Island, this 14th century cloister was brought to the tropics by William Randolph Hearst.

Romantic Resorts

Cable Beach Area

Breezes Bahamas, (800) 859-SUPER, (242) 327-6153; fax (242) 327-5155. $

- beachfront
- all-inclusive
- adults over 16 only
- tennis
- buffet dining and Italian restaurant
- watersports
- rollerblade and jogging track
- circus workshop

This may just be the all-inclusive bargain of the Caribbean. Part of the SuperClubs chain, Breezes is a moderately priced property offering only slightly less than others in the chain. Unlike the sprawling resorts of the SuperClubs chain, the Breezes properties (there are also two Breezes in Jamaica) are somewhat smaller and charge a fee for some premium activities. Breezes offers all the amenities of the Super-Clubs chain, including excellent meals (one of our tastiest meals in Nassau was a buffet lunch at this property), watersports, bars and nightclubs, and even free weddings (see "Island Weddings" in "Before You Leave Home").

The 400-room resort emphasizes fun and relaxation. No one under 16 is permitted in this resort for singles and couples only.

Breezes is decorated in bright tropical pastels, from its open-air lobby to the rooms located in the lemon yellow hotel.

Compass Point, (800) OUTPOST, (242) 327-4500;
fax (242) 327-3299. $–$$

- oceanfront (next to Love Beach)
- watersports, dive shop
- freshwater pool
- casual restaurant

You won't find many resorts that list "state-of-the-art recording studio" among their features, but here's one, thanks to owner Chris Blackwell. The creator of Island Records has a string of small, fine hotels in the Caribbean, including Jamaica and Young Island in St. Vincent and the Grenadines.

Located about 25 minutes west of Nassau, Compass Point is away from the hustle and bustle of Cable Beach on a quiet stretch of the island near the upscale Lyford Cay, where stellar residents such as Sean Connery and Mick Jagger have residences in the private no-visitors-allowed compound. (You might get lucky and spot a familiar face at Compass Point, however. There's a dock for Lyford Cay residents to cruise up to the restaurant for a night out.)

Compass Point only has 18 rooms, but you can't miss this rainbow property. Look for the festive colors of the Bahamian Junkanoo festival: vibrant tones of purple, blue, yellow and red. Each individual cottage is decorated in a style that might be described as Caribbean kitsch meets "Gilligan's Island." Guests can choose from five cabana rooms (the only air-conditioned accommodations) or the larger, more private huts and cottages (which include a downstairs open-air kitchen and picnic-table dining room). Every room is hand-crafted and faces the sea. The two of you can complete your day in rocking chairs on your private porch that looks out to the sea, then come in to sleep beneath a ceiling fan in a hand-made bed covered with a Bahamian batik spread.

Marriott Crystal Palace, (800) 222-7466, (242) 327-6200;
fax (242) 327-6459. $

- beachfront
- casino
- fine and casual dining

Cable Beach's largest hotel is tough to miss. This large property literally glows in the dark, with colored lights over each balcony, giving the hotel the look of a seaside candy cane. This is one of the liveliest nightspots in town, thanks to its super-sized casino and glitzy revue (see "Nightlife").

Radisson Cable Beach, (800) 432-0221, (242) 327-6000; fax (242) 327-6987. $

• beachfront
• casual and fine dining
• adjoining casino
• pools
• shopping arcade
• golf, tennis, watersports

Sporting a new $15 million renovation, the Radisson Cable Beach offers round-the-clock action both on and off the beach. Every room in the high-rise hotel offers an ocean view. For real luxury, splurge with one of the junior suites located at the end of each floor. We did and enjoyed sunrise from the bedroom balcony and sunset from the living room balcony.

A shopping arcade (with surprisingly good prices) connects the Radisson with the Marriott Crystal Palace Casino.

The hotel's all-inclusive program, Splash, is available for US $89 per person per day. Participants wear a wristband that allows them unlimited use of all sports, plus all meals, drinks, snacks, and tips.

Sandals Royal Bahamian, (800) SANDALS, (242) 327-6400; fax (242) 327-1894. $$

• beachfront
• all-inclusive
• couples only
• fine and casual dining
• watersports
• freshwater pool

This new Sandals offers couples a romantic, elegant atmosphere with all the options of all-inclusives. Recently, Sandals purchased this hotel, converted it to a Sandals, added a signature pool, and gave Sandals fans an excellent Bahamian property to enjoy.

South Ocean Golf and Beach Resort, (800) 241-6615, (242) 362-4391; fax (242) 362-4310. $

- beachfront
- fine and casual dining
- golf, tennis
- watersports

For real peace and quiet, this is the place to be on New Providence. Located by itself on a wide swath of beach, this property is ideal for lovers who don't want the hustle and bustle of shops and casinos (or who are content with taking the hotel van to Nassau for a day of activity).

Accommodations here include rooms in the main house and on the beach, our choice. These rooms are decorated with Caribbean furnishings and pencil post beds, and have balconies or patios that look directly out to the shallow sea.

Downtown

Best Western British Colonial, (800) 528-1234, (242) 322-3301; fax (242) 322-2286. $

- small downtown beach
- freshwater pool
- shopping arcade
- bar

This pink behemoth sits at the head of Bay Street, a reminder of Nassau's early hotel days. It is a warm reminder of our early hotel days as well, as the site of our first visit to the Caribbean.

Sadly, the British Colonial (or B.C., as the taxi drivers say) is looking a little tired these days. Still, it's a bargain hotel situated in a great location. It has a small beach of its own, and it is just steps away from the duty-free shops (and the fast food restaurants if you are watching your pennies). Skip this property during spring break, however; it's one of the most popular with student tour groups.

Paradise Island

Atlantis Resort, (800) 321-3000, (242) 363-3000;
fax (242) 363-2493. $$

- beachfront
- casual and fine dining
- casino
- shopping arcade
- pools
- golf, tennis, watersports

This new resort truly transforms Paradise Island into Fantasy Island. Along with an elegant hotel, it brings to the Bahamas a water park unequaled in the Caribbean. Here you can walk through a 100-foot-long clear tunnel, surrounded by thousands of tropical fish, sharks, manta rays, and sea turtles in the world's largest open-air aquarium. From above, a lagoon bar and several bridges look down on these denizens of the deep.

The tunnel and the 14-acre water gardens surrounding it are the kind of place couples either love or hate. Don't expect to find peace and quiet here, or even a Caribbean atmosphere. This is Vegas-goes-to-the-beach, but if you're into non-stop fun it's the place to be on Paradise Island.

Atlantis is a fantasy vacation resort with pleasures for children (of which you will see many) and adults. The massive hotel is split between the Beach Towers and the Coral Towers (slightly more elegant). The best choice for couples who may not want to don a beach cover-up and shake off all the sand before traipsing through the plush lobby are the Terrace Rooms. These bungalow rooms are housed in two-story buildings with separate entrances and roomy balconies or terraces and are our choice.

Nearly a dozen restaurants are found at the resort, ranging from steak to Chinese to Northern Italian. Our favorite is Cafe Martinique, a French restaurant located right on the water's edge (see Dining). To trim costs, a Deluxe Dining Plan offers a full American breakfast daily and a choice of dinner at seven restaurants. The Gourmet Dining Plan adds three additional restaurants to the dinner offerings.

Ocean Club, (800) 321-3000, (242) 363-3000;
fax (242) 363-3524. $$$

- beachfront
- fine and casual dining
- swimming pool
- golf, tennis
- watersports

With the same owner as nearby Atlantis, Ocean Club offers a far different atmosphere than its larger cousin. This 71-room property is designed to pamper its discriminating guests with maid service three times a day, concierge service, baths with imported marble, reproduction European antique furnishings, and the air of a fine European hotel.

The hotel is home to the Versailles gardens with many marble statues and the Cloister, a fourteenth-century French cloister originally purchased by William Randolph Hearst.

Shopping

Bay Street is the Fifth Avenue of the Bahamas, a boulevard lined with shops stocked with names like Gucci, Lalique, Cartier, and Baccarat. Inside, display cases gleam with gold, diamonds, and emeralds, and travelers look for duty-free bargains.

Perfume prices are regulated by the government, so you will find the same prices at any of the many "perfume bars" in Nassau. Everything from French to American perfumes, colognes, and aftershaves are sold in the perfume bars, as well as in many clothing stores.

For authentic Bahamian souvenirs, head down Bay Street to the frenzied, open-air Straw Market. Every imaginable straw good is sold here, and if you don't see it, the nimble-fingered women will make it for you. Expect to haggle over prices here, but overall, prices and goods vary only slightly from booth to booth. Upstairs, wood carvers chip away at logs to produce sculptures of animals, birds, and anything else you might request.

Visitors may take home up to $600 in goods duty-free. You may also mail home gifts (marked "unsolicited gift") up to $50 in value duty-free. Items manufactured in the Bahamas are not dutiable.

Travelers may also take back two liters of liquor provided that one of the liters is a Caribbean product.

Dining

Although you will find any type of food in Nassau (including plenty of fast food), give Bahamian cuisine a try. One of the most popular dishes is conch (*konk*), a shellfish served chopped, battered, and fried in conch fritters. Grouper, a large fish caught in the waters just offshore, also appears on every menu, usually served with the ever-present side dish of peas and rice. For real traditional Bahamian food, try johnny-cakes and boiled fish—for breakfast. You might have a tough time looking at fish (usually grouper) early in the morning, but sample the cornbread-like johnnycakes.

The popular beer in these islands is Kalik, pronounced *ca-LICK,* like a ringing cowbell in a Junkanoo parade. For something a little stronger, a popular drink in the Bahamas is gin and coconut water.

Throughout the Bahamas, gratuities of 15% are usually added to your food and drink bills.

Cafe Johnny Canoe, Forte Nassau Beach Hotel, West Bay Street on Cable Beach. $–$$

This is one of our favorite Bahamian restaurants both for its festive atmosphere and its excellent food and service. Don't look for anything fancy; this is a diner-style restaurant decorated with Bahamian crafts and photos of the restaurant's long history. Diners can select from seating indoors and outside, a good choice on warm evenings, when you can share a drink beneath the multicolored Christmas lights and listen to live music.

Breakfast, lunch, and dinner are served in this popular eatery. We opted for an appetizer of conch fritters followed by grouper entrees. Prime rib, Bahamian fried chicken, fried shrimp, cracked conch, and burgers round out the extensive menu. Follow it all with Bahamian guava duff with light rum sauce.

Make reservations for dinner, (242) 327-3373, or be prepared to wait with both vacationers and locals who come to enjoy the excellent Bahamian dishes.

Cafe Martinique, Atlantis Hotel, Paradise Island. $$$$

One of Nassau's most elegant (and expensive) restaurants, this French eatery was featured in the James Bond movie *Thunderball*. The restaurant, located on the water's edge, offers candlelight dining with choices that include French dishes as well as Bahamian cuisine such as sautéed grouper topped with slivered almonds. Save this one for an extra special night out—unless you hit it big in the Atlantis casino.

Jackets are required, but the front desk keeps a supply on hand in case you packed light.

Graycliff, West Hill Street. $$$$

The best-known restaurant in Nassau is undoubtedly Graycliff. Diners in this elegant eatery have included the Beatles, Sean Connery, Kirk Douglas, Tony Curtis, Paul Newman, Princess Caroline of Monaco, and just about any other celebrity to visit this island.

Located in a 250-year-old house, the restaurant boasts an expansive wine cellar as well as what it terms the best Cuban cigar collection in the world. Bring a jacket and tie for this fine restaurant. For reservations, call (242) 322-2797 or (242) 328-7985.

Margaritaville, Radisson Cable Beach. $$

This is the only Tex-Mex restaurant in the Bahamas. As long-time Texans, we felt an obligation to check it out—and we're glad we did. The offerings are good and plentiful. Start with nachos and follow up with cheese enchiladas, fajitas, or tacos.

Rock and Roll Cafe, West Bay Street. $$

We're warning you: do not come to this cafe for a quiet dinner. It can't be done. Music played at a deafening level will put an end to any attempted conversation.

This Cable Beach eatery is a good spot for lunch, though, especially for lovers of rock 'n' roll. Choose from conch, fish, and burgers, all enjoyed in rooms filled with rock and roll memorabilia a la Hard Rock Cafe.

Festivals

The biggest blowout of the year is Junkanoo. Starting at 1 A.M. the day after Christmas (Boxing Day), lavish parades on the order of

Mardi Gras fill the streets and locals clang cowbells throughout the night. A second parade takes place at 4 A.M. on New Year's Day.

Romantic Activities

The heart of Nassau is Rawson Square. Make your first stop here at the **Visitors Information Center** for brochures and maps before starting off on busy Bay Street, the shopping district. Here gold and gems are sold down the street from straw baskets and T-shirts at the **Straw Market**, one of the most popular souvenir stops. Be sure to look behind the Straw Market for a glimpse at the cruise ships that dock at **Prince George Dock**. At Rawson Square, horse-drawn surreys wait for passengers, who pay $10 (be prepared to negotiate) for a two-person, half-hour ride along picturesque Bay Street.

Landlubbers who are curious about the creatures of the deep should consider a ride on the **Atlantis Submarine**. Following an island tour, visitors board the submarine for a look at marine life 80 feet below the surface. For 50 minutes, the submarine views coral reefs, tropical fish, a Cessna aircraft wrecked for the filming of *Jaws 2,* and even the Tongue of the Ocean, a wall that drops 8,000 feet into liquid darkness. The submarine departs from the far west end of the island near Lyford Cay at a dock built for the movie *Flipper.*

You can also see colorful marine life at **Coral Island**, a white tower easily spotted just west of downtown. Twenty feet below the surface, visitors view what Coral Island calls the world's largest man-made living reef, dotted with coral and colorful fish. At Coral Island you can also view sharks, sea turtles, and stingrays in pools.

Another popular attraction is the **Ardastra Gardens and Zoo**. The only zoo in the Bahamas, Ardastra features 300 species of animals and 50 species of birds including monkeys, iguanas, and marching pink flamingos. Stop here if you have time, but we felt that this is one stop that can be cut from busy itineraries. The caged animals are depressing to view, and the personnel here are far from friendly.

A better choice for us is the nearby **Botanical Gardens**, where you can walk hand-in-hand along blooming paths that feature tropical plants and flowers.

History lovers should head over to **Fort Charlotte** for a free guided tour of the largest fort in the Bahamas. Perched high on a hill overlooking Cable Beach, this fort never saw action but today sees plenty of activity as tourists come to enjoy a bird's eye view and a look at the fort's dungeons, cannons, and exhibits.

One of the most popular activities in Nassau is a day at **Blue Lagoon Island**, (242) 363-3577. This "uninhabited" island lies about half an hour from the dock at Paradise Island and offers some beautiful beaches, hammocks beneath towering palms, and plenty of watersports activity. For additional charges, visitors can parasail, swim with stingrays, or meet dolphins (make reservations early for this choice). One option includes feeding, petting, and swimming with the friendly mammals. (The dolphin encounters can also be booked as a separate attraction without a day at Blue Lagoon Island by calling (242) 363-1653. For our money, Blue Lagoon Island is only for those looking for a party, not for peace and quiet or anything resembling privacy. If you do make this trip, bring a towel and, to save money, your own snorkel gear.

Nightlife

Two casinos tempt visitors in Nassau. On Paradise Island, Atlantis boasts a 30,000-square-foot casino. Adjacent to the casino, Le Cabaret Theatre, (242) 363-SHOW, features Las Vegas-style revues with laser effects and fanciful costumed dancers. Cocktail and dinner shows are offered nightly except Sunday. The Joker's Wild Comedy Club features comedy acts Tuesday through Saturday.

On Cable Beach, Marriott's Crystal Palace boasts the island's largest casino. A Vegas-type revue called Jubilation, (242) 327-6200, ext. 6861, can be enjoyed as a dinner show (which we recommend for good food) or a cocktail show. Showgirls, comedians, and an illusionist who materializes tigers keeps the show moving.

If you are looking for something more Bahamian, check out the Kings and Knights Club, (242) 327-5321, at Forte Nassau Beach Hotel on Cable Beach. For over 35 years, this delightful show has entertained visitors with Bahamian songs, dances, steel bands, fire eaters, limbo dancers, comedians, and even a few bawdy calypso tunes.

Bar hoppers can enjoy a look at three bars aboard Majestic Tours Bar Hop, available through hotel tour desks. Visit Green Shutters, an English pub that dates back to the 18th century and offers real pub grub; Drop Off, a Bahamian nightclub; and Billabong, an Australian pub in a package that includes three tropical drinks.

OUR IMPRESSIONS OF NASSAU

- a cosmopolitan destination that offers world-class shopping
- plenty of attractions

ROMANCE IN NASSAU

- take a surrey ride for two in Rawson Square
- shop for international treasures along Bay Street

$\mathscr{B}$arbados

Language	English
Currency	Barbadian dollar (fixed at US $1 = about BDS $2; U.S. dollar accepted)
Population	263,500
Driving	left
Best romantic features	beaches, elegant English atmosphere, history

George Washington slept here. Really. This tiny island has been welcoming tourists since the days before the American Revolution. George himself came to enjoy the healthful climate (much needed by his tuberculosis-stricken brother, Lawrence) back in 1751, and visitors have been coming to this island in the far eastern Caribbean ever since.

The reasons are easy to see. An idyllic climate. An atmosphere that combines tropical casualness with British formality, where high tea on a hot afternoon makes perfect sense. A history that includes not only presidents but pirates, and greathouses that recall the days of vast plantations and a jungle of sugar cane.

Today Barbados exudes the most British atmosphere found in the Caribbean. As you drive through the island, look for both men and women in cool white suits on the cricket fields. In the afternoons, take time to enjoy high tea. And listen to the voices of the Barbadians or Bajans (rhymes with Cajun): their accent is almost British.

If the two of you like to maintain a regular exercise routine, you will feel right at home on Barbados. When the sun's first rays peek out over the Atlantic (around 5 A.M.), Barbadians hit the roads for some early morning jogging, power walking, and strolling to enjoy this special time before the day's heat sets in.

A Little History

The history of Barbados goes back far before the days of English rule which has left such a strong mark upon its character. The earliest residents of this island were the Arawaks, a peaceful tribe who lived here around 400 B.C. As on many other islands, these inhabitants were wiped out by the fierce Caribs, who ruled here for 300 years.

European influence on the island dates to about 1536, when Portuguese explorer Pedro a Campos was believed to have sighted the land and named it Los Barbados, Spanish for "the bearded ones," a moniker given because of the island's Spanish moss that hangs from the trees.

The British came to the island in the 1600s and soon began farming sugar cane, which became the principal source of wealth for the island. Huge plantations covered the island and flourished until the abolition of slavery in 1807.

A reminder of those plantation days remains in Barbados: the chattel house. These small homes, usually built on blocks, were designed so that a man, when moving from area to area, could break down the house and move it by wagon. Today, these small dwellings are still found on the island, and many are in use as small shops.

For years, the island reigned as one of the crown jewels of the Caribbean, vying with Jamaica for top honors in the British empire. Finally, in 1966, the island became independent, although it still retains a very British atmosphere.

Compass Points

Barbados is a pear-shaped island with gentle rolling hills. Agriculture rules much of the landscape, and cane is still king. Although sugar prices have dropped severely in recent years, the crop is a Barbadian mainstay. A drive through the island will take you through a jungle of cane, often with nothing but the road before and behind you visible during the peak of the growing season.

The most easterly of the Caribbean islands, Barbados has strongly differentiated east and west sides. On the Atlantic side, currents are strong, and jagged cliffs and sea caves are carved by the water's force.

In contrast, western beaches offer placid Caribbean waters with excellent visibility, little current, and a gentle trade breeze.

Just the Facts

Getting There

American Airlines, BWIA, and Air Canada offer service from the United States and Canada. Charter service from Detroit is available during high season from Travel Charter International, (800) 521-5267.

Departure tax is US $12.50 for adults; children 12 and under are free.

Cruise ship passengers arrive at the Bridgetown port facility, recently renovated for US $6 million. The enhanced terminal, designed to resemble an island street, now offers 19 duty-free shops, 13 local retail stores, and many vendors as well as tourist information booths, car rentals, and dive shops.

Getting Around

Taxis are prevalent, but not inexpensive. A drive from the airport to the Speightstown-area hotels will run you close to US $30.

Rental cars are available; a Barbados drivers license (US $5) is required. Many visitors rent "Mini-Mokes," a cross between a jeep and a dune buggy for about US $50 daily. And, don't forget, driving is on the left side of the road.

Island tours are offered by several operators. Highland Outdoor Tours, Inc., offers adventure excursions, including a horseback trek across the island, safari rides, and plantation tours. Bajan Tours, 437-9389 or e-mail: bajan@caribnet.net, offers a complete island tour with stops at Holetown, Speightstown, the East Coast, Sam Lord's Castle, and other places of interest.

Entry Requirements

A passport or birth certificate and driver's license or identification card is required of United States citizens.

For More Information

Contact the Barbados Tourism Authority, (800) 221-9831; fax (212) 573-9850. In Canada, the Barbados Tourism Authority can be reached at (800) 268-9122 in Ontario.

For the Marriage-Minded

Your first step in obtaining an application for a marriage license is to stop at the Ministry of Home Affairs office. Bring along the following documentation in English or with a certified translation: valid passports or birth certificates, copies of applicable marriage certificates, death certificates for previous marriages that ended with spouse's death, original decrees or certified copies of divorce judgments, and a letter from the authorized officiant who will perform the service. There's no waiting period—just say "I do!"

The price of a wedding license is about US $62.50 or $125 Barbados dollars. Of that amount, $12 is for a revenue stamp that can be obtained at any post office in Barbados.

To have a Roman Catholic wedding on island, couples must show proof of a premarital interview with signature by the couple and the home parish priest, a Statement of Freedom to Marry signed by the home parish priest, certified copies signed, dated, and stamped by the home parish official of baptismal certificates issued within the past six months indicating freedom to marry, certificate proving participation in a marriage certification program, permission to marry or dispensation from disparity of cult issued by the Bishop of the Catholic party if one member of the couple is Catholic, record of confirmation, copies of applicable declarations of nullity or death certificates of previous marriages ending with spouse's death, and testimonial letters from the couple's archdiocese. These documents should be sent to the bishop of Bridgetown, St. Patrick's Presbytery, P.O. Box 1223, Jemmott's Lane, Bridgetown, West Indies, (246) 426-3510. A fee of US $98 is required for use of the church, as well as an additional fee of US $40.40 for an organist.

For those not utilizing resort matrimonial facilities, two popular wedding sites are the Andromeda Gardens and the Flower Forest. These beautiful gardens are in bloom with tropical color year-round.

Romantic Resorts

Almond Beach Club, (800) 425-6663, (246) 432-7840;
fax (407) 872-7770. $$$$

• beachfront
• all-inclusive
• watersports
• fine and casual dining
• freshwater pools and Jacuzzis

You have your choice between two resorts: Almond Beach Village and
Almond Beach Club. The Club is a couples-only resort, so it is favored
by honeymooners and lovers looking to spend time together. A
full-time wedding specialist can help couples arrange weddings during
their stay.

Guests at both resorts enjoy reciprocal privileges, and they also
have the chance to participate in a unique dine-around program. Vacationers who remain at the resort for a week can enjoy visits to local
restaurants as part of their all-inclusive program. Transportation
between the resort and the restaurants are provided.

Almond Beach Village, (800) 425-6663, (407) 872-2220;
fax (407) 872-7770. $$$$

• beachfront
• all-inclusive
• watersports
• fine and casual dining
• freshwater pools and Jacuzzis
• golf
• children's program

Similar in many ways to its sister property, Almond Beach Club, the
Village caters to both families and couples. You can still enjoy a
romantic vacation while traveling with your family, thanks to the children's program here, where the little ones will enjoy supervised fun
while the two of you play a round of nine-hole golf, enjoy watersports
right on property, or lounge around the long expanse of sand. The
Village also has a romantic wedding site: a stone sugarmill. We watched

a wedding during our stay here when vows were exchanged in the historic setting.

Glitter Bay, (800) 283-8666, (246) 422-5555; fax (246) 422-3940. $$$

- beachfront
- casual and fine dining
- freshwater pool
- watersports, dive center
- tennis, golf
- fitness and massage center

You will feel the elegance and refinement of Barbados and Britain at Glitter Bay, constructed as the home of shipping magnate Sir Edward Cunard. The Mediterranean-style structure, with white stucco walls and Spanish clay roofs, is located on a half-mile-long beach. Glitter Bay's sister resort is the Royal Pavilion (see below), and guests enjoy reciprocal privileges and services of both resorts. You can also golf at the island's new golf course, the Royal Westmoreland.

Marriott's Sam Lord's Resort, (800) 223-6388, (246) 423-7350; fax (246) 423-5918. $$

- beachfront
- casual and fine dining
- health club

This resort is more than a hotel, it's a regular tourist attraction. Built in the 19th century, this castle was the property of the pirate Sam Hall Lord who, according to legend, lured passing ships onto the east coast rocks. Of course, no real castle would be complete without its resident ghost, and at Sam Lord's they say his truly still rests on his four-poster bed.

The 234 guest rooms here are much more peaceful than Sam Lord's old quarters. Guests have access to several restaurants on site, including The Queen's Dinner, a seven-course banquet that commemorates the 1976 visit of Queen Elizabeth to the castle. The two of you can enjoy this feast on Wednesday evenings (reservations required).

Wedding packages are available that include a bouquet and boutonniere, wedding cake, champagne, minister, and all paperwork.

Royal Pavilion, (800) 283-8666, (246) 422-5555;
fax (246) 422-3940. $$$$

- beachfront
- casual and fine dining
- watersports, dive center
- tennis, golf

This elegant property is designed for guests looking for the finest money can buy: from a grand entrance lined with fine boutiques such as Cartier, to the 72 junior suites that overlook the sea. In your room, you will be pampered with twice-daily maid service, a private terrace or patio, and a decor that combines elegance and tropical splendor. Children are not permitted at Royal Pavilion during high season.

The sister property of this resort is Glitter Bay, and guests share facilities and services with that property. Guests also enjoy golf privileges at the Robert Trent Jones, Jr.-designed course, the Royal Westmoreland.

Sandy Lane Hotel and Golf Club, (800) 225-5843, (246) 432-1311; fax (246) 432-2954. $$$$

- beachfront
- fine and casual dining
- watersports, tennis
- children's program
- freshwater pool

One of the Caribbean's most expensive resorts, Sandy Lane is for those looking for the highest level of luxury and style.

Shopping

The primary shopping area on the island is found in Bridgetown along Broad Street. Here the two of you will find fine goods of every variety: luggage, designer clothing, china, crystal, silver, cameras, the list goes on. Barbados is a tax-free haven, so you will enjoy savings. Only liquor must be delivered to the airport or the cruise port; other purchases can be carried out from the store.

In Bridgetown, Cave Shepherd Shop offers china, crystal, fine clothing, electronics, and perfumes. Located on Broad Street, this shop has been serving Barbados visitors and residents since 1906. Today it includes a Colombian Emeralds International outlet with fine jewelry, as well as two restaurants, an activities desk for island tours, photo lab, and American Airlines office. Other Bridgetown shopping malls include Sunset Mall and DaCostas Mall, with over 35 shops offering everything from perfumes to china to cameras.

For island crafts, drop by the Medford Craft Village in St. Michael. Hand-carved items such as birds, boats, clocks, and fish are made here from local mahogany.

Dining

Although you will find cuisine from around the world represented on Barbados (especially at the luxury resorts), make time for a meal of local favorites like flying fish, *cou-cou* (a cornmeal and okra dish), pepperpot stew, and *jug-jug* (a dish made of Guinea corn and green peas).

The most popular drinks are Banks beer and Mount Gay Rum, both local products.

La Cage, Prospect. $$$$

Located in the Summerland Greathouse, this restaurant is one to save for your most special night out. The menu presents dishes from the Caribbean as well as China, France, and India, with choices including crispy and aromatic duck, steak au poivre, fish in banana sauce, and rack of lamb. Finish off the meal with bananas flambéed with Barbadian rum.

The Cliff, Derricks. $$$

A view of the sea competes with the bounty of the menu at this West Coast restaurant featuring fish, steak, and pasta.

Nico's Champagne and Wine Bar, Derricks. $$$

This informal restaurant (with a menu chalked on blackboards) features starters such as Martinique paté and continues with favorites including Caribbean lobster, lasagna, and deep-fried blue Brie with passionfruit sauce.

Olives Bar and Bistro, Holetown. $$

This casually elegant eatery offers indoor and courtyard dining in a two-story Barbadian structure. Choose from entrees that range from potato rosti with smoked salmon and sour cream, to Jamaican jerk pork to gourmet pizza. Follow it up with an espresso at the upstairs bar.

Ragamuffins, Holetown. $$

West Indian and European cuisine highlight the menu of this restaurant and bar which has been recommended by many U.S. gourmet publications.

Festivals

The biggest blowout of the year is the Crop Over Festival, held late June through the end of August. This island-wide celebration includes six weeks of competitions and festivities that exhibit Barbadian arts, foods, music, and dance. Look for the calypso and steel band competitions, folk concerts, and craft exhibitions and markets.

Music lovers head to the island in mid-January for the Barbados Jazz Festival, where world-class artists such as Ray Charles, Roberta Flack, and others have headlined. Other major events include February's week-long Holetown Festival to celebrate the arrival of the first settlers on the island, and April's Oistins Fish Festival with fish boning competitions, boat races, dances, and crafts. Or, jump in the Caribbean's longest conga line at DeCongaline Carnival, an 11-day street festival held in late April.

Romantic Activities

Barbados is home to many romantic beaches where couples can snorkel in calm Caribbean waters or enjoy windswept vistas on the Atlantic shoreline. Swimmers should definitely head to the Caribbean coast; precautions should be taken not to get over waist deep in the often-dangerous Atlantic currents. These Atlantic waters are preferred by windsurfers and sailors, but swimmers are better off with the calm waters found on Mullins Beach, Crane Beach, and Dover Beach.

The natural beauty of Barbados can also be enjoyed in many of its other attractions. Hold hands and enjoy a ride into **Harrison's Cave,** where damp rooms reveal hidden formations, waterfalls, and pools. A sea cave rather than a cavern, the **Animal Flower Cave** is named for the sea anemones found in its pools.

History lovers should make plans to be in Barbados on Sunday to participate in one of the walking tours sponsored by the **Barbados National Trust**. Starting at 6 A.M. and 3:30 P.M., the walks are a good way to learn more about the culture and history of this rich island.

History buffs will also appreciate a tour of the greathouses. **St. Nicholas Abbey**, built in 1650, is one of only three houses of Jacobean architecture that remain standing in the Western Hemisphere. With Dutch gables and coral finials, the estate combines European and Caribbean styles and is well worth the meager admission price.

Sam Lord's Castle, located in St. Philip on the eastern shore, is another must-see. Now a Marriott hotel, the "castle," built in 1820, is rich with tales of piracy on the high seas and stories of Sam Lord allegedly luring ships onto the eastern shore's rocky coastline. With elaborate plaster ceilings created by the same artist who crafted the ceilings of Windsor Castle, gilt mirrors, and fine mahogany furniture, this is a Caribbean gem of a home and now a hotel.

If you are wondering what lies in the ocean's depths, take a cruise aboard the **Atlantis Submarine**, which cruises to a depth of 150 feet below sea level. It is an excellent way for non-divers to see the rich marine life and the wrecks that surround this island.

Golf lovers are in good shape; Barbados is home to a new Robert Trent Jones, Jr.-designed course. **Royal Westmoreland**, an 18-hole championship course, is the best known on the island. Other popular choices are the 18-hole **Sandy Lane** course, and nine-hole courses at **Almond Beach Village** and **Club Rockley** hotels.

And, if all this touring whets your thirst, take the **Mount Gay Rum Tour** for a look at the place where the oldest rum in the world is produced. Luncheon tours include a Bajan buffet, transportation to and from your hotel, and, of course, a complimentary miniature bottle of the distillery's product. Regular, 45-minute tours are offered on weekdays every half hour and include a taste of Mount Gay Rum at the conclusion of the tour. Or, for a little different taste, stop by **Malibu Visitors Centre** in St. Michael to tour the distillery that produces Malibu Caribbean White Rum with Coconut. After the tour, enjoy a Bajan barbecue or take a swim on the beach. Other local product tours include **Cockspur Rum Tours**, scheduled for Tuesdays, Wednesdays, and Thursdays, and **Banks Breweries Tours**, offered Tuesdays and Thursdays.

If the two of you will be enjoying many excursions, check out the **Heritage Passport Program**, sponsored by the Barbados National Trust. Sixteen sites are included on the pass, which offers about a 50% savings on admission (a mini passport is available for fewer stops). The passport includes admission to Harrison's Cave, St. Nicholas Abbey, Mount Gay, and many other sites.

Nightlife

The Sherbourne Center, Barbados' convention center, offers a folklore dinner show, "1627 and All That," every Thursday and Sunday night. Along with dinner and an open bar, guests enjoy a show featuring the Barbados Dance Theater.

"Rum shops" or businesses licensed to sell alcohol are found through the island. The hottest spot in Speightstown is Fisherman's Pub, a rollicking bar tucked on the waterfront. On Friday nights, this bar fills with local men, who traditionally come by to enjoy some rum and dominoes.

Some other hot nightspots include Sandy Bank Nightclub, which schedules nightly shows such as steel pan, comedy, and, every Monday, Bajan Fun Night with a limbo contest, fire eating, steel pan, and dancing. Reservations are required; call 435-1234. Harbour Lights Night Club, 436-7225, offers Monday night beach parties with beach limbo and an outdoor barbecue. The Plantation Restaurant and Garden Theatre in Christ Church offers a tropical dinner show on Wednesday, Thursday, and Friday evenings with buffet dinner, open bar, and Caribbean favorites such as fire-eating and flaming limbo shows. For reservations, call 428-5048 or 428-2986.

For nighttime fun on the water, the Bajan Queen provides sunset party cruises with complimentary drinks, live music, and a buffet dinner. Reservations are required; call 436-6424. Limbo Lady sailing cruises, 420-5418, offer sunset cocktail cruises every weekday with a singer onboard. L.E. Williams Tour Co. Lts., 427-1043, offers sunset cruises, with transportation to and from hotels.

OUR IMPRESSIONS OF BARBADOS

- excellent for independent travelers
- wonderful for a sophisticated atmosphere
- good for history buffs and golf players

ROMANCE ON BARBADOS

- stroll along the rugged Atlantic coastline
- share a kiss in the darkness of Harrison's Cave
- tour Sam Lord's Castle and hear tales of piracy on the high seas

British Virgin Islands

Language	English
Currency	US dollar
Population	17,000
Driving	left
Best romantic features	boating, intimate inns, safe atmosphere

Hoist the sails and gather way. Grip the wheel in your hands and cut a feather through aquamarine waters to a quiet Caribbean cove. Drop anchor and motor a small launch to an empty beach for a gourmet picnic on the white sand.

Sound like a boating fantasy? It is, but in the British Virgin Islands, it is also reality. Year-round, old salts and would-be skippers come from around the world to sail these calm waters and take advantage of a group of 50 islands that call themselves "Nature's Little Secrets." These Virgins are loved for their quiet getaways, empty beaches, and a romantic maritime atmosphere.

More than any other Caribbean destination, the British Virgin Islands ("the BVI" if you want to sound like a real salt) is a great choice for those who want to divide their vacation with a stay on land and on the sea. The island of Tortola is the home of the largest charter yacht company in the world, and many properties offer packages combining resort rooms with a few days on a crewed or bareboat yacht. You can set sail for paradise from just about any point in the BVI.

Tortola will probably be your first taste of these islands. It is the most active destination in the island chain, but don't expect big resorts, duty-free shopping, or cruise ship traffic. Here, traffic comes from a goat in the middle of the road or from boaters coming ashore for a full moon party at a side-of-the-road joint called Bomba's Shack. These are, as the tourist office likes to say, the Virgin Islands that are still virgin.

Tortola is a semi-arid, hilly island that is home to two primary communities: West End and the capital, Road Town. With such no-nonsense names, you would expect no-nonsense places, and that is exactly what these towns are. You won't need a road map to locate West End, a community visited by yachtsmen who come in to provision their vessels and to enjoy the local flavor at Soper's Hole, a marina splashed in shades of pink, sea green, and turquoise. This pastel shopping center offers Caribbean arts, crafts, and also one of the most picturesque photo spots in the islands, where waterfront buildings are as colorful as Easter eggs.

Another popular provisioning area is Road Town, named because most roads converge here. Government offices and banks line the streets of this capital city, along with a few shops and restaurants of special interest to travelers. In either town you can catch a water taxi to other islands in the chain.

Tortola is the largest of this chain of about 50 scattered islands and cays, many of which are uninhabited. The other prime destination is Virgin Gorda, home to both resorts and marinas. Separated from Tortola by the Sir Francis Drake Channel, Virgin Gorda is a quieter version of Tortola. Equally hilly, most activity and lodging here is clustered around the Spanish Town region and marina area.

The other islands are even less visited. Jost (pronounced *Yost*, rhymes with roast) Van Dyke was named for a Dutch pirate, and today the tiny island is a getaway for those seeking true tranquility, beautiful snorkeling waters, and a sometimes rollicking atmosphere. Peter Island is almost totally owned by a single resort operated by the Amway Corporation. If you read the tabloids you may have heard of Necker Island, a hideaway of the rich and famous, like Princess Di and Oprah. And there's Anegada, a quiet destination that rises barely 27 feet over sea level. Between these islands, tiny landforms dot the horizon. Look for Dead Chest, a tiny islet of bare rock where legend has it that Blackbeard marooned his men to fight over a single bottle of rum. (Remember "Fifteen men on a dead man's chest, Yo ho ho and a bottle of rum"? Now you know where that got started.)

The British Virgin Islands are different from their American cousins. Life is quieter here and more attuned to the sea. Days are not spent shopping, but sometimes, as the locals say, just limin' or hanging out and doing nothing at all. Nights are even quieter, beneath the stars that guided explorers here over 500 years ago. And when morning comes, if you stay at one of the small inns for which the BVI is known, your alarm clock may well be the rooster next door.

For some couples, this is true paradise. This was one of our first Caribbean destinations, and remains one of our favorites.

A Little History

The boating history of these islands goes back to the days of Christopher Columbus, who landed on Tortola in 1694. The multitude of tiny islands reminded Columbus of the tale of Saint Ursula and her 11,000 virgins, so he named these the Virgin Islands. Tortola was named for its numerous turtle doves.

The BVI was originally claimed by the Dutch (like the neighboring U.S. Virgin Islands), but soon were acquired by the British. Today the islands are still a dependency of Great Britain.

Compass Points

All the islands in the BVI are semi-arid, sprinkled with cacti and succulents, but dotted with tropical blooms. A drive around Tortola reveals numerous coconut palms and flowering hibiscus, mixed with tall organ and squat barrel cacti. Tortola and the other islands receive only about 16 inches of rain a year.

Tortola is the largest island with only 21 square miles. Don't let distance fool you, however. Because of steep hills, a car trip around or across the island is a slow undertaking.

Just the Facts

Getting There

Service to Tortola's Beef Island International Airport is available from San Juan on American Eagle. Other vacationers prefer to fly directly into St. Thomas and ferry over to Tortola (see "Getting Around"). Service into St. Thomas is available from American Airlines with flights from JFK/New York, Miami, and Washington/Dulles via San Juan. Direct service from Baltimore/Washington is available aboard USAir, and service from Atlanta is available on Delta. Direct flights from Miami are also available on Prestige Airways.

Getting Around

Island hopping is a way of life in the BVI and the most common way is aboard ferries. One-hour service from St. Thomas is available daily to Road Town and West End in Tortola aboard Smith's Ferry Service, (809) 495-4495. Service from West End to Cruz Bay, St. John, is available from Inter-Island Boat Service (809) 495-4166.

Entry Requirements

U.S. and Canadian citizens should bring a current passport or original birth certificate with photo ID. You will also have to show a return or onward ticket.

For More Information

Contact the British Virgin Islands Tourist Board at (800) 835-8530 in the eastern U.S. or (800) 232-7770 in the western U.S.

For the Marriage-Minded

Weddings in the BVI are simple to arrange. After three days on the islands, you can apply for a marriage license for $110 in BVI postage stamps. Bring a passport or original birth certificate and photo ID as well as proof of divorce or death of former spouse if applicable. No blood tests are necessary.

After application for a license, go to the Registrar's Office on Wickham Cay (weekdays 9–3:30, Saturday 9–12). The registrar also serves as marriage officer and will request the names, ages, and occupations of the two parties and the names of two witnesses. The registrar's fee for the ceremony is $50 if performed in the office; $100 if performed elsewhere.

Church weddings can be arranged, but you must publish banns on three consecutive Saturdays or Sundays in that church and make arrangements with the minister.

For more information on marriage license regulations, write the Registrar's Office, P.O. Box 418, Road Town, Tortola, BVI or call (809) 494-3701 or 494-3492.

Romantic Resorts

Tortola

Long Bay Beach Resort, (800) 729-9599, (809) 495-4252; fax (809) 495-4677. $$

- beachfront
- casual and fine dining
- tennis
- freshwater pool
- sailing

They call this resort Long Bay but we found that they might as well change the name to Long Beach. A mile-long white sand beach is the focal point of this 105-room resort located near West End. All rooms, both hilltop and beachside, have views of the beach and the quiet waters of Long Bay.

The Moorings, (800) 437-7880; fax (809) 494-2507. $–$$$$

- bareboat and crewed yacht charters

Ahoy mates, here's your chance to take to the seas on your own yacht. Well, the yacht's not technically yours, but for a few days it will be home for you and usually two or three other couples. You can rent a stateroom aboard a yacht and enjoy a luxurious trip around the islands (or for true luxury, rent the entire boat, complete with the services of a captain and a cook). The Moorings is the world's largest charter yacht company, an operation that started in tiny Road Town.

Sugar Mill, (800) 462-8834 or (809) 495-4355; fax (809) 495-4696. $$–$$$

- beachfront
- freshwater pool
- casual and fine dining

If you are a cooking aficionado, you may already be familiar with the Sugar Mill's owners, Jinx and Jeff Morgan. These *Bon Appetit* columnists and cookbook authors have brought their expertise to the Caribbean in the Sugar Mill Restaurant (see "Dining").

But the recipe for happiness for this former California couple included not just a restaurant but a complete resort. Since 1982, the Morgans have operated this 21-room inn and made it a prime destination for couples looking for peace and privacy.

The Sugar Mill is one of the finest small inns in the Caribbean, offering visitors a chance to enjoy a spectacular setting while at the same time feeling part of island life. The rooms are nice but not distinctive. In our second-floor room, air conditioning was provided by nature. We enjoyed a balcony and kitchen facilities and a simple room with a view of the lush grounds.

Those grounds draw the visitors to this Tortola site. This hotel is located on the ruins of the Appleby Plantation, which dates back to the island's days of sugar and slaves. Little remains of the early buildings except the ruins of a 360-year-old sugar mill, today part of the hotel's elegant restaurant. Another reminder of the location's sugar history is the swimming pool. This circular tank is built on the site of a treadmill where oxen once powered the machinery to crush the sugar cane that eventually became rum.

Honeymooners will find a seven-night package that includes a deluxe room, bottle of champagne, massages for two, a castaway beach picnic for two, a day sail to neighboring islands, car rental, and more.

Virgin Gorda

Biras Creek, (800) 608-9661, (809) 494-3555; fax (809) 494-3557. $$$$

- beachfront
- full American plan or FAP (all meals)
- watersports
- tennis
- fine and casual dining
- freshwater pool

Biras Creek makes a mighty tempting offer to lovers: they'll maroon you on a deserted beach for the day. Just the two of you, a picnic basket, and paradise.

Problem is, it's pretty tough to leave Biras Creek itself. This luxurious resort on Deep Bay combines beach resort and yacht club. The

32-suite property was purchased recently by Bert Houwer, who had vacationed at the hotel for 14 years. You cannot get a much better guest recommendation than that.

Biras Creek offers a complete wedding package with marriage license, registrar's fee, floral arrangement, wedding cake, champagne toast, and photographer. Pick from an outdoor ceremony or an intimate exchange of vows on a 47-foot luxury yacht.

Bitter End Yacht Club, (800) 872-2392, (809) 494-2746; fax (809) 494-4756. $$$$

- beachfront
- FAP (all meals)
- marina
- casual and fine dining
- sailing school

This 100-room resort is located at the "bitter end" of the BVI on the North Sound. Reached only by boat, this resort gives you the feeling of staying at a yacht club, where days are spent in close connection with the sea. The resort boasts 150 vessels, the largest fleet of recreational boats in the Caribbean. Many guests arrive via their own craft and simply dock for their stay. Those without a boat can stay in a resort room or aboard one of the club yachts. Spend the day in your "room" boating among the islands, then return to port at night and enjoy a quiet meal in the resort's elegant restaurant.

Lovebirds will find a seven-night honeymoon package here that includes a beachfront villa, a refrigerator stocked with orange juice and champagne, a sunset sail on the North Sound, a daysailer or outboard skiff to explore quiet coves, and more. Even if you don't take the package, there is plenty of romance at this resort, from mornings spent on the hillside hiking trails among orchids and island birds to afternoons spent learning to sail together.

Little Dix Bay, (800) 928-3000, (809) 495-5555; fax (809) 495-5661. $$$$

- casual and fine dining
- tennis
- watersports, dive shop
- Sunfish sailboats and kayaks

We have fond memories of our stay at Little Dix: lazing beneath a palm palapa, snorkeling just offshore, enjoying our rondoval guest room with a wonderful view in every direction, dining outdoors to the music of whistling tree frogs.

Apparently plenty of other couples also have good memories of Little Dix; it boasts a wonderful repeat business. Many customers have been coming since the days Laurance Rockefeller first developed this property in 1964. Today the hotel still has the same attention to service as it did in its Rockresort days; you will find that the ratio of employees to guests is one to one.

Toad Hall, (809) 495-5397; fax (809) 495-5708. $$$$

• freshwater pool
• music system and video players

This elegant inn offers its guests privacy; guests rent the entire property. These are one-of-a-kind rooms where you will truly feel like you are living outdoors. Scattered among the six and a half acres are three guest suites, bath cottages with stone showers tucked into screened gardens (and one with a whirlpool bath), dining room, kitchen, and living room. The real treat is the location: perched just above The Baths, this inn has the only private access to the park beach. The atmosphere of The Baths is felt here at the inn as well; granite boulders tumble from the sides of the swimming pool, mimicking the natural pools down the hill.

Peter Island

Peter Island Resort, (800) 346-4451 in U.S., (809) 495-2000; fax (809) 495-2500. $$$$

• beachfront
• casual and fine dining
• freshwater pool
• tennis
• yacht harbor
• watersports, dive shop
• fitness center and massage

This is true luxury: a resort that occupies an entire island. Owned by the Amway Corporation (a fact that most visitors are unaware of except for the can of Amway spot remover in the closet), Peter Island is truly a place where romance can flourish like the bougainvillea, hibiscus, and sea grapes that dot its hills. This 1,800-acre island is paradise for couples. It starts with your arrival by private launch from Tortola, and continues as you check in and see your guest room: a combination of Scandinavian and Caribbean styles.

Lovers can try the special Island Romance package, which includes a day sail to the Baths in Virgin Gorda, champagne on arrival, and a photo album. Other packages include scuba diving, a combination land and sea stay with two nights on your own private yacht with guide, crew, and cook.

For us, Peter Island's most memorable feature is its beach. Here we lazed away one afternoon in a hammock built for two beneath the shade of some of the most impressive coconut palms we have ever seen in the Caribbean. They were planted by the daughter of an early island family, and today they stand in tall, straight rows looking out on the turquoise waters dotted with nearby islands.

Shopping

Unlike the "other" Virgin islands, shopping is not a major attraction of the BVI. However, you will find a good variety of shops in Road Town and West End at Soper's Hole. Look for Pusser's Rum, spiced rum, or guavaberry liqueur; you may bring back one liter duty-free. Spices are also popular buys, from hot sauces to West Indian mustards to chutney. One of the best selections is at Sunny Caribbee, (809) 494-2178, on Road Town's Main Street. This store has a good collection of things Caribbean, including local crafts, cookbooks, and art prints.

For inexpensive buys, visit the open-air market on Main Street. Here you can haggle for jewelry, T-shirts, calabash bags, and straw hats. The mood is friendly, and you will be entertained most days by steel band musicians.

Another popular Road Town stop is Pusser's Company Store, located near the ferry dock. Here you will find plenty of Pusser's Rum as well as souvenirs bearing the name of this local drink.

Dining

Before dinner, many vacationers stop off at the resort or a local bar for a sample of a true BVI product: Pusser's Rum. The most popular drink is the Painkiller, made from Pusser's Rum, orange and pineapple juice, and coconut creme.

There is really no need to worry about a painkiller though, because dinner in the BVI is a painless affair. Restaurants here are typically very casual, usually outdoors, and feature excellent cuisine. Fresh fish as well as lobster and conch are specialties in most restaurants. Curried dishes are favorites as well.

Skyworld, Tortola. $–$$

Perched at one of the island's highest points, this restaurant offers couples a beautiful view of Tortola, along with refreshing tropical drinks and lunches and dinners featuring local seafood. Call (809) 494-3567 for directions.

Sugar Mill Restaurant, Sugar Mill, Tortola. $$

This restaurant is housed in the remains of a former sugar mill. The stone walls form a backdrop for Haitian artwork and for couples enjoying a candlelight dinner. The menu here changes daily, starting with appetizers such as smoked conch pâté or smoked scallops followed by roasted corn soup or West Indian tania soup. Entrees range from tropical game hen with orange-curry butter to fresh fish in banana leaves with herb butter to roasted pepper stuffed pork tenderloin with pineapple chipotle sauce. This is our choice for the BVI's most romantic restaurant. Reservations suggested; call (809) 495-4355.

Festivals

Not surprisingly, many BVI special events are boat races. One of the biggest is the BVI Spring Regatta in early April. Sailors from around the globe come to compete in this yachting event.

In late June, windsurfers take the stage at Hook-In-Hold-On (HIHO), billed as the world's greatest windsurfing adventure.

For fun out of the water, drop by the BVI Summer Festival, held in late July and early August. We were lucky enough to be in Tortola during this special event held in Road Town. We danced in the moonlight to steel pan bands and watched locals betting on a game of chance we never could understand. With all the atmosphere of a small town festival, this event is popular with locals and visitors alike and shouldn't be missed.

Romantic Activities

A top destination in the BVI (or, for that matter, in the Caribbean) is **The Baths**. This 682-acre park is located on Virgin Gorda, and it is so unique that once you visit it you will be able to spot this park in any Caribbean video or magazine. Unlike most Caribbean beaches, which are mostly flat, this site is scattered with massive granite boulders. As smooth as riverbed stones, these gargantuan rocks litter the sea and the beach. They form shadowy caves where you can swim in water lit by sunlight filtering through cracks. This special site is unspoiled (just one or two concessionaires and no hagglers) and is a fun snorkeling spot.

Hikers should save time for a visit to **Sage Mountain National Park** on Tortola. The BVI's highest point has an altitude of 1,780 feet and is lush with greenery that can be viewed from its many gravel walkways.

Divers will find plenty of activity in the waters off any of the British Virgin Islands. The best-known dive spot is the wreck of the **RMS Rhone**, a mail steam packet that broke up in a storm. You may be familiar with this wreck—it was used in filming *The Deep*. The bow lies just 80 feet below the surface, making it an easy wreck dive (and usually visible to snorkelers). Other top dive sites include Alice in Wonderland, a deep dive with mushroom-shaped corals; the *Chikuzen* wreck, a 246-foot fish-filled wreck just 75 feet below the surface; and Santa Monica Rock, located near the open ocean and a good place to spot large fish.

Nightlife

One of the BVI's best nightspots is also a good place during the day, albeit a little quieter. On Jost Van Dyke, Foxy's Tamarind Bar,

(809) 495-9258, is a legend throughout the Caribbean, thanks to the boats that frequent this beach bar and pass the word on to other boaters. The yachties so love this joint that many have even removed clothing—shoes, tee shirts, even bras—and stapled them to the posts and underside of the palm-thatched roof.

Whether you come by for lunch or dinner, you will have your choice of West Indian specialties like curried chicken rotis or burgers and plenty of drinks. But the real treat is Foxy himself.

Foxy, AKA Philicianno Callwood, is a one-man show, greeting incoming guests with impromptu songs that may feature a political viewpoint, the president of the United States, the person at the next table, or Foxy himself. Sung to a calypso beat, these off-the-cuff tunes bring Foxy's loyal fans back for more. Every year, Foxy's really celebrates with Foxy's Wooden Boat Regatta in early September.

Over in Tortola, the hottest spot is Bomba's Shack, (809) 495-4148, best known as home of the full moon parties. These blowouts are some of the best-known parties in the Caribbean.

OUR IMPRESSIONS OF THE BVI

- excellent for sailing buffs and anyone looking for an unspoiled island atmosphere
- limited nightlife, shopping
- one of the most scenic destinations in the Caribbean
- excellent for independent travelers

ROMANCE IN THE BVI

- do some limin' on a palm-shaded beach
- kiss in the shadowy pools of The Baths
- search for your favorite beach bar
- sail the islands, just the two of you, a captain, and a cook

Cayman Islands

Language	English
Currency	Cayman dollar (fixed at US $1 = CI $.80); US dollar widely accepted
Population	28,000
Driving	left
Best romantic features	snorkeling and scuba diving, fine dining

For the American traveler, perhaps no other Caribbean island offers the comfort and "this is almost like back home" feeling of the Cayman Islands, especially the most popular destination: Grand Cayman. This island, together with its smaller cousins, Cayman Brac and Little Cayman, enjoys the highest per capita income in the Caribbean, is friendly, safe, and tailor-made for couples looking for a slice of home on their vacation. Here you will find all the comforts of the United States, as well as an American standard of service in many restaurants, bars, and hotels, from the many stateside ex-pats who make their home in these lovely isles. For some visitors, this Americanized atmosphere is as welcome as eating a Big Mac in Paris; for others it is a familiar way to experience the islands.

Comfort comes at a price. The Cayman dollar is stronger than its U.S. equivalent; at present US $1 is worth only 80 cents CI. Prices in hotels, restaurants, shops, and attractions reflect that unfavorable exchange rate and high standard of living; we have paid as much as US $36 for breakfast for two in a hotel restaurant.

These lofty price tags do not deter the nearly 300,000 U.S. vacationers and businesspeople who fly into these islands every year. The vacationers are drawn by protected waters as clear as white rum and teeming with marine life, offering one of the best snorkeling and scuba vacations in the region. The business world is also attracted to these small islands for an entirely different reason: tax-free status. (Remember *The Firm?* Portions of that movie, based on the John Grisham book, were filmed here.)

A Little History

Cayman Brac and Little Brac, also known as the Sister Islands, were spotted by Christopher Columbus on his last journey to the New World in 1503. He called these islands "Las Tortugas" after the many sea turtles he found there.

About 150 years later, the British took control of the isles when Jamaica was captured from the Spanish. The British decided to rule the Cayman Islands as a dependency of Jamaica, and the neighboring islands maintained that relationship for close to three centuries. Jamaica gained its independence from England in 1962, but the Cayman Islands decided to remain a British Crown Colony. Today, the islands are ruled by a Governor appointed by the Queen.

Compass Points

Located in the westernmost reaches of the Caribbean, about 180 miles west of Jamaica, the Cayman Islands are composed of three islands: Grand Cayman, Cayman Brac, and Little Cayman. Grand Cayman is the largest of the trio, spanning 76 square miles. The Sister Islands are located about 80 miles east-northeast of Grand Cayman, separated by seven miles of sea.

These three islands are actually the peaks of a submarine mountain range, the Cayman Ridge, part of a chain running from Cuba to near Belize. The islands are limestone outcroppings with little soil, so vegetation is not as lush as on some islands. Most of the rain is quickly absorbed in the porous limestone, and there are no rivers on these islands. That means little runoff and therefore greater visibility in the waters surrounding the islands. Divers rave about the visibility, often 100 to 150 feet.

Beyond the reaches of land, each island is surrounded by coral reefs, producing some of the best snorkeling and scuba diving in the Caribbean. Divers have a chance to spot a wide array of marine life, partly because of the deep water located nearby. The deepest waters in the Caribbean are found between this nation and Jamaica, depths that plunge into inky blackness over four miles beneath the ocean's surface.

The Cayman Islands have taken strict measures to protect the marine life of these waters. Today the sea turtle is protected and no one may disturb, molest, or take turtles in Cayman waters without a license. Other marine conservation laws prohibit the taking of any marine life while scuba diving, or damaging coral with anchors. Over 200 permanent boat moorings prevent further coral damage by anchoring.

Just the Facts

Getting There

You will arrive in the Cayman Islands at Owen Roberts International Airport, a stylish facility that resembles a Polynesian structure. The principal carrier into this port of entry is Cayman Airways, (800) G-CAYMAN, the national carrier with flights from Miami, Tampa, Atlanta, and Houston. Air/land packages are also available from Cayman Airtours, (800) 247-2966. Service is also available from American Airlines from Miami (and Raleigh-Durham during high season), Northwest Airlines from Miami, USAir from Charlotte and Tampa, and America Trans Air from Indianapolis.

Direct flights to Cayman Brac are available from Miami, Tampa, Atlanta, and Houston or from Grand Cayman.

Departure tax is US $10 per person.

Cruise ship passengers arrive in George Town, a wonderfully charming community brimming with shops and restaurants along its clean waterfront.

Getting Around

Transportation around Grand Cayman is easy. Take your pick from taxis and group tours as well as rental cars, vans, jeeps, and scooters (a scary option to us, considering the left side driving and considerable traffic in George Town).

Entry Requirements

U.S. and Canadian citizens need to show proof of citizenship in the form of a passport, birth certificate, or voter registration card. Visitors must also show a return airline ticket.

For More Information

Contact your nearest Cayman Islands Department of Tourism Office: Miami, (305) 266-2300; New York, (212) 682-5582; Houston, (713) 461-1317; Los Angeles, (213) 738-1968; Chicago, (708) 678-6446; and Canada, (416) 485-1550.

When on Grand Cayman, visit the Cayman Islands Department of Tourism office at Elgin Avenue in George Town or call (345) 949-0623.

For the Marriage-Minded

Getting hitched in the Cayman Islands is now a simple process. Couples arrange for a Marriage Officer and apply for a special marriage license for non-residents (US $200) at the Chief Secretary's Office, Fourth Floor, Room 406, Government Administration Building, George Town, or call (345) 949-7900. The simplest way is to contact the Chief Secretary's office before your visit to obtain the name of a Marriage Officer (who will need to be named on your application form). Complete the form with your names, occupations, permanent addresses, and your temporary address while staying in the Cayman Islands.

You will also need to present the following:

- valid passports or birth certificates verifying that you are at least 18 years of age (the minimum age for marriage without parental consent);
- the original (or a certified copy) of a divorce decree or death certificate if applicable;
- a letter from the authorized Marriage Officer who will officiate at your ceremony;
- a Cayman Islands International Immigration Department pink slip showing proof of entry (or, for cruise passengers, a boarding pass

proving you are in port legally. If you are arriving on a cruise ship, contact your Purser and ask him to call ahead to the ship's agent for assistance);

• two witnesses.

No residency period is required.

Write for a copy of the free brochure, "Getting Married in the Cayman Islands," from Government Information Services, Broadcasting House, Grand Cayman, or call (345) 949-8092; fax (345) 949-5936.

Another option is to contact wedding packagers at Cayman Weddings, (345) 949-8677; fax 949-8237. Owned by a husband-wife team of Marriage Officers, this company produces weddings that range from barefoot beach ceremonies to elaborate rites with arrival on a beach or at a tropical garden by limousine.

Romantic Resorts

Most visitors to Grand Cayman stay along Seven Mile Beach just outside of George Town. Okay, it's only five and a half miles long, but with this kind of beauty, who's counting? Along this busy stretch you will find luxurious hotels, fine restaurants, nightclubs, and most of the activity on the island.

Holiday Inn Grand Cayman, (800) 421-9999, (345) 947-4444; fax (345) 947-4213. $$

• beachfront
• pool
• restaurant and bar
• dive shop and watersports center
• shopping
• children under 18 stay free with parents

The 215-room Holiday Inn has garnered a great deal of attention because of its nightclub singer: the Barefoot Man. The Caribbean tunes of this performer are known throughout the islands and were heard in *The Firm*. Couples will find plenty of other reasons to like the Holiday Inn, including a nightly poolside barbecue buffet and a comedy club.

Hyatt Regency Grand Cayman, (800) 233-1234, (345) 949-1234; fax (345) 949-8528. $$

- casual and fine dining
- near beach with private beach club
- pool and hot tub
- dive shop
- tennis
- 24-hour room service

One of Grand Cayman's most beautiful resorts, the Hyatt is not located on the beach but does offer its guests use of a private beach club with full watersports. You may recognize parts of this resort from the movie *The Firm* (it's the place where Gene Hackman and Tom Cruise stayed). The 235-room hotel includes many levels of rooms and suites plus luxury villas (where, of course, Gene's and Tom's characters were stationed). Our favorite part of the hotel is the beautiful landscaping and the freeform swimming pool, complete with bridges and pool bar.

Radisson Resort Grand Cayman, (800) 333-3333, (345) 949-0088; fax (345) 949-0288. $$

- beachfront
- casual and fine dining
- pool and hot tub
- dive shop, wave runners, windsurfing
- shopping
- full service spa

Two miles from George Town and about four miles from the airport, this convenient property is on a beautiful stretch of Seven Mile Beach. Swimmers and snorkelers can enjoy calm waters and a small coral reef just offshore, learn scuba diving, or book dive trips through the on-site shop. Oceanfront rooms include private balconies with good beach views and are worth a somewhat long walk to the elevators in this 315-room hotel.

Treasure Island Resort, (800) 327-8777, (345) 949-7777; fax (345) 949-8489. $$

- beachfront
- two freshwater pools

- two whirlpools
- tennis
- dive operation
- shopping
- informal dining, bar, lounge

This 280-room resort includes an offshore snorkel trail.

Westin Casuarina Resort, (800) 228-3000, (345) 945-3800; fax (345) 949-5825. $$

- beachfront
- casual and fine dining
- pools, whirlpools
- tennis, fitness facilities, massage
- beauty salons

The newest hotel in Grand Cayman is built on a strip of beach bordered by willowy casuarina trees. The hotel has 340 guest rooms, most with breathtaking views of the sea from step-out balconies.

Shopping

The Cayman Islands are a duty-free port, so after 48 hours out of the States, Americans can return home with up to $400 in purchases without paying duty. (Families can pool their exemptions. A husband and wife can take an exemption of $800, a family of four $1600.) Cayman crafts are exempt from this allowance, as are works of art, foreign language books, caviar, and truffles.

Duty-free shopping is especially popular in George Town, where you can choose from china, perfumes, leather goods, watches, crystal, and more. Jewelry (mostly gold) is a popular buy and available at stores such as 24 K-Mon Jewellers (Treasure Island Resort), Savoy Jewellers (Fort Street. and Church Street, George Town), and The Jewelry Center (Fort Street in George Town). For china and crystal, check out the Kirk Freeport Centre (Albert Panton Street, George Town).

If you are looking for something uniquely Cayman, check out the Caymanite jewelry. Made from a stone found only on the eastern end of Grand Cayman and on Cayman Brac, Caymanite resembles tiger's eye and is often sold in gold settings.

Another popular island purchase is the Tortuga Rum Cake, (800) 444-0625, made using five-year-old Tortuga Gold Rum. Sealed in a red tin, the cake is the product of a 100-year-old family recipe. Or, if you want to skip the cake, take home a bottle of Tortuga Rum, Blackbeard, or Cayman Gold.

Dining

Grand Cayman is filled with restaurants of every description, from fast food joints to fine dining. Check your bill before paying as some restaurants automatically add a 15% gratuity to the total.

Lantanas, $$

This elegant restaurant has an excellent menu featuring spicy Cuban black bean soup, jerk pork tenderloin, grilled yellow fin tuna with cilantro linguine, and more, followed by tropical coconut cream pie with white chocolate shavings and mango sauce or frozen Cayman lime pie with raspberry sauce and whipped cream. Need we say more?

Lighthouse at Breakers, $$

On the south shore about 25 minutes from George Town, this picturesque restaurant offers good seafood and Italian cuisine and an even better view. We dined on the open air back deck, a romantic spot for dinner or lunch.

Lobster Pot, $$$

Save this restaurant for your most special night out on Grand Cayman, thanks to an excellent view, an attentive staff, a good wine list, and a romantic atmosphere. We enjoyed a romantic dinner of, what else, Caribbean lobster tail at this casually elegant restaurant overlooking the sea. Other popular dishes include cracked conch, island seafood curry with shrimp, fish, scallops, and lobster, Cayman turtle steak, and steak. Call 949-2736 for reservations.

Festivals

The Cayman Islands observe special holidays throughout the year. The month of June is Million Dollar Month, when fishermen from around the globe come to try their luck. Mid-June is also the Queen's Birthday, a date observed with bands and colorful parades.

At the end of October, it's shiver-me-timbers time during Pirates Week. The islands celebrate their buccaneering history with treasure hunts, parades, and plenty of excuses to dress as pirates and wenches.

Romantic Activities

There's no doubt that one of the top draws of Grand Cayman is the unparalleled **scuba diving** in its clear waters. Visibility often exceeds 100 feet and this is a diver's paradise with over 130 sites to select from near Grand Cayman. Wall and reef dives, many less than half a mile from shore, are available from operators including Bob Soto's Diving, (800) BOB-SOTO, Don Foster's Dive Cayman, (800) 83-DIVER, Red Sail Sports, (800) 255-6425, Treasure Island Divers, (800) 872-7552, Tortuga Surfside Divers, (800) 748-8733, and many more.

The top attraction on Grand Cayman is **Stingray City**, the place for you to act out your Jacques Cousteau fantasies. It is an area where numerous operators (including many of the scuba operators named above) introduce vacationers to one of the most unique experiences in the Caribbean.

Following a short boat ride, visitors don snorkel gear and swim with the stingrays just offshore on a shallow sandbar. Accustomed to being fed, the stingrays (which range in size from about one to six feet across) are docile and friendly, brushing against swimmers and even allowing themselves to be held and petted. About 30 stingrays frequent this area.

But you don't even have to get wet to enjoy the underwater sights of the Caribbean. The **Atlantis Submarine**, (800) 253-0493, offers hourly dives six days a week. For 50 minutes, you will feel like an underwater explorer as you dive to a depth of 100 feet below the surface. It's a unique opportunity to view colorful coral formations and sponge gardens, and identify hundreds of varieties of tropical fish. The submarine has individual porthole windows for each passenger, plus cards to help you identify fish species. A pilot and copilot point out attractions during the journey.

Just a portion of the attractions on Grand Cayman lie below the water's surface. To experience the entire island, consider an **island tour**. We signed up for a tour with Burton Ebanks, (345) 949-7222, a local with an extensive knowledge of the entire region. We headed off for the day to view the 76-square-mile island.

Outside the city of George Town, the population is sparse and the atmosphere is rural. The least populated region is called North Side. Located about 25 minutes from George Town, this remote area is home to the **Queen Elizabeth Botanical Park**, (345) 947-9462, a 65-acre park filled with native trees, wild orchids, birds, reptiles, and butterflies. We enjoyed a self-guided tour and a quiet look at the flora and fauna that make the Cayman Islands special.

From the North Side we traveled to the East End, home of the **Blow Holes Park** and walked down to the rugged coral rocks carved by rough waves into caverns. As waves hit the rocks, water spews into the air, creating one of the best photo sites on the island.

Just under 30,000 people populate the island, and almost half live in the capital city of George Town. Save time for a tour of the **Cayman Islands National Museum**, (345) 949-8368. This excellent two-story museum traces the history of the Cayman Islands, including the islands' natural history. **George Town** bustles with life any time of day as a center for shoppers and diners. Among historic government buildings, you will find plenty of shops selling Cayman souvenirs and restaurants featuring Caribbean cuisine and international dishes.

Continuing past George Town lies the world's only **Turtle Farm**. Here you will have a chance to get up close and personal with green sea turtles, viewing them as eggs, hatchlings, and in various sizes as they work their way up towards adulthood. Some reach 600 pounds, and can be viewed slowly swimming in an open-air tank in the center of the farm.

The **Links at SafeHaven**, (345) 947-4155; fax 947-4001, is the only championship 18-hole golf course in the Cayman Islands. Rates average about US $60 for 18 holes. Shoe and cart rental are available.

One of the best ways to enjoy Grand Cayman is in its waters. To feel like one of the pirates of the Caribbean, consider a cruise aboard the **Jolly Roger**, (345) 949-8534, an authentic replica of a 17th century galleon. Cruises, starting at US $15, take couples on a romantic sunset sail, a rollicking pirate excursion, and an elegant dinner cruise.

A sunset cruise may be pure heaven, but one of Grand Cayman's top tourist spots is pure Hell. This odd attraction is actually a community named **Hell**, a moniker derived from the time an English commissioner went hunting in the area, shot at a bird, missed, and said

"Oh, hell." The name must have seemed appropriate for the devilishly pointed rocks near town, a bed of limestone and dolomite that through millions of years eroded into a crusty, pocked formation locally called ironshore.

Today, Hell trades upon its unusual name as a way to draw tourists to the far end of West Bay. The **Devil's Hangout Gift Shop** (open daily) is manned by Ivan Farrington, who dresses as the devil himself to greet tourists who come to buy the obligatory postcard and have it postmarked from Hell.

Nightlife

Nightlife is busy in the Seven Mile Beach area. Just past George Town at the start of the beach The Wharf, (345) 949-2231, is a favorite with couples. This seaside restaurant and bar is open for lunch on weekdays and dinner nightly with a menu featuring continental and Caribbean cuisine, but the Wharf is best experienced as an unbeatable romantic sunset spot. Located right on the water's edge, the open-air bar is casual and oh-so-romantic with an uninterrupted view of the setting sun. A school of huge tarpon linger below the deck, waiting for scheduled handouts, and live music is offered most evenings. For the nuptial-minded, this spot is available for weddings and receptions.

For live music, another popular spot is the Holiday Inn and its Coconut's Comedy Club, (345) 945-7000, open nightly except Monday and Thursday. Reservations are suggested for these popular acts. Holiday Inn is also home of Barefoot Man and his band (you may recognize them from *The Firm*), performing Caribbean music several times a week. Treasure Island Resort is also popular for nightly entertainment, with Long John Silver's Nightclub and Tradewinds Lobby Bar, featuring a steel drum band.

OUR IMPRESSIONS OF GRAND CAYMAN

- excellent for vacationers looking for an American atmosphere
- excellent for snorkeling and scuba
- poor for those on a tight budget
- a safe, friendly atmosphere

ROMANCE ON GRAND CAYMAN

- a sunset cruise
- a sunset cocktail at a beachfront bar on Seven Mile Beach
- a quiet stroll through the Botanical Gardens
- snorkeling at Stingray City

$\mathcal{C}$uraçao

Language	Dutch, Papiamento, English widely spoken
Currency	Antillean guilder (US $1 = ANG 1.77); U.S. dollar accepted
Population	170,000
Driving	right
Best romantic features	beaches, quaint shopping areas, friendly international atmosphere

Just the name *Curaçao*—derived from the Portuguese word for the heart—speaks of romance. Add to that a historic capital city with tiny twinkling lights and picturesque European-style structures, fine cuisine from around the globe, tranquil beaches and rugged coastline, and you have all the ingredients for a romantic getaway.

Curaçao is part of the Netherlands Antilles, along with the islands of Sint Maarten, Bonaire, Saba, and St. Eustatius. The Netherlands Antilles, the island of Aruba, and Holland comprise the Kingdom of the Netherlands. Ruled by a governor appointed by the Queen, each island has autonomy on domestic affairs. Curaçao is the capital of the Netherlands Antilles, and here you will find most of the governmental, financial, and industrial positions.

Tucked into the far southern reaches of the Caribbean, less than 40 miles from the coast of South America, Curaçao is very much an international destination. Dutch is the official language, and you will hear many Dutch-speaking vacationers. Many South Americans also enjoy the island where most residents speak Spanish. We found that most Curaçao residents speak an amazing total of five languages: Dutch, Spanish, English, Papiamento, and either French or German.

Papiamento is the local language spoken on the streets, a veritable cocktail of tongues. Spanish, Portuguese, French, Dutch, Indian, English, and some African dialects combine to form the lingua franca of the Netherlands Antilles. Even between the islands the language varies slightly, each with its own slang and accent. (Ask a Curaçaoan, and he will tell you that in Bonaire they talk with a sing-song accent.)

That ease with multiple languages seems to translate into a comfort with many nationalities. Over 70 nationalities are represented on the island and, with such a true melting pot on this 184-square-mile piece of land, there is a true welcoming spirit for tourists, wherever their homeland. When Curaçaoans says "Bon Bini," they mean welcome in any language.

A Little History

Discovered by the Spanish in the late 15th century, Curaçao became a Dutch territory in the mid-17th century. England tried to rule the island and did briefly, but it was returned to the Dutch by the Treaty of Paris in 1815. Since 1954 the island has been the capital of the Netherlands Antilles, part of the Kingdom of the Netherlands.

Compass Points

Some say the island of Curaçao looks like a bikini top, pinched in the center. On one side lies the capital of Willemstad, by Caribbean standards a major metropolitan area with a harbor consistently rated about the fifth busiest in the world. This truly international city boasts streets lined with Dutch-style architecture as colorful as a candy store.

The city is divided into two sides: Punda, the original settlement, and Otrabanda, literally the "other side." Both sport picturesque harborfront buildings, and are connected by the largest bridge in the Caribbean, a free ferry, and the Queen Emma Pontoon Bridge for pedestrians, locally known as the "Swinging Old Lady" because of the way it moves out of the way for harbor traffic.

Beyond Willemstad, Curaçao becomes a countryside dotted with tall cacti and trimmed with windswept and tranquil coastlines. The Atlantic shoreline of the island is rugged and wild, with pounding surf, shady sea caves where you can steal a kiss, and evidence of past volcanic action. Swimming is prohibited in the dangerous waters, but lovers will find plenty of calm waters along the placid Caribbean side of the island.

Just the Facts

Getting There

Curaçao International Airport lies just minutes from Willemstad and nearby resort hotels. American Airlines serves the island from Miami, and ALM arrives from Atlanta twice weekly. Air Aruba flies from Newark daily, Tampa four times a week, and Baltimore three times weekly. Guyana Airways offers service from NY-JFK twice weekly.

Departure tax is US $12.50 per person.

Entry Requirements

U.S. and Canadian citizens need to offer proof of citizenship in the form of a passport or a birth certificate and a photo ID. Travelers also need to show a continuing or return ticket.

Getting Around

For most properties, rental jeeps are the best option. Hertz, Avis, Budget, National, Dollar, and other firms offer rentals.

Taxis are widely available, but they are not inexpensive. In downtown Willemstad, you can ride the trolley bus for stops in town as well as the Princess Beach Hotel and the Seaquarium. Fare is US $0.56.

When traveling in the downtown Punda area, if you have questions or need directions, look for burgundy-suited men and women, members of the Curaçao Hospitality Service. Stationed throughout the shopping area, these friendly assistants provide help in many languages.

For More Information

Call the Curaçao Tourist Board at (800) 3-CURAÇAO. Once you're on the island, stop by the Visitors Information Booth at the airport (just past customs) for brochures and maps.

For the Marriage-Minded

Curaçao requires a two-day residency before applying for a marriage license, after which there is a 14-day waiting period. A passport, birth certificate, travel documents, and divorce papers (if applicable) are necessary. At present time, the marriage license fee is US $167.

Romantic Resorts

Lion's Dive Hotel and Marina, (800) 223-9815, (011) 599-9-618100; fax (011) 599-9-618200. $

- beachfront
- fine and casual dining
- dive shop

Especially popular with divers, this hotel has everything scuba enthusiasts could want: a five-star dive center, dive courses, snorkel and boat dive trips, rentals, and a complete dive shop. Its 72 guest rooms are all air-conditioned, each with a balcony or a patio. The hotel also operates a shuttle to Willemstad and offers free admission to Seaquarium.

Princess Beach Resort and Casino, (800) 327-3286, (011) 599-9-367888; fax (011) 599-9-614131. $$

- beachfront
- casual and fine dining
- casino
- freshwater pools
- shopping arcade
- children's program
- watersports, dive shop

Located near the Seaquarium, this resort is nestled along a wide stretch of beach protected by a man-made breakwater. The three-story resort features rooms in Caribbean colors, as well as three restaurants, four bars, and a casino.

Sonesta Beach Hotel and Casino, (800) 766-3782, (011) 599-9-368800; fax (011) 599-9-627502. $$

- beachfront
- freshwater pool, hot tub

- casino
- children's program
- casual and fine dining
- tennis, watersports
- shopping

This elegant hotel holds the position as the island's best, stretched along a wide swath of beach a short ride from either the airport or the city. Built in 1992, the 248-room property is designed in the style of Netherlands Antilles architecture. Cool lemon walls contrast with chile pepper-colored roofs, all framed by stately palms. The property is a veritable oasis on this dry island, just down the beach from the desalinization plant (the world's largest), where unsightly smokestacks distract slightly from the view but don't interfere with the enjoyment of this romantic property.

We especially liked the low-rise, open-air quality of this resort, starting with the lobby, where you arrive to a view over a cascading fountain across a palm-shaded pool and out to the sea. Every room includes either a balcony or patio (ask for a ground floor room for direct beach access) and at least a partial view of the ocean.

Dining

With its numerous nationalities, Curaçao enjoys many cuisines. Indonesian *rijsttafel* or rice table is especially popular. Local specialties include *stoba di cabrito* (goat stew), fried plantains, seafood, and conch or *karko*. Amstel beer, Dutch gin, and local rums such as San Pablo are choice drinks. For an after-dinner liqueur, try Senior Curaçao's Blue Curaçao (it comes in several other colors as well). Made from a bitter orange grown on the island, the choice of flavors includes orange, chocolate, rum raisin, and coffee.

Fort Nassau (Otrabanda), Willemstad. $$$

The most romantic night view in Willemstad is from this historic fort. Dine indoors or out on continental dishes at your table lit by candlelight. Enjoy dishes as varied as saltimbocca (veal cutlets with sage and prosciutto) or fried sunfish breaded with pecan nuts, served with a choice of excellent soups such as mustard or rich coconut.

Landhuis, Brievengat, Banda Riba. $$$

Rijsttafel, an Indonesian feast, is served in this historic country house. Diners sit outdoors beneath a web of tiny lights strung in the trees. Come with a big appetite to this spread. The meal begins with an appetizer of egg rolls followed by main courses such as *sateh ajam* (skewered chicken covered with a spicy peanut-flavored sauce), *kerrie djawa* (beef curry), *daging ketjap* (beef braised in soy and ginger sauce), and *telor* (egg in spiced coconut sauce). You can work off the calories on the dance floor, then return the next day to tour the *landhuis* which is furnished with period antiques.

Mambo Bar, Seaquarium Beach. $

Casual fun is the order of the day at this beachside joint, where the tables are located right on the sand. Choose from pasta dishes or look for lighter dishes like tuna, shrimp, and crab on a baguette.

Portofino, Sonesta Beach Resort and Casino Curaçao. $$$

One of very few Italian restaurants on the island, this elegant eatery features Northern Italian cuisine including cheese ravioli with a tomato basil Alfredo sauce, double-baked tortellini, grilled swordfish, salmon filet, and garlic-roasted shrimp in balsamic vinegar.

Old Market, Breede Straat (Punda), Willemstad. $

Don't expect anything fancy at this cafeteria called Grandma's Kitchen by many locals. Located behind the post office and within walking distance of the Punda's shops, this is where residents come for Curaçaoan dishes like *kadushi* (cactus) soup, *steak di weja,* and *giambo* (gumbo). Diners line up and order from the cooks, who ladle generous helpings out of gargantuan pots. Wash it down with a glass of cold Amstel. Open for lunch only, daily except Sundays.

Romantic Activities

Independent travelers love Curaçao: it's easy to get around and it's simple to move beyond the resort to experience the stream of everyday life. This is an island without hasslers or pushy vendors, a place where the two of you can walk hand-in-hand along the streets, dine at sidewalk cafes, and be greeted by friendly Curaçaoans.

Start with a visit to **Willemstad**, a historic city that bustles with activity but takes a slow pace in its shopping district. Here you can take a guided tour aboard an open-air trolley or a self-guided walk for a look at **Fort Amsterdam**. And you can't miss the historic harbor-side shops, as colorful as Easter eggs.

Stroll through the streets and alleyways, then walk across the **Wilhelmina Bridge** to the **Floating Market**, one of Willemstad's most colorful sites. Here Venezuelans sell fresh fish and vegetables (a real commodity on an island without much agriculture). Stroll along the waterway booths and buy exotic tropical fruits or watch fishermen cleaning their catch for a buyer. Behind the stalls, colorful schooners make an excellent photo.

While you're in the city, make time for a visit to **Seaquarium**, one of the Caribbean's finest marine exhibits. Along with tanks of local fish, coral, and sponges, the aquarium has several outdoor tanks with larger species—including sharks, sea turtles, and stingrays. Divers and would-be divers can take a dip here and feed the sharks through holes in an underwater Plexiglas wall. Complete instruction and equipment are provided. For those who want a drier look at these toothy denizens, just walk down into the **Seaquarium Explorer**, a semi-submarine parked by the shark tank. The Seaquarium has been the site of an underwater wedding as well as four deep-sea proposals. Divers popped the question by writing on underwater clipboards.

After Seaquarium have a dip at **Seaquarium Beach**, a full-service beach with watersports, restaurant, bar, and plenty of action. There's a small admission charge. This is the beach where Curaçaoans and visitors come to see and be seen, and topless bathing is popular. Waters as calm as a lake make swimming inside the breakwaters easy and safe.

Curaçao has over three dozen additional beaches from which to choose, all located on the Caribbean side of the island. Some of the most popular are **Knip Bay** and **Barbara Beach**.

Curaçao may be a dry island, but you will find plenty of other natural attractions. One of the most romantic is **Boca Tabla**, a sea cave carved by pounding Atlantic waves. Located on the road to Westpoint, the cave is a short walk off the road (wear sturdy shoes!) but it rewards lovers with one of the region's most breathtaking sights. Kneeling in the darkness of the sea cave, you will watch the surge of crystal blue waves as they come within feet of you, roaring into the cave and back out to sea. Above the cave, walk on the volcanic rock (stay on the pebble path) to the seaside cliffs for excellent photos.

If you want to venture into a cavern, take a tour of **Hato Caves**, open daily except Monday. Guided tours take the two of you through the stalactite- and stalagmite-filled rooms, several of which include pools or waterfalls.

Nature lovers should save time for a visit to **Christoffel National Park**, on the western end of the island. This wildlife preserve includes the island's highest point and 20 miles of trails that wind through local flora and fauna. Don't be surprised to see some native wildlife in the park; it is home to iguanas, donkeys, small deer, rabbits, and many bird species.

Curaçao is also home to many man-made attractions. The *cunucu* or countryside is dotted with *landhaisen* (landhouses) where you can tour, dine, or enjoy a cold brew. Stop by **Landhuis Jan Kock**, built in 1650 (and supposedly haunted) for a cold Amstel. If you drop by on a Sunday, enjoy Dutch-style pancakes.

For a look at all these attractions, consider an island tour. Tours can be booked through hotel desks or call Taber Tours, 011-599-9-376637, for a rundown of their packages which include east and west end tours, Hato Cave tour, jeep safari, and sailing and sunset cruises.

Shopping

Curaçao's shopping opportunities keep many travelers busy, especially in downtown Willemstad. The prime shopping district is in Punda, just across the floating bridge. Cross the bridge and continue up Breede Straat, where you will find most of the shops and boutiques aimed at vacationers, along with some charming sidewalk cafes.

The most obvious shop in Punda is the J. L. Penha and Sons department store, housed in a beautiful lemon-tinted colonial building constructed in 1708. You will find just about everything in this department store, from perfumes to fine jewelry to collectibles.

Down Breede Straat, shops such as Sunny Caribbee (Caribbean collectibles, spices, and crafts), La Perla (fine clothing), Little Holland (sportwear, linens, cigars), Little Switzerland (fine jewelry, china, watches), and more offer high-ticket items. The Gomezplein plaza, a couple of blocks up from the bridge, offers picturesque boutiques and a relaxed shopping atmosphere.

For lower-priced purchases, take a turn off Breede Straat and enjoy a stroll down Heeren Straat or Keuken Straat. These streets are filled with electronics, inexpensive clothing, and housewares. It's a fun atmosphere where you will have a chance to mix with residents.

These streets end at the water, where you will find an entirely different shopping opportunity: the Floating Market. Schooners from Venezuela bring exotic fruits, vegetables, spices, and plants to this open-air market that's very popular with older residents. To reach the Floating Market, walk across the bridge at Columbus Straat. We highly recommend the market to enjoy a slice of island life and, for photographers, to capture one of Curaçao's most colorful sights.

You are allowed to return to the United States with $600 worth of purchases (per person) before paying duty.

Festivals

Curaçao parties with special events such as Carnival, which starts New Year's Day and comes to a fevered pitch the day before Ash Wednesday. Every month, Willemstad throws a giant block party called the Ban Tupa Street Fair with a rollicking island spirit.

Nightlife

Discos, live music, and casinos offer nightlife to restless visitors, especially in the Willemstad area and in the major hotels. The Sonesta Casino offers one room of slots and table action.

The Papaya Plantation House is open Thursday and Friday nights with an open-air barbecue and music by local bands.

OUR IMPRESSIONS OF CURAÇAO

- excellent for independent travelers
- wonderful island atmosphere
- friendly reception for tourists from around the world
- does not offer tropical beauty often associated with the Caribbean

ROMANCE ON CURAÇAO

- rent a jeep and explore the countryside or *cunucu*
- watch the lights come out in Willemstad at twilight
- kiss in a misty sea cave on the Atlantic shore

$\mathcal{D}$ominican Republic

Language	Spanish
Currency	Dominican Republic peso (exchange rate varies about US $1 = RD $12.5)
Population	7.5 million
Driving	right
Best romantic features	pulsating music and nightlife, economical

For lovers on a tight budget, the Dominican Republic or Dominicana (not to be confused with Dominica, a somewhat remote island known for its eco-tourism) is an excellent choice. The Dominican Republic (DR) has long been heralded as one of the least expensive Caribbean destinations; some sources estimate it to be as much as 50 to 70 percent cheaper than its neighbors. Except such resorts as Casa de Campo where jetsetters come to relax (and where Michael Jackson and Lisa Marie Presley wed), the island boasts inexpensive prices and bargain resorts. With the favorable exchange rate, Americans can enjoy a stay on the north shore for under US $100 per person per day, including all meals, tips, and watersports.

Although values abound on this festive island, you need not worry that you will be shortchanged in beauty or fun. The Dominican Republic has ancient history, mountain-covered vistas, and a party atmosphere that's as fun as any found throughout the Caribbean.

Well known to European travelers, the Dominican Republic's tumultuous neighbor, Haiti, may be more familiar to Americans. To be honest, news accounts of trouble in Haiti almost made us reconsider our trip to the Dominican Republic. But we soon discovered that, even though the two nations share the same island, Hispaniola, geography is about all that unites Haiti and the Dominican Republic. The second-largest Caribbean island (only Cuba is larger), Hispaniola is a land of rugged mountains, palm-lined beaches, and two diverse cultures. Haitians speak French; Dominicans, Spanish. The leadership of Haiti has frequently been torn by assassinations and military takeovers while the citizens of the Dominican Republic enjoy the relative tranquility of a stable, freely elected government. And while life has become a struggle for Haitians, Dominican Republic days are far more carefree, with plenty of time to dance to the throbbing sounds of merengue and to enjoy a glass of "Dominicana gasolina," the nickname for locally produced rum.

Many resorts are found on the Dominican Republic's north side, a region dubbed the Amber Coast. The Dominican Republic boasts the fastest-growing tourism business in the Caribbean, with over two million visitors a year. Over 60 percent of the vacationers are European.

For visitors, the two primary destinations in DR are Puerto Plata on the island's north shore, and the capital city, Santo Domingo, on the southern coast.

About 20 minutes from Puerto Plata's La Union international airport lies the resort area of Playa Dorada. This horseshoe-shaped complex contains over a dozen resorts, numerous restaurants, a casino, a two-story shopping mall, and a Robert Trent Jones-designed 18-hole golf course, all tucked between the backdrop of the lush mountains and the palm-lined Atlantic beach. The sea here is choppier than its Caribbean counterpart on the south shore, but a gentle breeze makes it popular with windsurfers, boogie boarders, and families that enjoy playing in the surf. Other guests are content to lie on the beaches lined with majestic palms.

Santo Domingo is located on the island's southern shore. Here history buffs will find a wealth of Spanish Renaissance architecture to explore. The city was the first permanent European settlement in the New World and has been honored for its cultural landmarks by a United Nations proclamation.

Near Santo Domingo is located the nation's most lavish resort: Casa de Campo, as well as a host of other first-rate vacation destinations.

A Little History

Columbus named Hispaniola ("Little Spain") following his discovery of it on his first voyage in 1492. His son, Diego, became the first Spanish viceroy of the West Indies and oversaw the construction of Santo Domingo as the capital of Spain in the New World. Fueled by the riches of the colony's gold mines, Santo Domingo's influence lasted until gold production dropped a century later. French pirates successfully colonized the western end of the island and by 1700, Hispaniola had been divided between the French and Spanish. Another 150 years passed with the two nations sparring over the island. Ever since the current configuration of Hispaniola between Haiti and the DR, politics in the DR has remained somewhat unstable. The northern city of Puerto Plata, founded by Nicholas de Ovando in 1504, is also rich with history.

Compass Points

The island of Hispaniola is the second largest in the Caribbean; the Dominican Republic occupies the eastern two thirds. Haiti occupies the western portion. The Dominican Republic is 235 miles long and 165 miles wide at its largest point. Much of the country is mountainous; the remainder is fertile farmland and sandy beaches. Pico Duarte is the tallest peak in the Caribbean soaring 10,417 feet. Since the DR is such a large country, it offers more varied destinations to the traveler than do small islands. It boasts the most hotels in the Caribbean, six international airports, and several large tourist zones.

Just the Facts

Getting There

Puerto Plata is served by American and Continental Airlines. Santo Domingo is served by American and Dominicana Airlines. Casa de Campo boasts its own air service from American Airlines, the only resort that can make that claim.

Entry Requirements

U.S. citizens should bring proof of citizenship, either a passport or an official birth certificate with photo ID.

Upon departure, vacationers are required to pay a departure tax of US $10 per person.

Getting Around

With 12,000 miles of roads, getting around the Dominican Republic can be achieved many different ways. You can rent a car from a major agency at the airports and in the larger cities. You will need your driver's license and a major credit card. You will also need good reflexes to deal with the frequent displays of driving machismo you will encounter. One fortunate thing: driving is (more or less) on the right side. Taxis are a safer bet, but are fairly expensive and are unmetered; negotiate a price before you embark. A variety of buses are available from luxury lines to those with few creature comforts. The most basic transportation in the DR are the *guaguas*, unregulated taxi/buses which are usually crowded with locals. If you speak Spanish, riding the guaguas can be a good way to get the lowdown on what's happening.

For More Information

For brochures on Dominican Republic attractions, call the Tourist Information Center at (800) 752-1151 on weekdays from 8:00 to 5:00, eastern standard time.

For the Marriage-Minded

A marriage license is not required to get married in the Dominican Republic. You will need to bring a notarized letter from someone who knows you both stating that you are both presently single and of good moral character.

Upon arrival in the Dominican Republic, present this letter with your birth certificates and any divorce decrees (if applicable) or death certificates (if widowed) to the County Clerk. A civil ceremony can be arranged in the office. For more information, call the Dominican Republic Tourist Office, (800) 752-1151, or the Dominican Republic Consulate office in New York, (212) 575-4966.

Romantic Resorts

Casa de Campo, (800) 223-6620, (809) 523-3333;
fax (809) 523-8548. $$

- golf, tennis
- horseback riding
- polo
- fine and casual dining
- pools

The Dominican Republic's most lavish resort is also one of the most activity-oriented in the Caribbean. You name it, you can do it at the plush resort sprawled over 7,000 acres. Located in La Romana, American Airlines offers direct flights into Casa de Campo's own airport.

Jack Tar Village, Puerto Plata, (800) 999-9182, (809) 320-3800;
fax (809) 320-4161. $

- beachfront
- all-inclusive
- casino
- golf, tennis, watersports
- children's program

This resort is easy on the pocketbook and still offers couples plenty of activity. The rooms here are separated from the beach by the golf course, but some days you hear the waves rolling in on this Atlantic side, which is too rough for snorkeling but nice for a romp in the surf.

Melia Bavaro, (800) 33-MELIA, (809) 221-2311;
fax (809) 286-5427. $$

- beachside
- pool
- shopping arcade
- fine and casual dining
- disco

Located in Punta Cana on the eastern end of the island, this 57-acre resort offers rooms in two-story bungalows and a two-story hotel for a total of nearly 600 rooms.

Renaissance Jarangua Hotel and Casino, Santo Domingo,
(800) 331-3542, (809) 221-2222; fax (809) 686-0528. $$

- spa
- tennis
- pool
- disco, showroom
- fine and casual dining

Pamper yourself at The Wellness Place, a European-style spa that epito-
mizes the elegant body holiday that this resort offers. After that, how
about a walk through tropical gardens, beside beautiful lagoons and
cascading waterfalls? Finish off the day with a spin around the disco
floor or a lavish show.

Shopping

The most unique purchase in the Dominican Republic is amber, avail-
able at gift shops along the north coast. Amber prices vary from
US $3 for small earrings to US $200 for a mosquito encased in amber
to several hundred dollars for large, chunky necklaces or amber set in
gold. The color of the amber affects the price as well. Generally the pale
blonde amber is the least expensive.

Amber resembles plastic, so avoid buying from street vendors and
check your item before purchasing. Amber possesses a slight electro-
magnetic charge, so genuine amber, when rubbed on a piece of cloth,
should attract particles. Better stores, such as the Amber Museum
Shop, have an ultraviolet light for testing. Genuine pieces will glow
under the light. Also, amber will float in salt water while plastic
will sink.

Other popular souvenirs are Brugal rum (US $3 to $4 per liter),
Dominican cigars, merengue cassette tapes, and larimar, a blue stone
similar to turquoise.

---

*D*o not exchange more dollars than you will spend while in the
Dominican Republic. Upon departure, you may only convert 30 per-
cent of your pesos back to dollars with proper receipts.

Dining

Casa del Rio, Altos de Chavon. $$$

Experience the 16th century re-created village of Altos de Chavon at this romantic restaurant. Call (809) 523-3333 for reservations; long pants and collared shirts are required of men.

Meson de la Cava, Santo Domingo. $$

Located in a cave (yes, a cave), this romantic setting is the perfect place to enjoy an intimate dinner. Jackets are required in this restaurant, which is open daily.

Restaurante Chopin, Melia Bavaro Hotel. $$$

Here's a romantic evening for you: take a nature walk through a rain forest to an elegant, open air restaurant. Following a quiet meal, all the lights go out except for tabletop candles. Suddenly you hear the sounds of strings—members of the Symphony Orchestra of Belgrade. Floating in gondolas and circling the restaurant by waterway, the musicians play classical songs accompanied by a show of lights beneath the trees. Truly magical.

Festivals

The vast majority of the population of the DR is Roman Catholic, and many of the national festivals are religious in nature. Carnival begins the week before Independence Day, February 27. Christmas festival begins in early December and ends on Epiphany Day, January 6. Of a more secular nature, the Merengue Festival celebrates the national music of the DR with band performances during the third week of July in Santo Domingo and the second week of October in Puerto Plata. The Puerto Plata Cultural Festival highlights the arts, crafts, and music of the northern region. It is usually held in late January and early February. In addition, many of the towns of the DR commemorate their patron saint's day with a large celebration. The dates of these festivals vary from town to town. Being in an area during a celebration can provide added color and fun to your vacation. One problem: many businesses close during festivals and this can be frustrating if you are caught unawares. It's best to check the dates with a local tourist board before you arrive, just to make sure.

Romantic Activities

Look for amber-encased mosquitoes, termites, ants, fern, cockroaches, and even a tiny lizard, at the **Amber Museum** in Puerto Plata. This Caribbean nation is one of only a few sites on the globe where amber is found. The popularity of *Jurassic Park*, where fiction gave scientists the ability to use DNA found in the mosquito blood to spawn dinosaurs, brings visitors flocking to this museum on the north shore of the island.

Dating back to the 16th century, the **Fortaleza San Felipe** still stands guard over the city and the harbor. Built by the Spaniards to protect the city from pirates, in this century it was used as a prison. The doors within the fort are only four feet tall, built to slow would-be attackers (and keeping tourists alert). The fort includes a small museum with a collection of period weapons and cannonballs.

Another fort stands at the top of **Pico Isabel de Torres**, one of the highest points in the Dominican Republic. The dome-shaped fortress is topped with a statue of Christ similar to one that overlooks Rio de Janeiro.

Today the fortress is a gift shop for visitors who take the cablecar ride to the summit. The 18-person car travels up the mountain daily except Wednesday. Be warned that lines to board the cars can be long.

The ride up the mountain is slow, but the view from the summit makes it worth the wait. Through a gentle mist you look down on **Puerto Plata**, so named for its "silver port," making it easy to see why Christopher Columbus wrote back to Queen Isabella, "This is the most beautiful land that human eyes have seen."

When we toured the mountain, our guide pointed west in the direction of Haiti and explained why the neighbor that shares one third of this island has had so many difficulties. "In Haiti, they have more people than land." He gestured out over the Dominican mountains, green with vegetation and devoid of human habitation. "We have more land than we have people."

The steep mountainsides are used for growing coffee, and the flatlands along the Amber Coast are rich with sugar cane. It is used in the production of another amber-colored product, this one produced at the **Brugal Rum Factory**. Open weekdays, the factory takes visitors through the process of making 9,000 bottles of rum daily, 95 percent of which stay on the island.

In Santo Domingo, historic attractions fill the Colonial Zone. Tour sites such as the **Catedral Santa Maria la Menor**, the first cathedral in the Americas and, according to some historians, final resting site of Christopher Columbus.

At Casa de Campo, **Altos de Chavon** is well worth a visit. This romantic recreation of a 16th century art colony, complete with Spanish wrought ironwork and hushed courtyards, speaks of colonial style in a way no museum ever could.

OUR IMPRESSIONS OF THE DOMINICAN REPUBLIC

- excellent economic choice
- good variety of vacation experiences
- some language difficulties beyond the resort areas

ROMANCE IN THE DOMINICAN REPUBLIC

- hop waves on the Amber Coast
- view Puerto Plata from atop Pico Isabel de Torres
- stroll hand-in-hand in historic Santo Domingo

$\mathcal{J}$amaica

Language	English
Currency	Jamaican dollar (US $1 = J$34.5; rate fluctuates); U.S. dollar accepted
Population	2.5 million
Driving	left
Best romantic features	friendly atmosphere, live music, natural beauty

For us, Jamaica means romance. Maybe it's the mountains covered in lush tropical vegetation. Maybe it's the plush resorts where couples are welcomed in an atmosphere that promotes romance. Or the people, who make visitors feel like they are returning home, a home where hummingbirds dart from bloom to bloom, where waters teeming with colorful marine life lie just steps from your room, where the island's own music makes nights pulsate with a tropical beat.

Jamaica was one of our first Caribbean destinations, and so, for us, a trip back to this island is indeed a homecoming. We try to make time for a meal at our favorite jerk stand, a stop by our favorite souvenir stand, a bamboo hut painted in Rastafarian colors and, as we drive the sometimes bumpy roads filled with wild drivers, we pass by many of our favorite resorts and restaurants, and relive romantic times we've shared in Jamaica over the last decade.

We have to admit, however, that Jamaica is not for everyone. Many travelers, including some fellow travel writers, prefer to skip this island because of the problems that inevitably reveal themselves even to the casual traveler. Drugs are a problem on this island, and you will be hassled by ganja-selling entrepreneurs. Although the resorts restrict their grounds and beaches above the high water line to guests and employees only, when you step outside the boundaries of the resort, be prepared to be approached. "I have something special for you" is a frequently used line that you can ward off with a friendly but firm "No, thank you."

In general, we have found that Jamaica has some of the friendliest inhabitants of the Caribbean. The service, even in all-inclusive resorts where tips are not even a question, is unsurpassable. Taxi drivers are proud to tell you about the island, and we've even had drivers jump out of the car and pick herbs and plants along the route to tell us more about their uses in the Jamaican household.

Jamaica's motto is "Out of Many, One People" and a quick look around the island confirms its multinational history. The predominately African heritage has mixed with that of South America, India, China, and Europe. You will also see a mixture of city and country life throughout the nation. In Montego Bay, trade with the rest of the world takes place in modern office buildings. Out on the roads that wind their way through the countryside, trade takes place from push carts made of discarded automobile parts, and transportation for many residents means walking, often with a load balanced on their heads with the grace of ballet dancers.

Along those roads you will see the diversity of Jamaican life. Around one bend lies a palatial home; around another corner a shanty without doors or windows. Towns are frenetic centers of activity, filled with pedestrians, street vendors, colorful fruit markets, and neighbors who take time to visit friends as they go about their day's duties. The roads are rushed and filled with endless honking given, not out of anger, but as a warning, a hello, or just for the heck of it. Jamaicans often stop their vehicles to talk to someone in the oncoming lane; others politely wait for the conversation to end.

As you wind through the communities in the Jamaican countryside, you will notice many churches in every small town. Religion is an important part of Jamaican life. The Church of Jamaica, formerly the Church of England, has the largest following. Methodists, Baptists, Presbyterians, Roman Catholics, Seventh Day Adventists, Christian Scientists, and other groups also have significant memberships. Rastafarianism, the religion that believes in the divinity of the late Haile Selassie, emperor of Ethiopia, is also practiced. You will see many

dreadlocked Jamaicans (usually wearing crocheted tams) who are prac-
titioners of this religion which mandates vegetarianism, a strict code
of peace, and, the best known facet of the religion, the smoking of
ganja or marijuana.

Jamaica's diversity comes from its visitors as well, guests from
around the globe that make this tropical island home for a short while.
Some of those visitors have become residents, most notably Errol
Flynn, Ian Fleming, and Noel Coward. Flynn came to the island in
the 1940s and remained until his death in 1960. The actor hit upon the
idea of putting tourists on bamboo rafts on the Rio Grande, which
today remains one of the most romantic rides in the Caribbean.
Fleming, creator of the James Bond series, wrote from his home named
"Goldeneye," located in Oracabessa near Ocho Rios. Today the home
is owned by Chris Blackwell, founder of Island Records. At about the
same period, Noel Coward arrived on the island, building a home
named "Firefly" near Port Maria.

With such a group of stellar residents, it is not surprising that
the island has always been a favorite with Hollywood movie pro-
ducers. Some films produced here include *20,000 Leagues Under the
Sea, Dr. No, The Harder They Come, Papillon, Live and Let Die,
Club Paradise, Clara's Heart, Cocktail, Wide Sargasso Sea,* and, of
course, *Cool Runnings,* the story of Jamaica's legendary Olympic
bobsled team.

A Little History

The Caribbean's third-largest island was visited by Christopher Columbus in 1494 on his second voyage to the New World. When the Spanish arrived in Jamaica, it was the point of no return. The Arawak
Indians, inventors of the hammock, welcomed the visitors, but were, in
return, executed or taken as slaves. Before all the Arawaks were killed,
however, they did pass along the name of this island: Xaymaca, or "land
of wood and water."

The Spanish lost the island in 1655 to the English. Soon slavery
increased as sugar became a booming industry.

In 1692, an earthquake struck the city of Port Royal, which was
located on a peninsula near Kingston. The entire city was lost to the
sea, and today efforts are underway to recover artifacts of what had
been termed "the richest, wickedest city in Christendom."

During these years, the English tried to tame an area of the island in the Blue Mountains that they nicknamed "the land of look behind" because of the necessity that soldiers ride two to a horse, one looking forward and one backward. Those soldiers feared an attack by the Maroons, descendants of slaves who had escaped from the Spanish and lived in the mountains. In 1739, the British gave the Maroons autonomy, and even today they retain a separateness from Jamaican authority.

In 1834, slavery was abolished although the sugar industry continued. Later it was joined by the banana industry and by the turn of the century, visitors began to arrive aboard those banana boats. The tourism business grew to become Jamaica's largest.

Jamaica has been an independent nation since 1962.

Compass Points

Because of its size, over 4,000 square miles, Jamaica has a little bit of everything: rivers, mountains, plains, forests, caves, and, of course, a beautiful coastline.

The most mountainous area is the eastern end, home of the Blue Mountains. This is the most rugged, unsettled region of the country, the home of the island's famous Blue Mountain Coffee as well as the world's second-largest butterfly, the *Papilio homerus*. With peaks that top 7,500 feet above sea level, visitors can find themselves grabbing for a jacket.

The mountains run like a backbone down the island's center from east to west, and along the journey they create a quiltwork of 160 rivers and cascading waterfalls.

Jamaica is a patchwork of communities. The capital city is Kingston on the south shore, a metropolitan area that is visited primarily for business rather than pleasure. The resort communities lie on the north shore. Quiet Port Antonio, once a hideaway for Hollywood stars, lies to the east. Heading west, the garden city of Ocho Rios is a popular favorite with couples. Montego Bay or Mo Bay is the first taste most visitors have of the island as it is home of the north shore airport. To the far west, Negril was once a hippie haven, but today it's the preferred vacation spot for anyone to enjoy its laid-back atmosphere and unbeatable sunset views.

Perhaps more than any other Caribbean island except St. Lucia, Jamaica is incredibly lush and fertile. Fruits, orchids, bromeliads, hardwoods, and ferns all thrive in this rich soil and bountiful environment. Sugar remains a major product, and during the summer months don't be surprised to see fires across the island as farmers burn off the stubble of harvested crops. During this time, the air sometimes becomes heavy with smoke and burnt sugar.

Just the Facts

Getting There

Service into Montego Bay's Donald Sangster International Airport is available on American Airlines, Continental, Air Canada, USAir, Air Jamaica, and Northwest Airlines. Service is available from New York, Newark, Baltimore/Washington, Philadelphia, Atlanta, Miami, Orlando, Los Angeles, Tampa, and Toronto.

Jamaica greets over 40,000 newlyweds every year and has one of the friendliest programs for new couples. Upon arrival at the Sir Donald Sangster International Airport, honeymooners are greeted with the "Honeymoon Trail," tagged with hibiscus markers. This walkway leads to an express route through customs and immigration, and couples make their entry into Jamaica by walking through a painted archway to be adorned with "lovebeads," a necklace of red and black seeds.

On return, you will pay a Jamaican departure tax of US $13 per person.

Most cruise ships arrive in Ocho Rios or Montego Bay. Both terminals are within easy distance of the craft markets and shopping centers.

Entry Requirements

Bring your passport or proof of citizenship: a certified birth certificate or voter registration card, and a photo ID.

Getting Around

Taxis are the easiest mode of travel and can be obtained at any resort. Look for red PPV license plates; these indicate legitimate taxis. Agree on the price with the driver before you depart.

Rental cars are pricey, and are available from most major rental companies. You must be 25 years of age to rent a car and show a valid driver's license and a major credit card. The speed limit is 30 mph in town and 50 mph on the highways, but be warned: Jamaica has some wild drivers! We have often seen two cars passing an auto at the same time, creating a three-lane, one-way road out of a two-lane, two-way highway. On top of that, you will be driving on the left side of the road and dealing with roundabouts at every intersection.

If you are staying in the Montego Bay area, consider a ride on the "Soon Come Shuttle." These colorful buses are designed to take vacationers from resorts to shopping and dining areas in central MoBay for just US $1 on the central route and US $2 on the eastern route, which runs out by Half Moon and Holiday Inn SunSpree.

For More Information

Contact the Jamaican Tourist Board at 866 Second Avenue, 10th floor, New York, NY 10017, or call (800) 233-4582.

In July 1997, Jamaica will be changing its area code from 809 to 876.

For the Marriage-Minded

With its bounty of couples-only resorts, Jamaica is one of the most popular wedding sites in the Caribbean. Jamaican law makes the job simple. You can marry after just 24 hours on the island if you have applied for your license and supplied all the necessary forms including proof of citizenship (either a passport or a certified copy of the birth certificates signed by a notary public), written parental consent for those under 21 years of age, proof of divorce with the original or certified copy of the divorce decree if applicable, and copy of death certificate if a previous marriage ended in death. Blood tests are not required.

Wedding consultants at all of the major resorts can help simplify paperwork and make sure that the process goes smoothly.

Romantic Resorts

Montego Bay

Breezes Montego Bay, (800) 859-SUPER, (809) 940-1150; fax (809) 940-1160. $$

- beachfront
- all-inclusive
- for adults over 16 only
- fine and casual dining
- watersports
- tennis

Part of the Breezes line, SuperClubs' budget all-inclusives, this property has plenty of offerings to keep couples busy, and it is convenient for those who will only be enjoying a short Jamaican vacation. Like other members of the SuperClubs chain, this property offers weddings as part of the complimentary package.

Holiday Inn SunSpree, (800) HOLIDAY, (809) 953-2485; fax (809) 953-2840. $$

- beachfront
- all-inclusive
- watersports
- fine and casual dining
- freshwater pool
- children's program

Over a decade ago, we spent our honeymoon at this resort located on the outskirts of Mo Bay. At that time, it was a standard Holiday Inn, albeit one with a private white sand beach, live entertainment every night, and restaurants that introduced us to Caribbean cooking.

Today this hotel is even better. Following a major recent renovation, the 516-room Holiday Inn SunSpree Resort is now all-inclusive, offering guests a package that includes all meals, drinks, non-motorized watersports, tennis, golf, daily activities, theme parties, shopping excursions, and a Greathouse tour. If you brought the family along, the KidsSpree Vacation Club accommodates infants through teens.

Jack Tar Montego Bay, (800) 999-9182, (809) 952-4340; fax (809) 952-6633. $

- beachfront
- restaurants
- pool
- watersports

Jack Tar emphasizes an all-inclusive package that is slightly less comprehensive than its competitors but more economical. Jack Tar, the nickname for British seamen, is a chain of all-inclusive resorts with locations in Mexico, St. Kitts, the Dominican Republic, and here in Montego Bay.

Guests will find a prime North Coast beach, both buffet and seated dinners, theme nights, unlimited drinks, no tipping, complimentary massage and sauna, and an array of activities in the all-inclusive package. Some sports come with a price tag, such as scuba diving, glass bottom boat rides, jet skiing, and golf.

Round Hill Hotel and Villas, (800) 972-2159, (809) 952-5150; fax (809) 952-2505. $$$

• beachfront
• tennis
• freshwater pool
• watersports

Located eight miles west of Montego Bay, this elegant resort is "old" Jamaica, a reminder of the time when guests came with their steamer trunks, brought the latest European fashions, and stayed for weeks. Today, this is where the rich and famous come to vacation; Ralph Lauren, Paul McCartney, and the Kennedys are often spotted on the guest register at this exclusive resort.

Sandals Montego Bay, (800) SANDALS, (809) 952-5510; fax (809) 952-0816. $$

• beachfront
• all-inclusive
• couples only
• casual and fine dining
• freshwater pool
• watersports

The Sandals chain was started in 1981 by Gordon "Butch" Stewart with Sandals Montego Bay, a resort located next to the city's Donald Sangster International Airport. This location has a potential negative, but Sandals turned the airport traffic to an advantage for romantically minded guests: every time an airplane flies overhead, guests kiss their partner. With Jamaica's increasing popularity, there's a lot of smooching going on at Sandals. The kissing must be working; Sandals Montego Bay has the highest return guest rate within the chain.

Sandals Royal Jamaican, (800) SANDALS, (809) 953-2231; fax (809) 953-2788. $$

- beachfront
- all-inclusive
- couples only
- casual and fine dining
- freshwater pool
- watersports

The atmosphere at nearby Sandals Royal Caribbean is slightly less lively than its neighbor, Sandals Montego Bay. What it may lack in liveliness, it more than makes up for in lavishness. Small touches—cool towels on the beach, herbal teas in the gym, aromatic saunas, continental room service—make this resort, styled after a Jamaican plantation, truly royal.

Along with lavish grounds, mini-suites with private balconies that overlook azure waters, and public areas that blur the boundaries between indoors and outdoors, this property boasts the only offshore restaurant in Jamaica. Bali Hai serves Indonesian cuisine, prepared by an Indonesian chef, in an authentic atmosphere. Guests are ferried out to the island (which by the day doubles as a nude beach) to enjoy a multicourse meal served family style. When the two of you arrive at the restaurant, the hostess offers two wraps for you to tie around each other's waist—simultaneously. It's a fun start to a romantic evening of dining by candlelight in a setting that is exotic and elegant.

The Sandals Royal Jamaican is one of our favorite properties in the Sandals chain, both because of its very friendly staff and its stylish accommodations.

Tryall Golf, Tennis, and Beach Club, (800) 742-0498, (809) 956-5660-7; fax (809) 956-5673. $$$$

- hillside
- golf, tennis
- pools
- fine and casual dining

This 47-room, 49-villa property is one of the finest in Jamaica with rooms tucked in private villas (with pools, natch) and a traditional greathouse.

Negril

Beachcomber Club Negril, (809) 957-4170-1;
fax (809) 957-4097. $$

- beachfront
- restaurant
- freshwater pool

Especially popular with European visitors, this resort is easy on your budget—and your body. Go from your suite to the beach to a palm-thatched palapa. Guest rooms here are either one- or two-bedroom suites, each with cool white tile floors, a living room and fully equipped kitchen, and private porches or covered patios. The resort is located right in the middle of Seven Mile Beach, and we found that it was easy to move from the hotel to area restaurants and shops.

A wedding package here includes champagne, witnesses, cake, flowers, and minister.

Grand Lido, (800) 859-SUPER, (809) 957-4010-4;
fax (809) 957-4128. $$$

- beachfront
- all-inclusive
- adults only
- casual and fine dining
- freshwater pool and hot tub
- complete watersports facilities
- nude beach

Just next door to Hedonism II lies another SuperClubs resort with a completely different atmosphere. This is SuperClub's "PG-rated" resort, a study in elegance and style aimed at achievers who are looking for pampering and the highest quality service. From the marble entrance to the elegant columns, this resort is a step above a typical beachfront hotel.

Standard offerings include 24-hour room service, private room valets, and direct dial phones.

Daily lessons are offered in snorkeling, sc
skiing at Grand Lido, plus private tennis lesso
strenuous, there's the white sand beach (plus
sunbathing or satellite TV back in the room. I
pering, guests can indulge with a complimenta

Grand Lido faces the clear blue waters o
during the days when whalers cleaned their catch here), ...
M./Y. Zein. This majestic 147-foot vessel was once owned by Aristotu
Onassis, who gave the yacht to Princess Grace as a wedding present.
Today Grand Lido guests enjoy cruises and specially arranged parties
and weddings aboard that honeymoon yacht.

Hedonism II, (800) 859-SUPER, (809) 957-4200;
fax (809) 957-4289. $$

- beachfront
- all-inclusive
- adults only
- freshwater pool, two hot tubs
- complete watersports facilities
- nude beach

More than any other resort in the Caribbean, everyone asks us about Hedonism II. Maybe it's the name. Maybe it's the wild reputation for late-night revelry in the nude hot tub. Maybe it's the stories (not unfounded) of wild swingers clubs that convene at the resort every year for annual conventions.

Whatever the reason, folks are curious about this Negril all-inclusive. We were as well. We checked in. Things looked pretty normal. Nice grounds. Nice room.

Then the maid knocked on the door and delivered white sheets. But these weren't for the bed.

They were for us to wear to dinner that night.

"No sheet, no eat" is the motto of the weekly toga party at this resort known for its adults-only atmosphere. Hedonism II attracts fun-loving couples and singles over age 18 who come to this western-most point of Jamaica for a vacation of sun, sand, and something more. These guests come to leave their inhibitions behind, seeking pleasure in the form of festivities like Toga Night, buffets to tempt the most devoted calorie counters, bars that remain open until 5 A.M., and non-stop adult fun.

On Toga Night, some guests fashion traditional modest Roman wraps, but variations abound, most revealing plenty of sunburned skin. Don't be surprised to see women lining up at the buffet wearing topless micro-togas or men leaning against the bar sporting getups rarely seen outside a sumo wrestling ring. Hedonism's credo is that "a vacation should be whatever you want it to be," and for some that means a break from the cares and even the clothes of the everyday world.

Although some form of dress is required in the dining room (no need to worry about packing a dinner jacket for this resort), many guests wear only suntan oil and shades on the beach. The wide, white sand beach has room for everyone though, whether prude or nude. Half is "formal," with swimsuit required. The rest of the beach is reserved for those seeking the total tan. The nude beach also includes its own hot tub, bar and grill cabanas, volleyball and shuffleboard courts, and, soon, its own swimming pool.

With its emphasis on unlimited pleasures, you might expect guests at Hedonism to be primarily college-aged. However, the average age here is 42. Over one third of the guests are returnees, coming back year after year to partake of the food, fun, and fantasy.

Nightly shows are organized by the resort's entertainment crew. Guests and staff strut their stuff during talent night (which might include an amateur strip-tease), fly through the air during the circus show, or bend over backwards for the limbo contest.

It's in these after-dark hours when the hedonists really get busy. Following the night's beach party, reggae dance, pajama party, or the ever-popular Toga Night, guests head to a disco that flashes with a $500,000 lighting system or to the nude hot tub for late night revelry. Others hang out at the bars, open until just before the Caribbean sun peaks over the horizon at 5 A.M. (If you're staying at another Negril resort and want to see Hedonism II for yourself, you can buy an evening pass.)

Even members of the party-'til-you-drop crowd eventually head back to their rooms, which at Hedonism are comfortable but not luxurious. Twin and king-size beds are available. Rooms do not have balconies or patios, although some rooms face the beach. In keeping with the adult atmosphere, there is one special feature in the rooms: mirrored ceilings above every bed.

Negril Cabins, (800) 382-3444, (809) 957-4350;
fax (809) 957-4381. $

- across from beach
- fine and casual dining
- freshwater pool

Negril is bordered to the east by the Great Morass, a swamp-land rich with peat, a substance that was considered as a possible energy source in the 1970s when scientists studied the feasibility of mining this resource. Environmental concerns about the possibility of damaging Negril's famous Seven Mile Beach put a stop to the mining plans.

During the study of the Morass, scientists lived in cabins in Negril. Today, Negril Cabins utilizes those original structures plus several new buildings and operates as a resort for those who want to combine the luxuries of a hotel with the natural experience of camping. Visitors enjoy Swiss Family Robinson-style accommodations in cabins perched on stilts. Lush grounds are filled with indigenous Jamaican flora and fauna and dotted with colorful hummingbirds. Negril Cabins offers tours to the Royal Palms Reserve, located directly behind the property.

Inexpensive wedding packages are available which include license, minister or justice of the peace, a best man and maid of honor if needed, a Jamaican wedding cake, flowers, champagne, and dinner.

Negril Gardens, (800) 752-6824, (809) 957-4408;
fax (809) 957-4374. $

- beachfront
- casual dining
- freshwater pool

Negril Gardens is popular with European visitors, so much so, in fact, that the daily news fax is also offered in Italian.

We enjoyed a stay in one of the beachside rooms (less expensive accommodations are available across the road). Like other guests, we sunned on the hotel's stretch of Seven Mile Beach, watching the continuous procession of traffic. Hair braiders, a cappella singers, craftsmen, and more worked their way along the beachfront (although they are restricted to within a few feet of the water's edge).

Here, we enjoyed one of our most romantic Jamaican dinners. One night a week, the hotel restaurant moves the tables out onto the sand, cooks a menu of local specialties, and serves guests by candlelight. We dined in semi-dark privacy, and were serenaded by musicians who came to our table. When they asked us for a request, we asked for anything by Bob Marley. Their choice fit perfectly with the romantic evening: "One Love."

An all-inclusive package is available at this resort and it includes weddings, providing a license, marriage officer, flowers, room upgrade based on availability, wedding cake, champagne, and services of a wedding coordinator.

Poinciana Beach Resort, (800) 468-6728, (809) 957-4100; fax (809) 957-4229. $$

- beachfront
- all-inclusive
- casual and fine dining
- freshwater pools, hot tub
- watersports, dive shop
- children's program

This charming 130-room resort has something for everyone, whether you are coming here as a pair of fresh-faced newlyweds or with your family to enjoy an annual vacation and squeeze in some private time for the two of you. Owned by a Jamaican doctor, this resort offers plenty of fun for adults, supervised activities for the children, a full selection of watersports, and nightly entertainment.

Many couples choose this lush resort as a vacation hideaway (and about one a week come here to tie the knot in a beautiful tropical setting), and it's a favorite with families who make use of the complimentary children's program. Unlike most other all-inclusives on the island, Poinciana caters to all guests: young and old, married and single. They try to place families on one end of the property. Some facilities such as the Jacuzzi are for adults only.

Across the street from the resort, Anancy Family Fun and Nature Park offers miniature golf, go-karts, a carousel, displays on Jamaican history and crafts, a small boating lake, and a fishing pond for youngsters. Admission to the park is free for resort guests.

Because it evolved over the years, Poinciana has an array of guest room categories. The 90 superior-class rooms include two double or one king-size bed. Older, less pricey villa accommodations feature one or two bedrooms and a living/dining area as well as a private balcony or terrace.

Twelve suites include a living/dining area with furnished kitchenette, refrigerator and stove, a fold-out queen-size sofa or a Murphy bed, and a wrap-around balcony. Four of these suites are designated as penthouse suites, and these third-floor rooms include vaulted ceilings, in-room check in, and valet service for errands such as laundry.

Sandals Negril, (800) SANDALS, (809) 957-4216; fax (809) 957-4338. $$

- beachfront
- all-inclusive
- couples only
- fine and casual dining
- watersports
- freshwater pool

On the southern side of Hedonism II lies Sandals, a couples-only resort especially popular with honeymooners. Don't look for a nude beach here, but instead an atmosphere focused on couples in love. Within the Sandals chain, this location is especially popular with sports-conscious guests.

Swept Away, (800) 545-7937, (809) 957-4061; fax (809) 957-4060. $$$

- beachfront
- all-inclusive
- couples only
- fine and casual dining
- watersports
- freshwater pool

While some vacationers love the spring break atmosphere at certain resorts, others are looking for a quiet retreat from limbo dances and reggae lessons. That's where Swept Away comes in.

Located on Negril's famous Seven Mile Beach, Swept Away focuses on quiet relaxation for couples who are fitness and diet conscious. Sure there are the requisite beach bars and buffets, but Swept Away also boasts a beachside veggie bar with pita sandwiches, grilled chicken, and pasta salads.

Swept Away is known as one of the top sports destinations in the Caribbean. Courts for tennis, racquetball, squash, basketball, plus an Olympic-sized pool, a fully equipped gym, and aerobics classes keep visitors busy.

All work and no play does not a vacationer make, so Swept Away also emphasizes romance. The 20-acre property offers plenty of room for private walks.

Wedding packages are complimentary and include the ceremony, license, minister's fees, cake and champagne.

Xtabi, (809) 957-4336; fax (809) 957-0121. $

- cliffside
- freshwater pool
- restaurant

Located on Negril's cliffs, this 16-room resort is an inexpensive way to enjoy Jamaica's western end. Each room is housed in an octagonal rondoval, most with uninterrupted views of the sunset. Take the ladder down to the sea to snorkel or sunbathe on the flat rock decks that spill into emerald-colored water, or explore the sea caves carved along the cliff's edge. This resort is a real bargain, and its exotic atmosphere will make you feel you've stepped off the beaten path.

Ocho Rios

Braco Village Resort, (800) 654-1337, (809) 954-0010-9; fax (809) 954-0020. $$

- beachfront
- all-inclusive
- adults only
- freshwater pool
- fine and casual dining
- tennis
- watersports, diving

This new 180-room all-inclusive was constructed to resemble a Jamaican village. Hungry? Get some peanuts from the peanut seller or pineapple from the local fruit vendor. Want to shop? Stop and watch the woodcarver or the potter as they ply their trade. Ready for lunch? Drop in the sidewalk cafe.

The guest rooms continue the theme of Jamaica with Georgian architecture, gingerbread trim, citron and pink interiors, ceiling fans, and porches.

An inexpensive wedding package makes ceremonies simple and includes a champagne cocktail reception, decorations, a wedding portrait, special wedding gift, a raft trip down the Martha Brae River on a bamboo float for two, and a candlelight dinner.

Jamaica Inn, (800) 837-4608, (809) 974-2514; fax (809) 974-2449. $$$$

- beachfront
- fine dining
- pool

Enjoy an old-money atmosphere at this elegant inn that recalls the sophisticated days of Caribbean travel. This is the kind of place where jackets come out in the evening hours and afternoon fun might include a round of croquet or high tea.

Breezes at Runaway Bay, (800) 859-SUPER, (809) 973-2436; fax (809) 973-2352. $$

- beachfront
- all-inclusive
- over 16 only
- fine and casual dining
- watersports
- golf

Formerly known as Jamaica-Jamaica, this resort is especially well suited to sports-minded couples. Just across the road from the resort, golfers can enjoy a golf school or a round on the beautiful 18-hole course which includes spectacular sea views.

Couples, (800) COUPLES, (809) 975-4271; fax (809) 975-4439. $$$

- beachfront
- all-inclusive
- couples only
- freshwater pools
- nude sunbathing island

- horseback riding
- watersports
- tennis

Formerly part of the SuperClubs chain, this elegant all-inclusive has something for every couple. You can start the day with continental breakfast in bed or order something from 24-hour room service. Then head off to explore the sports offerings: scuba diving, water skiing, windsurfing, canoeing, squash, racquetball, horseback riding, the list goes on and on. The resort has professional-class tennis courts (they host, appropriately enough, the Couples Cup, a professional doubles tennis tournament every year), not to mention plenty of more leisurely pursuits: daily trips to Dunn's River Falls, shuttles into Ocho Rios for duty-free shopping, glass bottom boat reef excursions, and sunset catamaran cruises, all part of the all-inclusive package.

And, for those looking for a total tan, Couples has a small island just offshore to enjoy the tropical sun au naturel. Just catch the transfer right off the beach and head out for a day of sunning and swimming (in the sea or the pool) on the private offshore island, one complete with a full bar.

Complimentary weddings are part of the package and include the license, marriage official, flowers, two-tiered cake, sparkling wine, musical accompaniment, and use of either of two wedding gazebos.

Plantation Inn, (809) 974-5601; fax (809) 974-5912. $$

- beachfront
- watersports
- tennis
- freshwater pool
- casual and fine dining

If you've seen *Prelude to a Kiss* with Meg Ryan and Alec Baldwin, then you've seen the Plantation Inn. This 63-room hideaway, styled like an antebellum plantation mansion, has plenty of activity. An all-inclusive plan is available if the two of you might try many activities or enjoy most of your meals at the hotel.

Sandals Dunn's River, (800) SANDALS, (809) 972-1610; fax (809) 972-1611. $$

- beachfront
- all-inclusive

- couples only
- casual and fine dining
- watersports
- freshwater pool with waterfall

Sandals Dunn's River is the largest of the Jamaica hotels, a high-rise by island standards with 256 rooms. Built in Italian Renaissance style, the resort has lavish public areas, including two swim-up bars, a replica of Dunn's River Falls, four restaurants, a disco, and the Forum, used for cabaret-style shows.

Sandals Ocho Rios, (800) SANDALS, (809) 974-5691; fax (809) 974-5700. $$

- beachfront
- all-inclusive
- couples only
- casual and fine dining
- watersports
- freshwater pool

Just down the road from Sandals Dunn's River, Sandals Ocho Rios is one of the most romantic resorts in the chain, located on lavishly planted grounds that bloom with bird of paradise and buzz with the sound of hummingbirds. Sandals' founder Butch Stewart grew up on these grounds; the building used for the piano bar was once his grandparents' home.

Sans Souci Lido, (800) 859-SUPER, (809) 974-2353; fax (809) 974-2544. $$$

- beachfront
- all-inclusive
- adults only
- casual and fine dining
- swimming pool with natural mineral water
- spa
- golf, tennis
- watersports

Like Grand Lido in Negril, this property is SuperClubs' top-of-the-line all-inclusive. The two of you will be pampered from the moment you arrive with gourmet meals, 24-hour room service, a nightclub, and plenty of activity. Located on a beautiful swath of beach, the resort also has mineral springs that fill the swimming pool and Jacuzzi. (According to legend, those springs were shared by an English admiral and a Spanish maiden, and today lovers who dip in their waters will feel the power of their forbidden love. Sounds like it's worth checking out.) Elegant and sophisticated, this resort is for those ready to be pampered.

Port Antonio

Trident Villas and Hotel, (800) 482-4734, (809) 993-2605; fax (809) 993-2590. $$$

- cliffside
- casual and fine dining
- freshwater pool
- tennis
- private beach

With only 26 rooms, this intimate hotel makes visitors feel like royalty, from afternoon tea to white-glove service. Each of the rooms is decorated with antiques.

Shopping

Jamaica offers plenty of shopping—but don't expect the endless alleys of boutiques that you find in St. Thomas, Aruba, or St. Martin. In Jamaica, shopping is generally concentrated around a shopping center, in hotel gift shops, at a crafts market or, our favorite, directly from the craftspeople themselves. This island has a wealth of arts and crafts, everything from colorful paintings to folk art wood carvings, not to mention batik T-shirts and crocheted tams in Rastafarian colors (yellow, red, and green). Shopping at the roadside stands or on the beach involves negotiating the price. It's part of the fun.

Our favorite purchases are the woodcarvings, both freestanding and wall hangings of local animal life, faces, fish, and just about everything else you can imagine. The finest pieces are carved from lignum vitae, or wood of life, a pale hardwood that is so dense it won't float and was originally used to construct ship's parts. If you get a wood carving, don't forget to ask the artist to sign it for you. The craftspeople have great pride in their work and most are happy to oblige.

Shopping centers are found in most resort areas, and here you will find the finest items: fine jewelry, china, crystal, collectible figurines, watches, and more. In the shopping centers, prices are firm just like at home.

In Montego Bay, the top shopping centers are City Centre, a block-long collection of duty-free shops, Holiday Village Shopping Centre near Holiday Inn SunSpree, and the new Half Moon Shopping Village, a compendium of fine stores where you will find shops selling designer wear, fine jewelry, perfumes, resort wear, local crafts, and more.

In Negril, the Hi-Lo Shopping Center offers a good selection of souvenirs, liquor, music, and sportwear stores. The Hi-Lo grocery itself is an excellent shopping stop; pop in to purchase spices, hot sauces, liquor, and Blue Mountain coffee at prices far lower than you will see in the hotel gift shops.

Ocho Rios is home to the Taj Mahal Shopping Centre, a complex of fine duty-free shops and other stores that sell souvenir items, liquor, and Blue Mountain coffee.

One of the most popular agricultural products is Jamaican Blue Mountain coffee, considered one of the finest coffees in the world. Gift shops at the resorts and the airport sell the coffee in small burlap gift bags for about US $1 per ounce (less than half the price found in American coffee shops). You can find the coffee sold for even cheaper at local markets.

Jamaica's rums and liqueurs are popular souvenirs. Appleton and Meyer's Rum, Tia Maria coffee liqueur, and Red Stripe beer are sold throughout the island. You can return to the U.S. with 1 liter without paying duty charges.

Dining

Jamaican cuisine is some of the most flavorful in the Caribbean. These spicy dishes trace their origin back to the earliest days of the island when the Arawak Indians first barbecued meats, ones that later were seasoned by Africans who came to the island as slaves in the days of Spanish rule. In the 17th century, English influences developed the Jamaican pattie, a turnover filled with spicy meat that's a favorite lunch snack with locals. A century later, Chinese and East Indian influences made their way to Jamaica, when indentured laborers who replaced slaves after emancipation brought their own culinary talents. Today, curried dishes grace nearly every Jamaican menu, using local meats such as goat, chicken, and seafood.

For breakfast, the national dish is ackee and saltfish. Ackee is a small fruit that is harvested only when it bursts and reveals its black seeds; before that time the fruit is poisonous. Ackee is cooked and resembles (and tastes) much like scrambled eggs.

But the best single dish in Jamaica, at least for us, is jerk. The meat—pork, chicken, or fish—is marinated with a fiery mixture of spices including Scotch bonnet, a pepper that makes a jalapeño taste like a marshmallow, pimento or allspice, nutmeg, escallion, and thyme. It is all served up with even more hot sauce (use with caution!), rice and peas, and a wonderful bread called festival, similar to hush puppies. Wash it down with a cold Red Stripe. Ya, mon!

Montego Bay

Le Chalet Restaurant, 32 Gloucester Avenue. $$

This casual restaurant offers a little of everything: Jamaican, Oriental, continental, and barbecue. Free transportation is available from area hotels and villas; call 952-5240 or 952-1760.

Pork Pit, 27 Gloucester Avenue. $

Our favorite Jamaican restaurant is a simple one. Step up to the window of this Rasta-colored octagonal building, select your order from the posted signs, then take your order to a shady picnic table. The Pork Pit has some of the best jerk in Jamaica, and it's a favorite stop with locals. Order some festival bread to cool the burn of the spicy jerk.

Don't be surprised if some uninvited guests show up during your lunch; Antillean grackles roam from table to table looking for handouts. Jamaicans call these shiny black birds "kling-kling."

Town House, 16 Church Street. $$–$$$

Built in 1765, this restaurant and tavern, where brick walls are decorated with local artwork, serves up red snapper papillot, stuffed lobster, shrimp, steaks, pastas, and Jamaican dishes, including many curried entrees. Open from Monday through Saturday for lunch and daily for dinner, the restaurant offers free round-trip transportation from local hotels; call 952-2660 for pickup.

Negril

De Buss, Norman Manley Boulevard. $

Located right on Negril's main road, Norman Manley Boulevard, this restaurant is easy to find: just look for the bus. The colorful double-decker transport once starred in a Bond flick; now it takes a lead role in casual Negril dining with jerk and other local favorites. Call 957-4405 for hours.

Rick's, West End. $$–$$$

Best known as Negril's top sunset spot, Rick's is also a popular restaurant with Negril vacationers. Filet mignon, kingfish, broiled lobster, jerk chicken, coco bread pizza, and blackened chicken breast are served in the open-air dining room. Get there early if you'd like a table by the edge for the best view.

Sweet Spice, Whitehall Road. $

This traditional Jamaican restaurant is no-frills. You will be cooled by a small fan and the breeze that comes through the open doorway. Artwork on the blue-tinted walls consists of framed towels with Jamaican axioms. But Sweet Spice is the real thing, not a hotel eatery. This is a Jamaican diner with food to match. Conch steak, curried goat, barbecued chicken, curried shrimp, and curried chicken are top offerings, served with rice. Cool off with a pawpaw daiquiri or a piña colada. For hours, call 957-4621.

Ocho Rios

The Ruins, DaCosta Drive. $$–$$$.

As the name suggests, this restaurant is perched beside a waterfall. Tables sit at the base of a 40-foot cascade, a wonderfully romantic site for lunch or dinner. The menu here is diverse: Oriental specialties such as lotus lily lobster and Far Eastern chicken, Jamaican specials, and even vegetarian dishes. Reservations are suggested; call 974-2442.

Sakura Japanese Restaurant, Half Moon Village. $$$–$$$$

Proof of the many cuisines Jamaica offers, this restaurant features hibachi grill-top cooking right at your table. With flying knives, the chef will prepare a meal of seafood, steak, or chicken that's as good as the show itself. Round-trip transportation from your local hotel to the restaurant is included. Reservations are required; call 953-9686.

Port Antonio

Trident Restaurant, Trident Villas and Hotel. $$$$

If you are ready for an extra-special night out, here's the place to go. Dinners here are enjoyed by candlelight and served on fine china and crystal. Continental and Jamaican entrees are prepared by European-trained chefs at what is one of Jamaica's most elegant restaurants. Jackets are required. Call 993-2602 for reservations.

Festivals

There are always plenty of reasons to visit Jamaica; a full list of festivals gives couples even more excuses.

One of the most elegant events is the Sugar Cane Ball, held in February at Round Hill Hotel in Montego Bay. For over two decades, this formal ball has raised money for local charities.

In April, Ocho Rios and Montego Bay celebrate with Carnival. Horse lovers can enjoy the Red Stripe Horse Show and Gymkhana at Chukka Cove in Ocho Rios, an annual event that brings in top riders from Jamaica, Europe, and the United States.

Negril celebrates Carnival in May, bringing further festivity to this already fun-loving town.

Summer brings plenty of music to the island, starting with the Ocho Rios Jazz Festival in June, a week of international performers from the United States, England, France, Holland, Japan, and the Caribbean. Jazz events take place in Ocho Rios as well as Montego Bay, with jazz teas, jazz festivals on the river, jazz barbecues, and more.

The biggest music event is August's Reggae Sunsplash, recognized around the globe as the top event for reggae buffs. Now held at Chukka Cove, the two-decades-old event features performances by the top names in the world of reggae.

Following Reggae Sunsplash, Reggae Sunfest is held in Montego Bay, also featuring top performers.

Golf events start in the fall, with October's Jamaica Open Golf Tournament and the Jamaica Pepsi Pro Am Golf Tournament at Montego Bay's Wyndham Rose Hall in October, and World Championship Golf, one of the largest purses in the golf world, held in December at Tryall Golf, Tennis, and Beach Club in Montego Bay.

Romantic Activities

With its lush tropical setting, anything can be a romantic activity in Jamaica: walking from your room to the restaurant, listening to the pip of tiny tree frogs hidden in the dense foliage at night, or sitting beneath a tall cotton tree and thinking of the centuries that magnificent tree has witnessed.

But if you are looking for something a little more planned, you will find an array of diversions across the island. Golf lovers are tempted with plenty of courses to challenge even the most dedicated. The best known course, and the home of the PGA's World Championship, is the **Tryall Golf Club** in Montego Bay. Other top courses include **Half Moon Golf Course** and **Ironshore Golf and Country Club** in Montego Bay; **Runaway Bay Golf Club**, **Sandals Golf and Country Club** in Ocho Rios; and **Negril Hills Golf Club**, just southeast of downtown Negril.

If golf's not your game, how about diving? The Negril area is especially popular with excellent visibility. **Montego Bay** and **Runaway Bay**, near Ocho Rios, also offer top diving.

Ocho Rios

In Ocho Rios, the most popular activity (one that just about every cruise ship passenger and resort guest enjoys) is **Dunn's River Falls**. This spectacular waterfall is actually a series of falls that cascade from the mountains to the sea. Here you don't just view the falls, but you climb up the cascading water. Led by a sure-footed Jamaican guide (who wears everyone's cameras slung around his neck), groups work their way up the falls hand-in-hand like a human daisy chain. Be prepared to get wet and have fun, but don't expect a quiet, private getaway. This is Jamaica for the masses, and, no matter what day of the week, the masses do come. At the end of the climb, you will be deposited into a hectic market for another opportunity to buy crafts, carvings, and the ubiquitous T-shirt.

West of Ocho Rios in the town of Oracabessa, 007 fans can visit the **James Bond Beach**. Located near Ian Fleming's home, "Goldeneye," the beach has plenty of options for a day of activity: waverunners, helicopter tours, and horseback rides as well as beach bar and grill.

If you are serious about horseback riding, check out the **Chukka Cove Equestrian Centre** between Runaway Bay and Ocho Rios. Well known for its world-class polo matches, the center also offers guided horseback trips along the beach and in the mountains.

Montego Bay

Several greathouses, which once oversaw huge sugar plantations, are today notable visitor attractions. **Rose Hall** is one of the best known and is an easy afternoon visit for Montego Bay guests. This was once the home of the notorious Annie Palmer, better known as the White Witch. According to legend, Annie murdered several husbands and slave lovers. Readers who would like to know more about the tales of Rose Hall can read the novel *The White Witch of Rose Hall* and take a guided tour of the greathouse.

Eco-tourists will find plenty of nature-related attractions that lie off the beaten path. Bird lovers should make a stop at the **Rocklands Bird Sanctuary** in the village of Anchovy. This is the home of octogenarian Lisa Salmon, Jamaica's best-known amateur ornithologist. Her home is a veritable bird sanctuary filled with grassquits, saffron finches, and, most especially, hummingbirds. Through the years, Salmon and her guides have hand-fed the birds, even the tiny hummers, and today visitors can come by during the afternoons, have a seat on the home's patio, and hand-feed the regular guests of this bird diner. A host will put birdseed in your palms and tiny finches will land in your hands. You can hold a bottle of sugar water and have the fast-as-lightning hummingbirds feed just inches from your face. This is truly a once-in-a-lifetime experience that any nature lover should plan to enjoy. Visitors are invited between 3:30 and 5 P.M.

Negril

Negril visitors don't have to venture all the way to Ocho Rios to enjoy waterfalls; on this end of the island a much quieter alternative is found on Jamaica's southern reaches at **Y.S. Falls**. These spectacular waterfalls cascade in steps through a tropical forest. As spectacular (and far less crowded) as Dunn's River Falls in Ocho Rios, Y.S. is a Jamaican attraction that has remained unspoiled by hassling vendors and long lines. At the top, swimmers enjoy clear waters under a canopy of ferns.

The falls have been open to the public since the late 1980s, but this property has existed as a farm since 1684. Some say its unusual name (the shortest place name in Jamaica) came from the Gaelic word *wyess,* meaning winding or twisting. Others believe the name was formed from the initials of the farm's original two owners: John Yates and Lt. Col. Richard Scott.

Nearby in the community of Black River, enjoy the **Black River Safari Cruise**, a popular day trip for Negril vacationers looking for a little respite from sun and sand. This hour-and-a-half tour takes travelers up the Black River, at 44 miles the longest river in Jamaica. The waters here are home to snook and tarpon, some reaching as large as 200 pounds. Spear fishermen, using a snorkel, mask, and speargun, swim in the dark river (its waters stained by peat deposits) to bring in the day's catch. The fish go into the canoe, hand-hewn and burned out in a generations-old technique. Others search out tiny shrimp, sold by women in the St. Elizabeth parish along the roadside. Peppered shrimp, highly salted and spiced, are a popular snack with locals and visitors.

The biggest attraction on the Black River are the crocodiles. Once hunted, these crocodiles are now protected but remain wary. Loud talk causes the crocodile to take refuge. These reptiles can live as long as 100 years, so long that some have become known by local residents. One 15-foot-long specimen named Lester is seen nightly as he heads out to sea.

Along Seven Mile Beach, you will find plenty of chances to get out on the water aboard **sunset cruises**, usually with an open bar. During the day, catamaran trips take visitors out to small offshore cays.

For a look at the countryside the way it used to be around Negril, consider a day at **Belvedere Estate**, one of the first sugar cane plantations on the island. Located an hour from town between Negril and Montego Bay, this estate is set up as a living museum with costumed guides to show you the ruins of the 1800s greathouse, the sugar factory, and the sugar boiler where the juice of the cane is made into brown sugar. In the craft village, watch a weaver make coconut palms into baskets, talk to an herbalist about Jamaica's bountiful herbs, visit a canoe maker, and have a taste of island bread at the bakery. A traditional Jamaican lunch is included with the tour. For reservations, call 952-6001 or 957-4170.

Port Antonio

The top activity in quiet Port Antonio is a **romantic raft ride aboard a bamboo float** powered by a pole-maneuvering captain. If at all possible, take the two- to three-hour excursion down the Rio Grande; it's an experience the two of you won't forget. Call 993-2778 for reservations.

Nearby, **Boston Beach** is the place to go on the island for jerk, slow-cooked in pits.

Cool off with a dip in the **Blue Lagoon** (remember the Brooke Shields movie?). The beautiful swimming hole that's been termed "bottomless" because of its uncanny blue hue is actually a lagoon about 180 feet deep.

Nightlife

For most vacationers, nightlife is found in the resorts, most of which feature nightly shows that range from reggae performers to Super-Clubs' Elvis impersonator (don't laugh—he's good!) to island night with fire eaters, limbo dancers, and contortionists.

Those looking for more nightlife will find plenty of it. In Negril, evenings start about an hour before sunset at Rick's, the most popular sunset spot on the island. Located on the cliffs of the town's West End, this open-air restaurant and bar is a favorite with American visitors. The action starts with daredevil cliff divers who leap from the rocky crags to the aquamarine depths below, to the cheers of onlookers. As the sun begins to set, the attention turns to the west and couples look for the green flash, a natural phenomena that only occurs when the sun sets on a cloudless evening. Under the right conditions, as sunset cools into the sea, comes a momentary green sizzle on the horizon that science explains as the refraction of sunlight through the thick lens of the Earth's atmosphere. Island lore links it to romance: couples who witness the flash are guaranteed true love.

In Negril, probably the most festive of the resort areas, you can boogie down until the wee hours with a night pass at Hedonism II; call

(809) 957-4200 to reserve this popular, but pricey, night pass. A half-million-dollar disco pulsates until 5 A.M. with laser effects, flashing lights, and all kinds of music.

The top tunes in Jamaica are reggae and dancehall, a lively mix that's part rap and part reggae. One of the best places to find live music is Kaiser's, an open-air venue that has hosted some of Jamaica's top performers.

In Montego Bay, a popular night excursion is An Evening on the Great River, (809) 952-5047, held every Sunday and Thursday. With pickup at your hotel, the evening includes a boat ride up the torchlit river, an open bar, Jamaican dinner, reggae band, and a native floor show with limbo dancers.

Mo Bay is also the home of Lollypop, 953-5413, an open-air bar on Sandy Bay. This popular spot has reggae shows and Jamaica night weekly with a Jamaican buffet.

OUR IMPRESSIONS OF JAMAICA

- one of the most beautiful Caribbean islands
- excellent array of resorts for all budgets
- not the best place for independent travel because of hasslers

ROMANCE ON JAMAICA

- kiss in the shade of a centuries-old cotton tree
- climb hand-in-hand up Dunn's River Falls
- dance to a reggae beat
- float down river on a bamboo raft built for two

$\mathcal{P}$uerto Rico

Language	Spanish and English
Currency	US dollar
Population	3.56 million
Driving	right
Best romantic features	lavish hotels, casinos, shows, eco-tourism

Ready for a fiesta? Then set your course on Puerto Rico. Here, in the capital city of San Juan, you will find a pulsating atmosphere that can't be topped anywhere in the Caribbean. Casinos ring with the clink of slots; showgirls kick up their heels in lavish revues; couples out on the dance floor shake to the sounds of salsa and merengue.

Beyond the boundaries of San Juan, the sounds change to the slap of waves on the honey-colored shore or the peek of the tiny coqui (*co-kee*), a frog that's a national symbol of Puerto Rico. (It is said that the coqui can survive only on the island, so to be as Puerto Rican as a coqui is a declaration of national pride.)

Puerto Rico is an easy destination to like. It's simple to reach—just 2½ hours from Miami and under four hours from New York; there's a wide variety of attractions no matter what your interest; it's the United States while at the same time offering the intrigue of a foreign destination.

Your first introduction to Puerto Rico will probably be arrival in San Juan. This high-rise city hugs the coastline like a Caribbean version of Miami (but with casinos) and offers all the amenities you expect in a metropolitan area this size. It's so large that it's divided into several districts. Tourists typically visit Condado, Isla Verde, and Old San Juan, the historical heart of the city. Here you will find buildings so old and quaint they look more like a movie set than part of a modern down-town district.

Beyond San Juan, the city gives way to beautiful countryside rich with agriculture, over 200 miles of coastline, and a spirit that welcomes visitors with a hearty "Buenos dias."

A Little History

Puerto Rico has witnessed a rich history that started with the Taino Indians before the landing of Christopher Columbus in 1493. The explorer termed the isle San Juan because St. John the Baptist was chosen the patron saint of the island. Later, San Juan became the name of the capital city and the island Puerto Rico or "rich port."

Puerto Rico remained a Spanish territory until after the Spanish-American War in 1898 when it was ceded to the United States. Today the island has commonwealth status, although the issue of statehood has arisen in the last few years.

Compass Points

Puerto Rico is a large island, spanning 110 by 35 miles. Within those boundaries, you will find plenty of environmental diversity, from dry areas to the only tropical rain forest in the U.S. Forest Service. The Caribbean caresses the southern shoreline; along the north shore are the somewhat less calm waters of the Atlantic.

Mountains form a rugged ridge from east to west. These mountains, the Cordillera Central and the Sierra de Luquillo, loom at about 3,000 feet above sea level and ease into rolling hills before reaching the coastal plains. The rainiest area is in the northeastern mountains in the El Yunque rain forest, an area rich with tropical lushness ranging from breadfruit to mahogany trees to orchids. On the opposite end of this large island, the southwestern side sports cacti and succulents because it receives only a fraction of the rain forest's total precipitation.

Rincón, on the island's northwestern end, is the surfing capital of the Caribbean. From January through April, surfers are joined by migratory humpback whales, so even if you're not ready to hang ten the two of you can head out from Rincón on a whale-watching excursion.

Off Puerto Rico's shores, the islands of Mona, Culebra, and Vieques offer quiet getaways for those willing to take an extra hop.

Just the Facts

Getting There

Puerto Rico boasts excellent air service via the Luis Muñoz Marin International Airport in San Juan. The airport serves as the American Airlines hub for Caribbean flights. Service to San Juan is also available from the other major carriers: Carnival, Towers Air, Kiwi, Continental, USAir, United, Delta, Northwest, and TWA.

Daily nonstop service to San Juan is available from Atlanta, Baltimore, Boston, Charlotte, Chicago, Dallas, Detroit, Hartford, Miami, Nashville, Newark, New York, Orlando, Philadelphia, Raleigh-Durham, Tampa, and Washington D.C.

Getting Around

You will have many of the same options in Puerto Rico as you do at home. Rental cars from the major agencies are available from AAA, Avis, Budget, Discount, Hertz, National, Thrifty, and other companies, especially in the San Juan area. Driving is on the right and signage, while bilingual, is like that at home. However, realize that San Juan is a major metropolitan area and just as difficult to maneuver as any other city its size. The Old San Juan area is especially congested, with old, narrow streets.

Taxis are a popular choice, especially within the San Juan area. A new Taxi Turisticos program sets specified rates within certain zones. These taxis are white and bear the words Taxi Turisticos and a drawing of El Morro. These taxis are an excellent choice for first-time visitors. The drivers have received special training to serve the tourist zones. A drive from the airport to the Isla Verde area costs $8; a trip from the airport to Old San Juan runs $16.

Entry Requirements

As a U.S. commonwealth, passports are not required of American citizens. Luggage is inspected upon departure for agricultural reasons.

For More Information

Contact the Puerto Rico Tourism Company at (800) 223-6350.

For the Marriage-Minded

As part of the United States, marriage procedures in Puerto Rico are simple and require just a one-day residency period. Couples can accomplish much of the work by mail before the trip. You will need an ID card or passport, original birth certificate, and, if applicable, a divorce decree or former spouse death certificate. You will also need a health certificate reviewed by a resident practitioner in Puerto Rico, including a venereal disease blood test within the last ten days. There is a $2 stamp fee for a certified copy of the marriage license.

To obtain a wedding license, write the Department of Health, Demographic Register's Office, P.O. Box 11854, Fernandez, Juncos Station, Santurce, PR 00910, and allow two months for delivery. You can also obtain the license in person at 1913 Fernandez Juncos Avenue, Second Floor, Santurce, PR. Call (787) 728-7980 for more information.

Best Weddings of Puerto Rico, (800) 697-2904, can assist with obtaining the marriage license, finding a site, and coordinating any food, flowers, and photo needs. Fees start at $175.

Romantic Resorts

El Conquistador, (800) 468-5228, (787) 863-1000; fax (787) 860-3280. $$$

- near beach
- fine and casual dining
- golf, tennis
- private island
- casino
- watersports and dive shop

Perched atop a 300-foot cliff, this is one of the grandest resorts in the region. With 918 guest rooms, it's not the place for those looking for privacy and to get away from the crowds, but you will find just about everything else at this $250 million resort. Choose from an 18-hole championship golf course, a private marina with rental boats and charters for deep-sea fishing, scuba facilities, six swimming pools, seven tennis courts, a nightclub, casino, fitness center, salon, and luxurious shops. Not to mention a 100-acre private island, Palomina, where guests can be whisked on complimentary ferries. On secluded Palomina, couples can enjoy snorkeling, nature trails, and siestas in hammocks stretched between tall palms.

El Conquistador also offers two wedding packages, including one that features a ceremony in Palomina Island's 50-seat wedding chapel.

El San Juan Hotel and Casino, (800) 468-2818, (787) 791-1000; fax (787) 253-0178. $$$

- beachfront
- casual and fine dining
- freshwater pool
- casino

Located just minutes from the airport, this hotel could symbolize the elegance of San Juan. A lobby paneled in rich woods greets visitors, and just steps away the most elegant casino in the Caribbean offers games of chance managed by croupiers in black tie. A new cigar bar, the only one in the Caribbean, recently opened off the casino.

The pool area is beautifully landscaped with tropical gardens, the perfect place to relax after a morning of touring or shopping in San Juan.

El San Juan also offers wedding packages, and the concierge will work with couples before their stay to select services such as limousine rental, pianist, and photographer. A hotel doctor can assist with blood tests.

Hyatt Cerromar, (800) 233-1234, (787) 796-1234; fax (787) 796-4647. $$$

- beachfront
- golf, tennis, in-line skating, biking
- freshwater pool and hot tub
- complete watersports center
- windsurfing center
- casino
- casual and fine dining

The Hyatt Cerromar is for couples looking to combine the glitz of San Juan with the peacefulness of the Puerto Rico countryside. Located 22 miles from the city, this high-rise resort has just about everything lovers could want—from luxurious massages to a float along what the hotel deems the world's longest swimming pool.

The hotel works in close conjunction with its sister property, nearby Hyatt Dorado Beach. The two resorts share 1,000 acres west of San Juan, and guests enjoy reciprocal privileges at the two resorts. Connected by a free shuttle system, guest cards are honored at both resorts.

For the more adventurous, watersports are available on Cerromar's strip of beach. At the Windsurfing School and Watersports Center (Puerto Rico's only certified windsurfing school), lessons are offered by Lisa Penfield, two-time women's windsurfing champion and former member of the U.S. Olympic team. Guests learn in the reef-protected calmer waters of nearby Hyatt Dorado. These placid waters are also enjoyed by Cerromar snorkelers and ocean swimmers who arrive at the neighboring property via the free shuttle.

Hyatt Dorado Beach, (800) 233-1234, (787) 796-1234; fax (787) 796-2022. $$$

- beachfront
- casual and fine dining
- freshwater pools and hot tub
- tennis, golf
- complete watersports facilities
- windsurfing
- casino

Located on a former grapefruit and coconut plantation, the Hyatt Dorado Beach is our favorite type of Caribbean property: a low-rise hotel with easy access to the beach. Apparently this style appeals to others as well; the Hyatt Dorado Beach boasts the highest repeat visitor rate of any properties in the popular chain.

The atmosphere is open-air and elegantly casual here. The guest rooms are decorated in a West Indian style, with furniture inspired by Caribbean antiques. The most romantic accommodations are the 17 casita rooms with split-level elegance that includes a private lawn and marble shower beneath a clear skylight.

You might find that the public areas are some distance from your guest room and from the golf shop and tennis center. A complimentary shuttle transports guests between these areas every half hour, and bell-men pick up guests in golf carts anytime on request.

Two beaches include both wave action and calm pools created by a ring of boulders just offshore.

Palmas del Mar, (800) 468-3331, (787) 852-6000; fax (787) 852-2230. $$

- beachfront
- casino
- casual and fine dining
- golf
- watersports
- tennis program
- children's program

For vacationers looking to get away from the glitz of San Juan, Palmas del Mar is a good choice. Located 45 minutes from the capital city, the resort lies tucked on the Caribbean side of the island near the town of Humacao. Actually a compendium of resorts that range from standard hotel rooms to a bed and breakfast inn to luxury condominiums, Palmas is a city in itself, with a staff of over 500 employees.

Three and a half miles of groomed beach (plus another six miles of nearly deserted beach) tempt vacationers to soak up sun and sometimes rolling surf, and the sports facilities offer plenty of opportunities to stay busy. The Palmas del Mar Golf Club features a championship course designed by Gary Player with holes offering views of El Yunque rain forest, the sea, and the nearby island of Vieques. The largest tennis center in the Caribbean has classes for players of every level, and nine restaurants make sure that, with all that activity, no one stays hungry for long.

Paradores, (800) 443-0266. $–$$

- bed & breakfast inns

If you enjoy bed & breakfast inns, consider Paradores, Puerto Rico's country inns. You will find restored estate houses and haciendas in this program, which features value-priced lodging at some of the island's off-the-beaten-track destinations.

Shopping

Shopping is a major activity for Puerto Rico visitors. Duty-free shopping is found at the Luis Muñoz Marin International Airport and at factory outlet shops in Old San Juan.

If you are looking for gold and jewelry or factory outlets, check out the shops on Calle Christo and Calle Fortaleza in Old San Juan.

Homesick for an American mall? Head over to Plaza Las Americas, which claims to be the largest shopping center in the Caribbean. Here you will find over 150 shops with everything from designer clothes to fine art to fine jewelry. The mall is located in the Hato Rey region, the main business district in San Juan.

If you're looking for an island product, popular purchases are *cuatros* (small handmade guitars), *mundillo* (bobbin lace), *santos* (hand-carved religious figures), rum, and cigars.

Dining

Don't leave Puerto Rico without a taste of the island's distinct cuisine, a blend of Spanish, African, and Taino Indian elements into dishes that will have you ordering more. Start with an appetizer of *tostones,* fried plantains, or *empanadillas,* little meat turnovers. Other Puerto Rico dishes include asopao, a chicken and rice soup, and mofongo, fried plantains mixed with fried pork rinds and seasoned with garlic. Save room for flan, a wonderful custard, or our favorite, tembleque, a custard made with coconut milk and sprinkled with cinnamon.

You won't go thirsty during a Puerto Rico stay; the island offers some of the Caribbean's best rums, Medalla beer, and stout Puerto Rico coffee.

Cafe Galeria, Old San Juan. $$

Dine with local businesspeople in this charming eatery located steps from the shops of Old San Juan.

La Dorada, Condado. $$–$$$

Puerto Rican cuisine is the specialty of this casual restaurant that features many seafood dishes. Choose from broiled halibut, red snapper in lobster and shrimp sauce, rice with squid, lobster asopao, or mofongo stuffed with seafood.

La Mallorquina, Old San Juan. $$$

Since 1848, this casual eatery has offered fine Puerto Rican cuisine: paella, fried rice with shrimp, chicken asopao, and even Puerto Rican-style beef tenderloin.

Restaurant El Coche, Ponce. $$$

An international menu is featured at this family restaurant. Specialties of the house include wiener schnitzel with German potatoes, smoked pork chops with sauerkraut, and lobster salad with fried plantains.

Su Casa, Hyatt Dorado Beach Resort, Dorado. $$$

Dine in an authentic hacienda, the former home of Dr. Alfred Livingston, the owner of the plantation on which the Hyatt Dorado now sits. You can dine on a balcony or in a romantic courtyard, surrounded by the Spanish Colonial style of this 1900 home. The restaurant, which features Puerto Rican and Spanish dishes, is open for dinner only during peak season; reservations are required. Call (787) 796-1234.

Festivals

If you're looking for a party, you're in luck: Puerto Rico enjoys fiestas throughout the year. In February, the Coffee Harvest Festival celebrates the end of the coffee harvest in the mountain town of Maricao, the capital of the coffee-growing region.

Classical music is the focus of the Casals Festival in late June and early July. Honoring the late cellist and composer Pablo Casals, this event features a month of romantic music.

If you are interested in art, make plans to attend the Barranquitas Artisans Fair in mid-July. The oldest crafts fair in Puerto Rico, shoppers will find everything from carvings to pottery to musical instruments for sale, plus plenty of local food and folk music to enjoy.

In late July, the town of Loiza, on the northeast end of the island, celebrates its African heritage with the Loiza Carnival. Look for parades, colorful floats, pulsating music, folk masks, and bomba dances (an Afro-Caribbean dance rhythm) at this lively festival.

Folkloric and classical music, ballet, modern dance, and musical theater are featured during the Inter-American Festival of the Arts, held in late September in San Juan. In early November, the Festival of Puerto Rican Music highlights classical and folk music. A special contest at this festival features the cuatro, a 10-string instrument shaped like a small guitar.

Christmas shoppers find over 100 artists and craftsmen selling their work at the Bacardi Artisans Fair, held on the grounds of the Bacardi rum plant in Cataño in early December. Along with plenty of shopping opportunities, the fair also includes a troubadour contest, rides, and plenty of old-fashioned Puerto Rican fun.

Romantic Activities

The attractions of Puerto Rico are as vast as the island itself, ranging from eco-tourism jaunts to historic sites that date back to the days of Spanish explorers. Undoubtedly, the most popular stop on the island is **Old San Juan**. Dotted with museums and historic sites and rich with the atmosphere of Spanish explorers and conquistadors, this region is a must for every visitor. You can take a self-guided walk among the historic streets, strolling hand-in-hand where lovers have literally walked for centuries. The city's best shopping is also found in this area.

The most recognized site in Old San Juan is Fuerte San Felipe del Morro, better known as **El Morro**. This fort, one of the most photographed spots in the Caribbean, contains a museum and is administered by the National Park Service. Built in 1539, the Spanish constructed this formidable structure to protect the entrance into San Juan Harbor, a point from which the Spanish monitored their shipping between the Caribbean and Europe. El Morro means promontory or headland in Spanish.

The park is open daily from 9 A.M. to 5 P.M.; there is no admission charge. Start with a video on the site then take a self-guided tour. You will find a map at the entrances, and exhibits throughout the park are posted in both English and Spanish. Even if you're not a history buff, this site is a romantic place where the two of you can look out on the sea and enjoy a gentle trade wind. Bring along your camera for this scenic stop.

Nearby, **Casa Blanca** contains exhibits on 16th and 17th century life and on its most famous residents: Ponce de Leon and his family. (Actually Ponce de Leon died before the home was completed.) Built in the 1520s, the home was the city's first fortress and is now open for tours Wednesday through Sunday.

Not all of San Juan's attractions are man-made; for a look at the natural beauty the island enjoys make a stop at the **Botanical Garden of the University of Puerto Rico**. This 75-acre garden blooms with 30,000 orchids as well as heliconias and water lilies. For a peaceful lunch away from the city crowds, bring along a picnic and enjoy it in grounds shaded by cinnamon and nutmeg trees. The garden is a popular site for wedding photos and for ceremonies, many of which take place in a small chapel on the grounds. For more information, call (787) 250-0000 ext. 6580.

If the two of you are history lovers, then make time for a trip south to the city of Ponce. Ninety minutes south of San Juan, Ponce boasts more than 500 restored buildings. The **Ponce Art Museum** features the most extensive collection in the Caribbean, with over 1,000 paintings and 400 sculptures. Ponce is also home to **Hacienda Buena Vista**, a restored 19th century coffee plantation open today as a museum.

If your interests run toward eco-tourism, you're in luck in Puerto Rico. One of our favorite excursions is a snorkel trip out to **Monkey Island**. More fun than a barrel of monkeys, this island of curious primates is located off the southeast coast of Puerto Rico. It's a sanctuary for hundreds of monkeys, and access to the island is prohibited. Visitors cannot actually step on land, but you can snorkel around the fringes of the island while excited primates hoot and holler at the intrusion. We found the snorkeling here excellent, full of colorful fans and bright corals. Coral Head Divers at Palmas Del Mar (787-850-7208) offer scuba and snorkel trips to Monkey Island.

Another natural attraction is **El Yunque National Forest**, the only tropical rain forest administered by the U.S. National Forest Service. Forty-five minutes east of San Juan (close to El Conquistador resort), the rain forest boasts 240 species of trees and flowers, including 20 varieties of orchids and 50 types of ferns. Walking trails carve through the dense forest, and guided tours are available.

If you are interested in a quiet walk beneath Puerto Rico, the island also offers what is called one of the finest cave systems in the world. The **Rio Camuy Cave Park**, located 2½ hours west of San Juan, was carved by large underground rivers. Today the park includes a new visitors center with reception area and cafeteria and a theater with an audio-visual presentation. Visitors reach cave level by trolley then follow walkways on a 45-minute guided tour.

Puerto Rico has earned a reputation as the "Scotland of the Caribbean" because of its many golf courses. Over a dozen courses, including those at **Hyatt Dorado Beach**, **Hyatt Regency Cerromar Beach**, **El Conquistador Resort and Country Club**, and **Palmas del Mar** offer golf enthusiasts a variety of golf experiences in a tropical setting.

Nightlife

The action doesn't stop when the sun goes down in Puerto Rico. In true Latin fashion, the city puts on its best clothes and gets ready to party during these cooler hours, starting with a late dinner. Evenings follow with dancing in the many discos in San Juan or in the luxurious casino hotels.

Several hotels offer lavish shows a la Las Vegas. Here you will find celebrity impersonators, costumed showgirls, and glitz revues to enjoy as dinner or cocktail shows. One of the best is the Hollywood Legends Show at the Sands Hotel and Casino Beach Resort, featuring celebrity impersonators (check out "Liza Minelli;" she's a ringer for the real thing).

Casino gambling is found at many Puerto Rico hotels. Most casinos open at noon and remain open until the early hours of the morning. Most have dress codes that require semiformal attire; leave the shorts, tank tops, and flip-flops in the room. This is your chance to dress up and party; with San Juan's lively atmosphere the rule of thumb is the tighter, the shinier, the better.

You may be surprised to learn that alcohol cannot, by law, be served in Puerto Rico's casinos. You will find bars in each hotel, but no drinks are served on the casino floor.

One of the most sophisticated casinos in San Juan, and, indeed in the Caribbean, is found at El San Juan Hotel. With a tuxedoed staff and an elegant European air, it's a favorite for couples looking for a fine casino.

El Conquistador offers a large casino with a view of the sea (yes—windows in a casino!). The entire casino is well-lit and bright, with pale paneling, beautiful views, and an airy atmosphere.

The casino at Hyatt Cerromar sports a recent expansion with a bright carnival theme, nearly 300 slots, and plenty of table games to test your luck and skill.

OUR IMPRESSIONS OF PUERTO RICO

- good gambling, shopping, nightlife, historic attractions
- simple to reach; numerous flights from the U.S.
- simple vacation: U.S. currency, stamps, driving laws
- not the true "Caribbean" atmosphere found on smaller islands

ROMANCE ON PUERTO RICO

- kiss on the lookouts at El Morro
- feel the Spanish colonial atmosphere at Old San Juan
- stay out past bedtime and merengue or salsa

$\mathcal{S}$t. Kitts and Nevis

Language	English
Currency	EC dollar (US $1 = EC $2.70 approx.); U.S. dollar accepted
Population	44,000
Driving	left
Best romantic features	plantation inns, lush flora, good beaches, friendly, small town atmosphere

Imagine a country inn where rooms brim with antiques and are cooled by a gentle breeze off a wide porch. You ease into a wicker chair, sip an icy drink, and enjoy a view unbroken by roads, electrical lines, or even fellow travelers.

This is St. Kitts, an island that offers all the country comforts and bed & breakfast luxury you might look for in a New England getaway. Here, however, palms replace pines and color comes, not from scarlet leaves, but from azure seas, beaches in shades of black and white, and verdant forests that engulf the island.

St. Kitts and Nevis, its partner in this two-island nation, boast one of the Caribbean's largest concentrations of plantation homes. The islands were once dotted with sugar plantations and greathouses, but today these stately manses have been transformed into elegant bed & breakfast inns especially popular with European vacationers and with Americans looking to experience a slice of the Caribbean "the way it used to be." Don't look for reggae lessons, limbo contests or mixology classes at these properties; instead, expect a sophisticated atmosphere similar to a fine country inn where the emphasis lies, not on providing fun for its guests, but in pointing the way for independent travelers to make their own discoveries.

Just two miles away from St. Kitts lies the tiny island of Nevis (*NEE-vis*). Columbus first named this island because of the ever-present cloud that circled Mount Nevis, giving it almost a snow-capped look. Today the cloud still lingers over the mountain peak. Home to only 9,000 residents, this country cousin has a charming atmosphere all its own, plus a good share of plantation houses where guests can enjoy a look back at Caribbean history.

A Little History

You might hear St. Kitts referred to as St. Christopher, its given name. In 1493 it was named by Columbus, not for himself, but for his patron saint and the patron saint of all travelers. He christened the neighboring island "Nuestro Señora de Las Nieves" or "Our Lady of the Snows" in reference to Mount Nevis, its cloud-covered volcano and the closest thing the Caribbean has to a snow-topped mountain.

Settled as far back as 1623, St. Kitts became the mother colony of the Caribbean. British ships first made landfall in St. Kitts before continuing their colonization efforts around the region.

For decades, the British and the French fought over St. Kitts, so much, in fact, that the English finally built one of the largest forts in the islands. Brimstone Hill, called the "Gibraltar of the Caribbean," guarded the island from a point over 400 feet above sea level. Apparently it didn't protect the shoreline well enough, however, because in 1782 the French captured the fortress and ruled the island. The next year the tables turned, and the losers were loaded onto British ships and sent back to the old country.

The British didn't mind transporting the French back home but they weren't about to take along their enemy's favorite pets: monkeys. Small vervet monkeys had been imported from Africa by the French. The British turned the monkeys loose on the island where they prospered. Today it is estimated that the monkeys of St. Kitts outnumber humans two to one. The monkeys have spread to Nevis as well and, if you get up early or go out after sunset, you will stand a chance of spotting one of the primates.

Compass Points

St. Kitts and Nevis are both mountainous by Caribbean standards and rich with undeveloped regions. Both islands are home to small rain forests, and visitors will find plenty of tropical foliage wherever they venture.

Shaped like a guitar, St. Kitts is the more developed of the two. Most of its 35,000 residents live in the town of Basseterre (*Bos-tear*) on the south shore (just where the guitar handle meets the body.)

South of Basseterre, the island slims, the land becomes drier, and the population scattered. This is the South Peninsula, an area that, until a few years ago, was accessible only by boat. Today a modern highway makes this region available to motorists. Here you will find some of the island's most beautiful, remote beaches and roadside overlooks with views of both sides of the island, the Caribbean Sea to the south, and the Atlantic Ocean to the north. Several hotel chains have purchased property in this area, but it remains, at least for today, remote and isolated. Animal lovers, the South Peninsula is your best chance for spotting vervet monkeys. Look in the underbrush and not in the trees. These monkeys don't have a prehensile tail so are usually spotted on the ground.

The north end of St. Kitts is the most lush, due to soil that owes much of its fertility to a volcano named Mount Liamuiga, a Carib word that means "fertile island." The remote reaches of Mount Liamuiga are home to St. Kitts' rain forest.

For all the tropical splendor of St. Kitts, Nevis is even more verdant. Tall coconut palms cover hills carpeted in tropical undergrowth.

Just the Facts

Getting There

Robert Llewelyn Bradshaw International Airport (formerly Golden Rock Airport) in St. Kitts has daily jet service from the United States. American Airlines provides daily service from the Caribbean hub in San Juan.

The small Newcastle Airport in Nevis is served by commuter flights from St. Kitts. Most visitors arrive by ferry. Ferry service is available several times daily between the two islands; the journey takes about 45 minutes and costs about US $8 round-trip.

When leaving St. Kitts and Nevis (but not to travel between the islands), visitors pay a departure tax of EC $27.

Getting Around

Rental cars are available on both islands, but be advised that driving is on the left side of the road. A visitors license is available from the Police Traffic Department for EC $30.

Excellent taxi and mini-bus service is available on St. Kitts and Nevis.

Many couples take a day trip to the other island aboard the passenger ferry The Caribe Queen. The 45-minute crossing costs about US $8 round trip. Air St. Kitts Nevis, (869) 465-8571, on St. Kitts; (869) 469-9241 on Nevis, whisks visitors from island to island in less than 10 minutes.

Entry Requirements

Passports are required of all visitors except U.S. and Canadian citizens who may present a voter's registration card, naturalization papers, or a certified birth certificate (not a copy).

For More Information

For a free tourist guide to St. Kitts and Nevis, call the Tourist Office at (800) 582-6208 or write 414 East 75th Street, New York, NY 10021.

For the Marriage-Minded

Getting married on St. Kitts or Nevis is a simple feat. Either the bride or groom must be a resident of the island for 48 hours prior to the wedding.

Bring along a valid passport or certified birth certificate and, if either party is divorced, present an absolute decree of divorce. If either the bride or groom is widowed, a death certificate is necessary. (If the documents are not in English, a notarized translation must be presented.)

To be married by a Catholic priest, you must bring a letter from your resident priest verifying that you are unmarried and have received necessary instruction. To be married by an Anglican minister, bring a letter from your minister verifying that you are unmarried.

The marriage license fee is EC $200 (US $80). If you have enjoyed a pre-honeymoon trip on St. Kitts or Nevis for at least 15 days prior to the marriage, the fee goes down to EC $50 or US $20.

Romantic Resorts

St. Kitts

Fort Thomas Hotel, (800) 851-7818, (869) 465-2695; fax (869) 465-7518. $

- downtown
- freshwater pool
- casual and fine dining

If you want to be in the heart of town, here's your place. Located in walking distance of restaurants and shops, this hotel is a good choice for the budget-conscious. Along with recently refurbished guest rooms, it offers one of the island's largest swimming pools, a shuttle to the beach, and a good restaurant.

Golden Lemon Inn and Villas, (800) 633-7411, (869) 465-7260; fax (869) 465-4019. $$

- beachfront
- freshwater pool
- fine dining

Fine dining and elegant accommodations lead travelers to the Golden Lemon, located on a black volcanic sand beach in the shadow of the island's volcano. Owned and managed by former *House and Garden* decorating editor Arthur Leaman, this 17th century greathouse and the 15 contemporary seaside villas are filled with West Indian antiques. For the ultimate in luxury, two suites offer plunge pools literally a step from the living room door. The hotel is located about 15 minutes from Basseterre, and most guests rent cars for their stay.

Horizons Villa Resort, (800) 830-9069, (869) 465-0584;
fax (869) 465-0785. $$

- hillside
- small beach
- pool

You will feel like the two of you have made your home on this beauti-
ful island during a stay in these lovely villas. Perched up on a hillside
with a path down to a crescent-shaped beach, the villas are comfortable,
cozy, and maintained by a friendly staff.

Jack Tar Village St. Kitts Beach Resort and Casino, (800) 999-9182,
(869) 465-8651; fax (869) 465-1031. $

- across from beach
- all-inclusive
- casino
- watersports
- golf, tennis

Renovated after Hurricane Luis, this all-inclusive resort is recom-
mended for couples looking for activity. Home of the country's only
casino, the resort offers plenty of organized fun and evening enter-
tainment as well as a modest golf course. All activities, along with food
and drink, are included in the price. Although it is not located on the
beach, it's just a short walk to the sand and surf. Jack Tar is recom-
mended for couples on a budget; it's one of the best-priced accom-
modations on the islands.

Ottley's Plantation Inn, (800) 772-3039, (869) 465-7234;
fax (869) 465-4760. $$$

- mountainside
- fine dining
- tennis, golf
- freshwater pool

Legend has it that this 18th-century greathouse is haunted, but that
doesn't stop the vacationers who come here looking for peace and
quiet. Guest rooms in the greathouse and in nearby cottages are nestled
on 35 acres of tropical grounds. Along with golf and tennis, guests

can explore a small rain forest on the grounds and search for vervet monkeys. Visitors have access to a nearby black sand beach.

Rawlins Plantation, Mount Pleasant, (800) 346-5358, (869) 465-6221; fax (869) 465-4954. $$

• mountainside
• freshwater pool
• restaurant

As far back as 1690 a plantation now named Rawlins began producing sugar. Nearly 300 years later the greathouse, burned in an early fire, was reconstructed and opened as an inn. Today Rawlins is in the hands of Cordon Bleu-trained chef Claire Rawson and her husband, Paul.

Along with dining, the chief activity around here is pure relaxation. With no phones or televisions in the 10 guest rooms, the emphasis is on leisure. The most romantic of the hideaway rooms is the honeymoon suite, housed in a 300-year-old sugar mill. Guests climb a winding stairway from the downstairs living room to the upstairs bedroom perch, its walls made of volcanic stone.

Nevis

Four Seasons Nevis, (800) 332-3442 U.S., (800) 332-3442 Canada, (869) 469-1111; fax (869) 469-1112. $$$$

• beachfront
• casual and fine dining
• freshwater pool
• golf, tennis
• watersports
• children's program

When word went out that the Four Seasons was coming to Nevis, doomsayers predicted the end of the quaint atmosphere for which Nevis is known. However, during the hotel's construction, Hurricane Hugo hit the island and the Four Seasons' bosses stopped building and put crews to work cleaning up the island. Today, even the island inns sing the praises of this corporate giant.

One of the Caribbean's most lavish hotels, the Four Seasons Nevis sprawls across grounds dotted with coconut palms and other carefully tended fauna. Guests can enjoy the Robert Trent Jones II-designed golf course, scuba, windsurf, order from around-the-clock room service, watch movies on VCRs or cable TV, hit the 10 tennis courts, lounge in two outdoor Jacuzzis, or sun around the pool, cooled by Evian sprayed on guests by mindful pool attendants.

Golden Rock Estate, (800) 223-9815, (869) 469-3346; fax (869) 469-2113. $$

- mountainside
- restaurant
- nature walks
- pool

Eco-tourists are attracted to Golden Rock because of the diligent efforts of its owner, Pam Barry. A fifth-generation Nevisian, Barry emphasizes local culture, history, and nature studies, offering her self-guided nature trails to guests and non-guests alike.

The most romantic room at this historic plantation inn is the two-story sugar windmill.

Hermitage Inn, (800) 742-4276, (869) 469-3477; fax (869) 469-2481. $$$

- mountainside
- fine dining
- freshwater pool
- tennis
- horseback riding

When magazines look for a classically Caribbean setting for fashion shoots, they often select the Hermitage Inn. This plantation inn is built around a 245-year old greathouse. Sprinkled around grounds bursting with tropical blooms are restored plantation cottages that serve as guest rooms for those looking for the ultimate in privacy.

Guests have access to a swimming pool and tennis courts as well as romantic pursuits such as carriage rides and horseback riding. Rates here include breakfast and a four-course dinner nightly.

Hurricane Cove Bungalows, (869) 469-9462; fax (869) 469-9462. $

- mountainside

If you're pinching pennies, don't despair. The enchantment of Nevis can still be enjoyed on a budget. The moderately priced Hurricane Cove Bungalows feature some of the most splendid views on the island. Each of the 10 hill-hugging cottages was constructed in Scandinavia, broken down and reassembled on a slope overlooking St. Kitts in the distance. Today they're all open-air and furnished with Caribbean artwork. One-, two-, and three-bedroom bungalows with kitchens are available, and guests can walk down to the beach. For our money, this is one of the island's best buys.

Montpelier Plantation Inn, (800) 223-9832, (869) 469-3462; fax (869) 469-2932. $$

- mountainside
- freshwater pool
- fine dining

You may have heard of Montpelier because of one of its most famous guests: Princess Diana. When Diana and her children visited Nevis, they opted for this hotel's quiet seclusion. Both royalty and honeymooners are offered peace and quiet in this very British hotel located on the slopes of Mount Nevis.

Princess Diana focused the eyes of the world on Montpelier, but it was hardly the property's first brush with royalty. On March 11, 1787 Admiral Horatio Nelson married Fanny Nisbet in front of a royal audience right on these grounds.

Today the plantation includes a 16-room inn that exudes a dignified British air appreciated by travelers who come to the Caribbean for peace and quiet. The inn provides shuttle service to the beaches and evenings here are spent at the open-air restaurant that features classical cuisine with many local ingredients.

Nisbet Plantation Beach Club, (800) 742-6008, (869) 469-9325; fax (869) 469-9864. $$$

- beachfront
- casual and fine dining
- freshwater pool
- tennis
- watersports

Nelson's bride, Fanny Nisbet, was a resident of Nevis, and lived on a beachfront plantation that today is the Nisbet Plantation Beach Club. This 38-room inn boasts a striking vista: a quarter-mile, palm-lined walk from the greathouse to one of the finest beaches in Nevis.

Guests stay in lemon-tinted bungalows scattered throughout the property. Couples can enjoy tennis, swimming in the sea or a pool, or that oh-so-British sport, croquet.

Shopping

Just one word of advice if you plan to make shopping your top reason to visit St. Kitts and Nevis: don't. While these sister islands boast many charms, good shopping isn't one of them.

The best shopping stop is St. Kitts' Caribelle Batik at Romney Manor. Here you can watch batik in progress and buy the finished product in the form of shirts, wraps, and wall hangings. (Even if you don't want to buy, it's worth a trip to Romney Manor to visit the stately greathouse and the grounds shaded by trees that date back hundreds of years.)

In Basseterre, duty-free devotees will find Ashburry's Duty Free Boutique (Liverpool Row), Little Switzerland (Pelican Mall on the waterfront) and A Slice of Lemon (at the Circus, the traffic circle in the center of Basseterre).

Shopping is even more limited in Nevis. One of the best stops is Nevis Pottery in Newcastle, where artisans craft the local clay soil into various vessels. The pots are finished over a fire of coconut shells behind the shop.

Stamp collectors will be familiar with Nevis because of its often-sought stamps. Stop by the Philatelic Bureau in Charlestown for the best selection.

Dining

A meal in St. Kitts and Nevis means traditional Caribbean fare such as snapper, grouper, salt fish, or even flying fish accompanied by side dishes such as breadfruit, pumpkin, yams, and the obligatory rice and (pigeon) peas. Everything will be flavorful and often spicy.

Wash down dinner with the local beer, Carib, or the island's own liqueur: Cane Spirit Rothschild or CSR. Made from cane, this clear liqueur was developed by Baron Rothschild and is manufactured in Basseterre.

St. Kitts

Fisherman's Wharf, Fortlands, Basseterre. $–$$

Relax in the informal seaside atmosphere at this open-air restaurant featuring local dishes. The restaurant itself is located on a wharf and offers romantic views of Basseterre at night.

Rawlins Plantation. $$

Guests and non-guests stop by Rawlins Plantation for the daily West Indian lunch buffet. The buffet features local favorites such as saffron rice, curried chicken, and flying fish fritters, followed by soursop sorbet. The dishes are prepared using fresh seafood and herbs and vegetables from the Rawlins' garden.

Royal Palm Restaurant, Ottley's Plantation Inn. $$

Often cited as one of the island's top restaurants, the prix fixe menu features dishes such as Kittitan Tomato Dill Bisque, pan-seared red snapper, and roast herb-infused tenderloin of prime beef.

Turtle Beach Bar and Grill, Southeast Peninsula at Turtle Beach. $

Located where the end of the island meets the sea, this laid-back bar and restaurant serves lunch daily and dinner on Saturday. Seafood and island barbecue are specialties. On Sunday afternoon, enjoy a buffet and sounds of the local steel band as well as a great view of Nevis.

Nevis

Sandpipers, Paradise Beach. $

Open for lunch and dinner daily except Tuesdays, this beach grill serves up Caribbean lobster, shrimp, and flying fish along a five-mile stretch of beach. Place your order, go out for a swim, and come back to dine in a truly relaxed atmosphere.

Romantic Activities

Couples should budget at least half a day for an **island tour**, which can be booked through any hotel. (Another alternative for those wishing more privacy is to hire a taxi driver by the hour.) On St. Kitts, an island tour includes a stop at **Brimstone Hill National Park** for a self-guided tour of this impressive fortress as well as stops at **Romney Manor** for a look at Caribelle Batik. Nevis island tours include a stop in the capital city of Charlestown, the ruins of the **Bath Hotel**, built in 1778 for wealthy Nevisians to bask in 108-degree waters (modest facilities are still open for visitors to "take the waters"), and the **Alexander Hamilton House**, the birthplace of the American patriot.

Most activity on these islands centers around the sea. Scuba divers will find a variety of trips including **reef and wreck dives**. On St. Kitts, call Kenneth's Dive Center, (869) 465-7043, Pro-Divers, (869) 465-3223, or St. Kitts Scuba, (800) 621-1270; on Nevis call Scuba Safaris, (869) 469-9518.

For those who want to stay above water level, the Spirit of St. Kitts, (869) 469-9373, catamaran offers **day sails** to Nevis and the Spirit of Mount Nevis takes couples on sunset cruises every Tuesday.

Golf is available at Golden Rock Golf Club, (869) 465-8103, Royal St. Kitts Golf Course, (869) 465-8339, and Four Seasons Nevis, (869) 469-1111.

Eco-tourists can visit **St. Kitts' rain forest** with Greg's Safaris, (869) 465-4121, on a half-day hike. For a very rugged adventure, Greg takes visitors on a **Volcano Safari**, climbing Mount Liamuiga to the crater rim to view the cloud forest.

Nightlife

The best advice for couples looking for nightlife on St. Kitts and Nevis is to make their own. Nights are often spent looking up at the moon or watching the sea on both quiet islands. Some restaurants feature local musicians and occasionally the local steel pan band.

On St. Kitts, the Jack Tar Village has a casino and disco for guests and non-guests alike. The casino includes slots and gaming tables.

For music, the Kittitian Monkey Bar on Frigate Bay Beach on the Southeast Peninsula sometimes has live music featuring island sounds. Similarly, the Cotton House Club and Disco, located 10 minutes from

Basseterre, offers music and is open Friday and Saturday nights. The club requires proper attire.

On Nevis, Club Trenim, located on Government Road in Charlestown, features disco dancing in an informal setting. Golden Rock Estate presents the music of David Freeman's Honey Bee String Band on Saturday nights.

OUR IMPRESSIONS OF ST. KITTS

- a quiet getaway
- great for history buffs and independent travelers
- excellent dining
- large selection of plantation inns

ROMANCE ON ST. KITTS

- dancing to a steel pan band at beachfront restaurants
- fine dining in open-air restaurants at a plantation inn
- taking a rental car down the peninsula to a deserted beach

OUR IMPRESSIONS OF NEVIS

- a quiet getaway
- large selection of plantation inns
- great for history buffs and independent travelers
- impressive mountain vistas and tropical lushness
- extra transportation (ferry or flight) required to reach the island

ROMANCE ON NEVIS

- a walk down an aisle of stately palms at Nisbet Plantation
- sunset at a beach bar
- limin', or just hanging out, in any island inn

$\mathscr{S}$t. Lucia

Language	English
Currency	EC dollar (US \$1 = about EC \$2.70 fixed rate); U.S. dollar accepted
Population	140,000
Driving	left
Best romantic features	tropical lushness, beaches

We heard St. Lucia before we saw it. Flying in from the States near the midnight hour, we stepped off the prop plane and instantly received a warm welcome from the humid night winds. Just yards away, we could hear the sound of the Caribbean lapping against the shoreline, right off the Vigie Airport runway.

But the next morning we learned what St. Lucia was really about. Jagged peaks clothed in velvety tropical plants. Honey-colored beaches shaded by towering palms. And everywhere, everywhere, colorful blooms and greenery that promised romantic walks in a true garden of Eden.

The two of you will feel like Adam and Eve in this wonderland, a place where every hill, valley, and roadside is a veritable garden. Orange, lime, lemon, mango (over 100 varieties, we learned), bread-fruit, plum, and coffee trees cover the landscape. Pineapples sprout alongside the highway. Spices like vanilla, nutmeg, and cinnamon grow in thick profusion.

But most evident are the bananas. Not just banana trees, but banana plantations. Miles of bananas that stretch to the horizon.

Along with its reputation as a drive-through grocery market, St. Lucia is also abloom with color. Tall flame flowers. Orchids. Hibiscus. Shrimp plants. Like an explosion of a thousand florist shops.

Romance comes easily in such a fertile environment. You will find plenty of excuses to kiss in the shade of a tall coconut palm, in the spray of a mountainside waterfall, or in a hillside lookout with a view of the mountains rearing from the sea.

St. Lucia's most famous attractions are the Pitons, twin peaks located in the southwest region of the island. Gros Piton, the shorter but fatter of the two, and Petit Piton are among the Caribbean's most recognizable landmarks.

A Little History

The Arawak and then the warlike Caribs first called this island Hewanorra or "where the iguana is found."

The island's European discovery is the subject of some debate. At first Columbus was believed to have landed here in 1502 and to honor that event Castries created Columbus Square. Later historians figured that Columbus really just did the equivalent of a quick drive-by, never actually making landfall. Castries decided to rename Columbus Square for Derek Walcott, a local Nobel Laureate.

For many years, the island passed between the English and French, who left their mark with Gallic names for almost every community and landmark. Even today, St. Lucia has a distinct French atmosphere, from its cuisine to its patois.

On Feb. 22, 1979, St. Lucia became an independent country.

Compass Points

Nicknamed the "Helen of the West Indies," St. Lucia is one of the most beautiful islands in the region. The 238-square-mile landform is rich with jagged mountains, lush valleys, rugged cliffs, and pristine beaches that come in various shades of black and beige.

The pear-shaped island becomes increasingly lush and mountainous the farther south you travel. The capital city of Castries, located on the northwest shore, is home to much of the island's industry, including a massive Hess oil plant. Farther south, the island's agricultural district offers miles of banana plantations.

On the southwest coast, the community of Soufriere stands just miles from the dense rain forest and in view of St. Lucia's two landmarks: Gros Piton and Petit Piton. These two peaks have been scaled by experienced climbers, who rate the ascent as difficult.

Just the Facts

Getting There

Unlike most Caribbean islands, St. Lucia is served by two international airports, so pay close attention here. More than one couple has booked flights into one airport only to discover that their hotel was across the island, over an hour's (expensive) taxi ride away.

The main airport is Hewanorra, located on the southern end of the island. It's the larger of the two airports, with jet service from American Airlines, Air Canada, BWIA, and several European carriers. Hotels near the Pitons are only a short taxi ride from the Hewanorra terminal.

On the northern end of the island lies Vigie International Airport, located in the city of Castries. This is closest to the bulk of the island's hotel properties, but it is served primarily by smaller carriers such as American Eagle, LIAT, and BWIA with daily service from New York and Miami.

Departure tax from either airport is US $11 per person, payable either in EC or US funds.

Cruise passengers arrive in Castries or Soufriere. The Castries port is in easy walking distance of duty-free shopping and the Castries market.

Getting Around

For years, St. Lucia was renowned for its poor roads, winding potholed terrors that made travel slow and uncomfortable. In 1995, however, the island completed a major road refurbishment project, and we are glad to say that we found travel from one end of the island to the other both speedy and easy.

Taxis are the most common means of transportation for vacationers, but be advised that a journey from the north end of the island to the Piton region is an expensive one: about US $50 one way. Rental cars are available from the airports and the major hotels; look for Avis,

Budget, or National Car Rental. You will need to obtain a local license from the immigration desk at either airport, police station, or from the larger rental dealers. You will also need to present your local driver's license.

Taxis can be rented by the hour for a private tour. Work out the price with the driver before you leave, but estimate about US $20 per hour.

Tour companies offer a wide array of guided full- and half-day tours of the island. Visit the rain forest in an open-air jeep (book early for this one since space is limited), take a bus tour to the volcano, the botanical gardens, and the waterfalls, or enjoy a combination tour with a drive down the coast and a catamaran ride back. Sunlink Tours offers a good selection of tours and we found the guides very knowledgeable about everything from island vegetation to history.

Entry Requirements

U.S. citizens need either a passport or birth certificate and a return or onward ticket.

For More Information

Contact the St. Lucia Tourist Board, 820 Second Avenue, 9th floor, New York, NY 10017, or call (800) 456-3984.

For the Marriage-Minded

To obtain a marriage license, the two of you will need to produce the following original documentation: passports, birth certificates, final divorce decrees if applicable, death certificate in case of widow/widower, original proof if name changed, and if under 18 years of age an original, notarized letter of consent from parents. All documents must be in English; if in another language an authenticated translation must be available.

If you don't stay at a resort where wedding fees are part of the package, here's the breakdown of cost: US $3 for a marriage certificate, US $112 for notary fees, and US $45 for registrar fees.

A resort wedding coordinator can handle applicable paperwork, or, if you do it yourself, you will need to work through a local lawyer to make application to the Attorney General. The marriage license is issued following the two-day residency requirement.

Weddings in St. Lucia are only valid if they take place between sunrise and sunset. We heard one story of a nervous groom who fainted just before the critical vows—and just as the sun was setting. The registrar and the bride quickly revived him in time to get out an "I do" before the sun vanished into the sea.

Romantic Resorts

Anse Chastanet, (800) 223-1108, (758) 459-7000;
fax (758) 459-7700. $$$

- beachfront
- fine and casual dining
- watersports, dive shop

A stay at Anse Chastanet is truly an experience that any couple will talk about for years. Tucked between one of St. Lucia's finest beaches and the Pitons, this hillside resort strips away the barriers between resort and nature. Here walls give way to scenic vistas and guests enjoy rooms where luxury means views uninterrupted by hindrances such as windows. Many accommodations in this 48-room resort have only two or three exterior walls, with bedrooms flowing directly onto terraces and out to the breathtaking scene beyond. Tiny birds make chattering roommates and just beyond the balcony railing flitting hummingbirds work the tropical blooms like oversized bees.

Anse Chastanet (*on-chas-tan-ay*) is perched right on the edge of the hillside, which translates into steep steps that wind from beachside to the main reception and dining area to the hilltop bungalows above. Not the place for visitors with walking problems—and leave the high heels at home for this destination. Casual is the order of the day, although in the evening men traditionally wear Bermuda length shorts or slacks.

We enjoyed room 7F, a truly unique room that cannot be compared to any other in the Caribbean. Like other rooms in the 7 block, this accommodation has an unbeatable view of Petit Piton and Gros Piton rising from the sea. From our king-size bed, we looked across our immense room (even the smallest room at Anse Chastanet measures 900 square feet), across a balcony rail, and straight at the Caribbean's most recognizable mountains. Even the shower (easily built for two) is replete with a view: a mirror offers you a look back over your shoulder and out the open wall where birds flit through the trees. You will feel like an intruder in Eden.

The toughest part of a stay at Anse Chastanet is the decision of whether to stay in your room and enjoy the breathtaking view or to venture down to the beach and perch beneath a palm-thatched palapa. You might compromise and make a stop halfway down at the Piton Bar, the open-air bar with a view of the mountains. While you're here, try the specialty: Stairway to Heaven, concocted with Seventh Heaven liqueur made of ginger and bois bandé (a local aphrodisiac), rum, coconut cream, and orange juice.

Anse Chastanet does weddings wherever the couple chooses: on the beach, in the Treehouse restaurant, or even on the patio of their guest room. And, to soothe muscles that might be tired from walking that steep hill, the resort offers a special massage course for couples.

Ladera Resort, (800) INSIGNIA, (758) 459-7323; fax (758) 459-5156. $$$

- mountainside
- restaurant
- freshwater pool
- shuttle service to Soufriere and beaches

Tucked above the sea between the Pitons, this intimate hillside resort features villas and suites, many with private pools. Each guest room is open on the west side to offer guests a breathtaking view of the Pitons and the sea. Rooms are decorated with 19th century French furniture and local artwork.

Weddings and honeymoon packages are available. Because of the size of this resort, the entire property can be rented by wedding parties for the week; special group rates are available.

LeSport, (800) 544-2883, (758) 450-8551; fax (758) 450-0368. $$$$

- beachfront
- all-inclusive
- spa
- golf school
- fine dining

LeSport differs from other all-inclusives; this resort doesn't emphasize a vacation from good wellness and nutrition habits with a week-long blowout of buffets, beach bumming, and boozing. Instead, this Moorish-style resort promotes the "body holiday," a chance to pamper your body with spa treatments, physical activity, and fine food. You will have an initial consultation then a program of treatments will be designed specially for you, ranging from the salt loofah rub to the hydro massage to Swedish massage to work out kinks after a round of tennis, a lesson in fencing, or a class at the golf school on the nine-hole course.

Rendezvous, (800) 544-2883, (758) 452-4211;
fax (758) 452-7419. $$$

- beachfront
- all-inclusive
- couples only
- fine and casual dining
- watersports, scuba diving
- tennis

If you only have a short time to enjoy St. Lucia, fly into Vigie Airport and make your stay at this all-inclusive resort, located about three minutes from the air terminal (it's right at the end of the runway, to tell the truth).

Rendezvous isn't the snazziest of all-inclusives, but it is comfortable and a good choice for those on a budget. You will get the full array of all-inclusive offerings: meals and liquor, nightly shows, plus a weekly excursion to Pigeon Point. Rooms here include ocean view accommodations with pink marble baths, island style furniture, and private porches. Approximately 70 percent of the resort's clientele is British, so you will notice a distinct international atmosphere here.

Sandals Halcyon, (800) SANDALS, (758) 453-0222;
fax (758) 451-8435. $$

- beachfront
- all-inclusive
- couples only
- fine and casual dining
- pools, whirlpools
- watersports

This Castries-area resort is one of our favorite Sandals properties. Rooms are nestled in one- and two-story buildings, most outlined in trailing vines and blooming tropical plants. Beautiful grounds offer couples plenty of quiet, shady nooks for time together.

This Sandals has the highest percentage of European guests within the popular chain, so the mood here is somewhat more reserved than at some Sandals hotels. You will still find basketball in the pool and volleyball at the beach, plus plenty of other activity thanks to those enthusiastic Playmakers, but couples who want to do nothing at all will feel at home here as well. Halcyon guests are a more adventurous group than at many properties; most book several off-property excursions during their stay. The tour desk can set up jeep tours to the rain forest, bus tours to the volcano, and catamaran excursions that trace St. Lucia's beautiful western shore.

Two specialty restaurants give Sandals guests a break from the main dining room; our favorite is The Pier. Built on a pier perched over the sea, this open-air eatery serves seafood in an elegant atmosphere.

Every room at Sandals Halcyon is identical; the only difference in category and price comes from the room view.

Sandals St. Lucia, (800) SANDALS, (758) 452-3081;
fax (758) 452-1012. $$

- beachfront
- all-inclusive
- couples only
- fine and casual dining
- freshwater pools
- watersports
- golf

The largest of the two Sandals properties on St. Lucia, this hotel is a veritable honeycomb of activity. Full-time Playmakers make sure that no one is left out of the fun and games. From the bars and billiards room in its elegant lobby to the tennis, golf, and watersports offerings on the 155-acre resort, guests have plenty of fun from which to choose. Of course, if you and your partner want to be alone, that's all right, too. You can hang out by the freeform pools, daysail in a Sunfish, or dine by candlelight.

Even more than most Sandals locations, this resort does things in a big way. The pool, which Sandals says is the largest in the Caribbean, includes a waterfall, bridges, and, of course, a swim-up bar where the two of you can order frozen and frothy concoctions.

Four restaurants keep guests well fed. Our favorite is La Toc, a French restaurant with a wine and sparkling wine list and white glove service. Although the restaurant is enclosed (not our choice in the Caribbean), the service is friendly and the atmosphere makes couples feel that they are enjoying a meal to celebrate a special occasion, even if that event is just another night on a vacation where the focus is on the two of you.

Shopping

Castries, the island's largest town, is also its top shopping area. Here you have a choice between malls and markets for everything from fine jewels to handmade crafts that capture the island spirit.

Gablewoods Mall, located near Sandals Halcyon, offers many gift shops such as Island Cotton.

Pointe Seraphine is the island's duty-free port. You will find well-known chains such as Little Switzerland, Colombian Emeralds, and Benetton. (Remember to bring your passport and return airline tickets to take advantage of the duty-free shopping. Items can be taken with you at point of purchase.) Pointe Seraphine is open weekdays, and on Saturdays, until 1 P.M. only. Like most shops in St. Lucia, the mall is closed on Sundays.

Outside of Castries, make a stop at Caribelle Batik for handmade batik shirts, wraps, and scarves. In Choiseul, stop by the Choiseul Arts and Crafts Center. This town is known as the crafts center of the island, and you will find straw, wood, and clay handcrafts, all manufactured locally.

Another local item that's a good reminder of your vacation is perfume. Caribbean Perfumes, located in Castries, captures the scents of the islands with perfumes for both men and women. Caribbean Perfumes are sold at shops across the island, including most resort gift stores.

Dining

Creole food is the order of the day in restaurants across St. Lucia. Spices liven up beef, chicken, pork, and lamb dishes, all served up with favorites such as rice and peas, dasheen (a root vegetable similar to a potato), and plantains. Enjoy it with a taste of local spirits such as La Belle Creole, Bounty Rum, and Piton beer.

Auberge Seraphine, Castries. $$–$$$

This seafood restaurant, with a sprinkling of French and Caribbean dishes, serves both lunch and dinner. Start with grilled calamari or Gros Islet-style fish cakes served with tamarind sauce, then try the breadfruit vichyssoise or Caribbean fish chowder. Entrees range from curried shrimp with coconuts to Caribbean lobster to St. Lucian-style chicken, stuffed with green bananas and served on a bed of callaloo. Reservations are suggested; call 453-2073.

Bang, Soufriere. $–$$

What a location! Tucked between the magnificent mountains, this waterfront restaurant specializes in jerk barbecue. Reservations are suggested; call 459-7864.

The Great House, Gros Islet. $$$$

On Friday nights, save time before the jump-up (see "Nightlife") for a run by this elegant plantation-style restaurant, located at Cap Estate. Enjoy a candlelight dinner of lime-grilled dorado, rack of lamb with mint sauce, jerk pork, or a local favorite: curried chicken and mango with rice. Finish off with truly sinful desserts: coconut cheesecake with tropical fruit toppings, passionfruit mousse, or soursop ice cream in filo pastry.

Jimmie's, Castries. $$–$$$

Tucked right beside Vigie Cove, this open-air hillside restaurant offers saltfish, black pudding, souse, green fig, and plenty of other local favorites. If you're a little less daring, you can fall back on seafood dishes such as conch (reputed to be an aphrodisiac), scampi, sautéed scallops, or even T-bone steak.

The Still, Soufriere. $

This is one of our favorite St. Lucian diners, a delightful local eatery that dishes out tasty local cuisine. Family-owned, the service is friendly and if you see something that you don't recognize, just ask. We dined on Creole chicken served with mango salad, rice, beans, and yam pie.

Don't expect anything fancy here, but this is the place to come for lunch or dinner for a true taste of Creole cooking at a very reasonable price.

The Treehouse, Anse Chastanet, Soufriere. $$$

Like its name suggests, this restaurant sits perched, tree level, on a steep hillside. Fortunately, the view is matched by the food here. We started with coconut-crusted local crab backs, then moved on to a creamy celery and bacon soup. Entrees include pork medallions with a light mustard sauce, vegetarian roti on curried lentils, grilled dorado, St. Lucian beef pepperpot, and other dishes using local products. The wine list here is excellent as well.

Festivals

St. Lucia's biggest events both occur in May. The St. Lucia Jazz Festival draws international superstars for four days of jamming before an outdoor audience at the Pigeon Island National Park. There's also plenty of music at Carnival, a jump-up that features calypso music, band contests, and plenty of partying.

Some other important dates include the International Food Fair in November, National Day on December 13th which celebrates with races and games, and the Christmas Folk Fiesta at Pigeon Island National Park.

Romantic Activities

Here's the toughest part of your St. Lucia vacation: trying to decide what to do. The choices are all so tempting that you can easily spend several days touring the island—and still have plenty of sights to justify a return visit.

On the northern reach of the island lies **Pigeon Island**, a 35-minute drive from Castries. No longer a true island but connected to the main island by causeway, Pigeon Island has a long history as everything from a pirate hideout to a military fort. The ruins of the fort can still be seen at Pigeon Island National Park, a popular day trip for north shore vacationers and the site of many of St. Lucia's festivals. North of Pigeon Island lies **Gros Islet**, known throughout the Caribbean for its Friday night jump-up (see "Nightlife").

Most guests stay on the northeast section of the island near Castries, the island's largest city with a population of 60,000. This capital city was destroyed by fire several times, but some colonial period wooden structures still remain. You will see several of them as you head south on **Government House Road**. This twisting, climbing slice of road is slow going but offers you a great view. Save time for a stop across from the Governor's House for a panoramic look at the city. From atop **Morne Fortune**, hill of good luck (not such good luck for the French soldiers who resided here in the 18th century; they were plagued with yellow fever), you will have a postcard view over Castries Harbour, Vigie Peninsula, and Pigeon Island.

Continuing south, the road soon drops into a veritable forest: the first of several **banana plantations**. Driving past this display of the island's number one crop, you will see blue plastic bags hanging from many trees. These cover the bananas themselves to shield the crop from insects and bruising by the banana leaves. The banana plant yields only one crop during its lifetime, a process that takes nine months to bear fruit.

Marigot Harbour, located just off the main road, is the next stop. This magical harbor, often considered to be the most beautiful in the Caribbean, is dotted with yachts from around the globe. If you don't have your own, don't worry. The Moorings, a company headquartered in the British Virgin Islands, can rent you a yacht with or without a crew to enjoy a sailing vacation of your own. Landlubbers will enjoy the scenic harbor as well, and may recognize it from the movie *Dr. Doolittle*.

South of Marigot, the road passes through many small communities and fishing villages. Make time for a walk around **Anse La Raye** (Beach of the Ray), a traditional St. Lucian fishing village. Enjoy a walk along the waterfront to view the hand-crafted fishing canoes painted in bright primary colors and the various fishing nets and traps used in these waters. In town, stroll past traditional Caribbean homes with lawns outlined in conch shells, past the large Roman Catholic church, and make a stop in the authentic Creole bakery for a treat.

The **Soufriere region** is the heartland of the island's many attractions. There's no denying that the most scenic part of the island is this south-central region. Starting with the rain forest and continuing down to the Pitons, this spectacular region is the breadbasket of the island.

Every tropical fruit and vegetable thrives in this rich region, which is sparsely populated.

For many visitors, the most fascinating area is the **rain forest**. You will need a guide to enter the restricted rain forest region, so sign up for a guided tour with one of the island's tour operators. Hiking tours are available with guides from the Forestry Department. You will walk through the dense foliage, swim in a tropical waterfall, and learn more about the plants that make up this fragile ecosystem. And, if you're lucky, you may have the opportunity to see the rare St. Lucian parrot.

This area is also home to a unique **Sulphur Spring volcano**, often called the "drive-through volcano." Actually, visitors cannot drive or walk through the volcano anymore (a few years ago a Rasta guide fell through a weak part of the crust—and fortunately received only severe burns). Groups walk only to the edge of the volcano, which last erupted two centuries ago. With the smell of sulphur heavy in the air, you will see jets of water black with ash and bubbling with gases released from deep in the earth's core. (Leave your silver jewelry back at the hotel for this trip. The gases can cause silver to tarnish.)

Near the volcano, the **Diamond Waterfalls and Gardens** bloom with tropical splendor. A self-guided walk through the garden leads the two of you past well-marked trees and flowers, and finally to the Diamond Waterfalls, a cascade that leaves a spray of "diamond" twinkles in the air. If you stop by on a Sunday, you can also enjoy a soak in the mineral baths. Originally funded by French King Louis XVI, these baths date back to 1784 when the king had the baths constructed for use by his troops.

Another major attraction of St. Lucia is its scuba diving. **Anse Chastanet** is considered to be the top dive spot on the island and one of the best in the Caribbean. The reason? Extraordinary fish life, coral formations, and sponge growth right off shore. Divers and snorkelers can enjoy spectacular underwater exploration just yards from the beach.

Night divers can also have the chance to see Anse Chastanet's unidentified sea creature known only as "The Thing." Frequently spotted on night dives, this shy creature, a 15-foot-long, worm-like being with hundreds of legs, has never been identified.

St. Lucia's beaches run from golden brown to a salt-and-pepper mixture of sand and volcanic elements. Some of the most popular beaches are Anse Chastanet, Anse Cochon, and Reduit Beach. Sunbathers take note: topless and nude sunbathing is prohibited throughout St. Lucia.

For fun away from the water, Trim's National Riding offers **horse and carriage rides** (which can be arranged for weddings as well). All levels of riders are accommodated on guided rides along the Caribbean or Atlantic beaches. For more information, call (758) 450-8273.

Nightlife

The hottest show on the island is Friday night's jump-up in the town of Gros Islet, on the northwest end of the island. Street side music blares and residents and locals alike jam to the sounds of reggae, soca, and calypso. This is a chance to enjoy a true Caribbean celebration.

Another jump-up (less crowded) occurs Fridays in Marigot Bay.

OUR IMPRESSIONS OF ST. LUCIA

- one of the Caribbean's most beautiful islands
- excellent outdoor activities from snorkeling to hiking

ROMANCE ON ST. LUCIA

- hike through a misty rain forest
- watch the moon rise over the Pitons
- stroll through the botanical gardens
- swim in a waterfall-splashed natural pool

St. Martin/Sint Maarten

Language	French/Dutch but English widely spoken
Currency	franc/florin (US $ accepted)
Population	60,000
Driving	left
Best romantic features	French side: fine dining, beaches; Dutch side: casinos, shopping, beaches

Fine French food. Topless French beaches. Dutch architecture. Casinos that ring with baccarat and roulette.

This is St. Martin, the island that calls itself "a little bit European and a lot Caribbean." Located 150 miles southeast of Puerto Rico, this 37-square-mile island is occupied by Dutch Sint Maarten and French St. Martin, the smallest land mass on the globe shared by two nations.

Today you will find that the line between the French and Dutch sides is the simplest border crossing you will ever make. No passports. No customs. No immigration. Just a simple sign marking the demarcation between two nations.

Although the border is almost superficial, there are distinctions between the two countries. Mention "St. Martin" and many visitors will immediately think of topless bathing that's de rigeur on the Gallic beaches. And on one mile-and-a-half stretch, au natural is the order of the day. Orient Beach or Baie Orientale is the home of Club Orient, a naturist resort. The public beach is an equal mixture of nudists and cruise ship gawkers, sprinkled with folks who just want to enjoy gentle surf and powdery sand the color of toasted coconut.

The most cosmopolitan area of the island is found on its Dutch acres. Most visitors arrive in Simpson Bay's Princess Juliana International Airport. Don't let the modest size of the terminal fool you—this is one of the Caribbean's busiest airports, with direct service from New York, Newark, Miami, Baltimore, and San Juan—not to mention Paris and Amsterdam. Regional air service to many small islands also travels through this hub.

All those visitors mean plenty of hotel rooms, and many are found along Simpson Bay. Each side of the island brims with 4,000 rooms (compared to just 200 on the Dutch side twenty years ago). However, the island was severely hit by Hurricane Luis in August of 1995, resulting in the rebuilding of many properties. For some hotels, the storm brought renovations, so many that the Sint Maarten Hotel and Motel Association boasts that the island shows a new face today, brought on by millions of dollars in refurbishments, many planned for years down the line until Mother Nature forced a change in plans.

Simpson Bay hops with vacationers who come to enjoy pristine beaches, the island's best snorkeling at Mullet Bay, and the only golf course on the island, but in nearby Philipsburg it's shopping that draws visitors. Duty-free shops line the busy streets, and pedestrians can spend an entire day popping from store to store in this commercial center. Cameras, electronic goods, perfumes, and fine jewelry are especially good buys.

A Little History

The island's Dutch influence goes back to 1631 when the Dutch decided to take a role in West Indian trade. Spain and Holland fought over the island for several years, and in the meantime, France slid into the picture. Finally, the Dutch and the French were left to work things out and to split the island between the powers.

No one knows exactly how the triangular island was divided, but the popular legend is that a Frenchman and a Dutchman walked in opposite directions around the perimeter of the island with the understanding that the points where they met would become the new border. One tale says the Frenchman carried water and the Dutchman beer, causing him to get sleepy and cover less ground. The R-rated version of the fable claims that the Frenchman enticed a young maid to divert the Dutchman for a few hours, helping the Frenchman claim 21 square miles to the Dutchman's 16.

C'est la vie.

Compass Points

St. Martin is not large, but winding roads mean that a trip around the island can be a slow undertaking. Steep hills weave their way through the island, making the trip from Philipsburg to the eastern side of the island a Caribbean roller coaster. (We had one van driver who had to back up a steep hillside at one point.)

Rain is somewhat sparse here, creating a scrubby undergrowth that is not tropically lush. The vegetation is secondary for most visitors, who come for the island's excellent beaches. Some of the best are Orient Beach, the clothing-optional beach on the French side, and Cupecoy on the Dutch side.

Sadly, the island is one of the most littered spots in the tropics. Household garbage is often tossed at the side of the road, spoiling what otherwise could be an island paradise.

On the northwestern side of St. Martin lies the culinary capital of Grand Case. Home to restaurants that perch at the pinnacle of Caribbean dining, both in taste and price, Grand Case also offers a true island dining experience at the Loos (*lows*). Wander among this stretch of outdoor stalls and order barbecue or lobster, freshly grilled and often highly seasoned.

South of Grand Case lies Marigot, home of the Saturday market. Here you can shop with locals for spices from throughout the Caribbean, as well as souvenirs such as batik clothing, wood carvings, and Haitian art, produced by the many Haitian refugees who relocated to this French island.

Continue south and soon you will reach the international border and Simpson Bay. This is the most cosmopolitan area of the island, dotted with high- rise hotels and condominiums, chic boutiques, and pulsating nightspots.

Just the Facts

Getting There

Air service to Princess Juliana International Airport, located on the island's Dutch side, is available through American Airlines and Continental Airlines. During peak season, service is also available from USAir.

A US $10 departure tax is levied on visitors over 2 years of age.

Getting Around

Taxis are the common mode of transportation, albeit an expensive one. A ride from the Philipsburg courthouse taxi stand to Mullet Bay runs US $12, across the island from Mullet to Dawn Beach runs US $26.

Entry Requirements

U.S. citizens need a current passport, an expired one less than five years old, or other proof of citizenship (a birth certificate with raised seal or a notarized copy, or a voter registration card along with driver's license) and a return or onward ticket. Immigration is in the airport only; there is no border check between the French and Dutch sides.

Canadian citizens need to present a valid passport as well as a return or onward ticket.

For More Information

For information on Sint Maarten, call the Sint Maarten Tourist Office at 800-ST MAARTEN, (800-786-2278). For information on French St. Martin, call the French West Indies Tourist Board, (212) 757-1125, ext. 227.

For the Marriage-Minded

Dutch Sint Maarten recently changed its marriage regulations, permitting non-resident couples to exchange vows on the island. (For more than a century, non-resident marriages were prohibited.)

Today, couples over 21 years of age must make a written request to the Lieutenant Governor to first obtain a temporary tourist permit not to exceed three months. The couple must also submit birth certificates, divorce papers (if applicable), and valid return or onward tickets. All of these documents must be translated into Dutch by an official sworn translator or a notary public.

The request should be mailed to the Lieutenant Governor, Government Administration Building, Clem Labega's Square, Pondfill, Philipsburg, Sint Maarten, Netherlands Antilles.

After approval by the Lieutenant Governor, there is a 10-day waiting period and a fee of 90 guilders, or about US $50.

On French St. Martin, marriage licenses are available after one partner has resided on the island for a 30-day period. Proof of citizenship, single status, and, if applicable, divorce papers are necessary. All documents must be translated into French. Both partners must show a medical certificate. including a blood test issued within three months of the marriage date. There is no fee.

Romantic Resorts

French Saint Martin

Club Orient Resort, (011) 590-87-3385; fax (011) 590-87-3376. $

- beachfront
- casual dining
- watersports
- nude beach

Located on the nude end of Orient Beach, Club Orient Resort is a naturist or nudist resort known throughout the world. Everything—from watersports to dinner—is available for guests to enjoy sans clothes. Just a look at the signs at the beach bar ("No tan lines, no problem") confirms the philosophy of this resort.

Cabins here are modest, camp-like structures with baths and fully equipped kitchens. Guests can stock up with supplies at a small store located on property or take their meals at Pappagallo's restaurant located right on the beach. The restaurant is clothing-optional (although waitstaff is clothed).

Club Orient received a direct hit from Hurricane Luis and at press time construction was still under way to rebuild this unique resort.

La Samanna, (800) 854-2252, (011) 590-87-6400;
fax (011) 590-87-8786. $$$$

- beachfront
- fine and casual dining
- tennis
- pool
- watersports

This 80-room resort is often cited as one of the Caribbean's most luxurious. A member of Rosewood Hotels and Resorts, whose other properties include Little Dix and Caneel Bay, this resort features rooms with cool white interiors, bamboo and mahogany furniture, and a genteel atmosphere. La Samanna was closed by damage from Hurricane Luis, but has reopened with a fresh face and restored grounds.

Dutch Sint Maarten

Holland House Beach Hotel, (800) 223-9815,
(011) 599-52-2572. $

- beachfront
- downtown
- restaurant

This 54-room hotel is the ideal location for serious shoppers. Especially popular with Dutch travelers in town to do business in Philipsburg, this charming European-style hotel is also perfect for those who are looking to do a little business of their own in the duty-free shops. The junior suite is an excellent value, a two-room accommodation with kitchen and living room and a large balcony.

Maho Beach Hotel and Casino, (800) 223-0757;
fax (011) 599-52-2690. $$

- beachfront
- casino
- fine and casual dining
- watersports

This 600-room hotel is located on a beautiful stretch of beach with calm waters that are perfect for beginning swimmers and snorkelers. There's plenty of action within walking distance for those who are looking for nightlife.

Shopping

In Philipsburg, shops line Front Street, the narrow boulevard nearest the waterfront. In these duty-free stores, electronic goods, leather, jewelry, and liquor (especially guavaberry liqueur) are especially good buys. (For the best prices, shop on days when the cruise ships are not in port.)

No duties are charged in or out of port, so savings run about 25 to 50 percent on consumer goods at this popular duty-free stop. Shop carefully, and know prices on specific goods before you leave home. Some items are not such bargains.

Most shops are found on Philipsburg's Front Street. Typically, shops open at 8 or 9 A.M. and remain open until noon, then reopen from 2 to 6 P.M. daily. When cruise ships are in port, most shops remain open through the lunch period.

On the French side, the best shopping is in the capital city of Marigot. A crafts market near the cruise terminal offers jewelry, T-shirts, souvenir items, carvings, and paintings (we were especially taken with the Haitian artwork available here). Marigot also is home to boutique shops open 9 A.M. to 12:30 P.M. and 3 to 7 P.M. that offer liqueurs, cognacs, cigars, crystal, china, jewelry, and perfumes, many from France.

Up to US $600 in goods may be brought back to the United States by every member of your party without paying duty.

Dining

Chesterfields Restaurant, Philipsburg. $–$$

Enjoy a yacht club atmosphere in this casual eatery which offers many excellent seafood dishes. Both indoor and outdoor seating is available.

Holland House, Philipsburg. $$

Dine on veal wiener schnitzel, beef brochette, duck a la orange, or Dutch pea soup at this waterfront restaurant located at the Holland

House Beach Hotel. We especially enjoyed the appetizers: miniature chicken parmigiani and spicy sateh skewers of pork.

The Rainbow, Grand Case. $$$$

Located on the waterfront, this fine restaurant is one to save for your most special night out. With Continental and French dishes, this eatery is the kind of place the two of you will talk about long after your vacation. Open nightly except Sundays.

Festivals

The Dutch Carnival in April is the island's biggest event, with over two weeks of parades, music, and celebration in downtown Philipsburg. The French side joins in to a lesser degree with calypso concerts, steel bands, and more.

Romantic Activities

Let's get this straight. We're not boaters. But we would name this boat race as one of our most exciting activities in the Caribbean. Our boat: the Stars and Stripes (yes, the same one that brought Dennis Conner to glory). Our mission: to win the America's Cup.

Well, maybe not THE America's Cup. This is the **12-Metre Challenge**, a race for both first-time sailors and salty skippers alike, held three times daily, six days a week from the Philipsburg marina. We learned that this was no pleasure cruise—we were there to work. For the better part of an hour we practiced our jobs, tacking and jibing, kicking up a salty spray and often leaning so far into the wind that half the crew enjoyed a cool Caribbean bath.

The division of labor was spread among the crew. A navigator kept us on the course (which ranges from 8 to 12 miles, depending on wind conditions that day). A timekeeper ensured that we started the race without penalty. A hydraulics expert operated the hydraulic primer to control the boom and keep the sails tight. Backstay grinders and trimmers moved sails and ropes, as did mainsail grinders and trimmers.

With the wind whipping as hard as 20 knots and swells churning up at six feet, we were quickly dowsed as we turned into position. "Red flag up! Start!" The race was on. We were now on course, racing upwind and zigzagging through the eye of the wind by tacking as fast as the crew could shout orders.

Minutes later, we jibed around the windmark and began sailing downwind. Canada II had pulled into the lead, but we were just a boat length behind. From our position we could see the masts, the height of an eight-story building, leaning into the wind.

For 45 minutes, we edged both Canadian vessels for the lead. Finally, on the last stretch, Stars and Stripes pulled ahead. With one last "Primary grinders, go!" instruction, we were leading.

And suddenly, there was one last shout. "Blue flag up!" Blue for Stars and Stripes. We had won.

Dennis would have been proud.

There's plenty of action on St. Martin's shores as well. Beaches such as **Cupecoy**, **Mullet Bay**, **Maho**, and **Dawn Beach** on the Dutch side attract sunlovers. On the French side, beaches are all topless and include **Baie Rouge** and **Orient Beach**, best known for its clothing-optional stretch. Orient Beach is lined with restaurants, beach bars, and souvenir stands, but on the nude beach photography is prohibited (although tour bus loads of gawkers come by daily). Chairs and umbrellas rent for about US $5 each.

Nightlife

Casino gambling is a prime activity on the Dutch side of the island. Here is your chance to enjoy slots and table games; the atmosphere is fun and relaxed at all the casinos. One of the biggest casinos is located at Maho Beach Hotel.

Cheri's Cafe, located near Maho Bay Hotel, is one of the island's hottest nightspots with live music nightly.

OUR IMPRESSIONS OF ST. MARTIN

- excellent duty-free shopping
- good nightlife
- poor for those looking for seclusion or off-the-beaten-path adventure

ROMANCE ON ST. MARTIN

- dine on fine French food
- shop for that perfect souvenir in Philipsburg
- spend an entire day on one of many beaches

$\mathscr{T}$rinidad and Tobago

Language	English
Currency	TT dollar (fluctuates, $1 US equals about 5.80 TT); U.S. dollar accepted
Population	1.3 million
Driving	left
Best romantic features	Trinidad: international atmosphere; Tobago: beaches, diving

Trinidad and Tobago may share membership in the same independent republic. They may share the Trinidad-Tobago currency, the TT dollar. And they may both enjoy the same idyllic climate, located south of the hurricane zone and rarely disturbed by the storms that can ravage other Caribbean islands in the summer and fall months. But that's where the similarities between these two islands stop. Like city and country cousins, Trinidad and Tobago each have their own unique personalities and their own distinct attributes.

Trinidad is by far the largest, both in terms of population and size. This anvil-shaped island bustles with activity in Port of Spain, the capital city that's also a capital in the world of Caribbean commerce. Here you'll hear accents from residents who have relocated from around the world to work in this modern metropolis. The Indian influence is stronger here than anywhere else in the Caribbean and is seen in the faces of islanders, the architecture, food, and religion of the island, where nearly one quarter of all residents are Hindu.

Both islands are especially popular with nature lovers. Trinidad is a favorite among the world's birders, who come to look for species such as toucans, hummingbirds, scarlet ibis, and the rare nocturnal oilbird. In Tobago, divers seek out giant manta rays near the village of Speyside.

A Little History

After Columbus landed here on his third voyage to the New World, Trinidad was colonized by Spain. Soon the island was caught in the middle of a tug of war between Spain, the Netherlands, England, and France, passing back and forth until the early 1800s. Slavery was abolished in Trinidad in 1833 and subsequently over 150,000 Hindu and Muslims were brought in to work the land, bringing with them a culture that remains strong today. In 1962, Trinidad and Tobago became an independent nation.

Compass Points

Trinidad's Port of Spain lies on the northwest coast, an area bordered by a mountain range to the north and a dense, wildlife-filled swamp to the south. On the south shore lies Trinidad's oil industry, a business that brought the island prosperity in the 1970s. At over 1800 square miles, the island is too large to be fully seen in one vacation; it tempts return visitors with promises of new discoveries.

In contrast, Tobago covers just over 100 square miles and the only bustling occurs in the city of Scarborough. Life here moves to a Caribbean beat, with a leisurely pace enjoyed by visitors primarily from Europe, especially Germany, as well as Trinidadians on holiday. Goats graze in every field; coconut palm-lined beaches offer quiet getaways; luxury resorts pamper guests with everything from dining to spa experiences.

Just the Facts

Getting There

Trinidad's Piarco International Airport is served by American Airlines and BWIA. The airport is located about a half-hour drive from Port of Spain, a taxi ride of about $20 US.

You can reach Tobago's Crown Point International Airport, near the town of Scarborough, via a 20-minute flight on Air Caribbean (809-623-2500). Air Caribbean passengers should reconfirm their flight arrangements the day before flying; these inter-island hops are very popular especially on holidays and weekends and many passengers are wait-listed for seats.

Departure tax is TT $75 (about US $15) per person.

A ferry travels from Port of Spain to Tobago, but the six-hour ride is usually taken only by visitors transporting autos to Tobago.

Entry Requirements

You must show a valid passport to gain admittance to Trinidad or Tobago.

No vaccinations are required for admission from the US, however, the Centers for Disease Control recommends a yellow fever vaccine for travelers who will be venturing to the remote areas of Tobago such as the rain forest. For more information, contact the CDC fax document service at (404) 332-4565. Request document 220150 for Disease Risk and Prevention in the Caribbean and document 221040 for yellow fever.

Getting Around

Taxis are a common means of transportation on both islands. Driving in Port of Spain is a little like participating in a stock car race, so most vacationers opt for a cab. Inexpensive options are the maxi taxis, vans which cover different areas of the island (locations are designated by the color of the stripe on the side of the vans). Maxi taxis stop anywhere along their routes.

In Tobago, taxis also frequent Scarborough's streets, but visitors on the north end of the island may find rental cars a better option. Thrifty Car Rental and several local companies offer rentals from Crown Point airport.

For More Information

Call the Trinidad and Tobago Tourist Office at (800) 595-1TNT.

For the Marriage Minded

Trinidad and Tobago recently revised its long-standing laws on marriage. Today, visitors need only be in the country for three days before applying for the wedding license. The two of you first register on the island and banns are posted announcing your upcoming ceremony. Passports are required, along with proof of divorce or widowhood if applicable. The cost is about US $20.

Resorts can arrange for weddings on site and help with paperwork requirements.

Wedding packages are also available from Pan Caribe Tours (512-266-7995), including air, transfers, minister, witnesses, documents, accommodations, champagne, and flowers.

Romantic Resorts

Trinidad

The Normandie Hotel, (809) 624-1181-4; fax (809) 624-1181. $

- downtown
- fine and casual dining
- shopping arcade
- freshwater pool
- nightclub

The Normandie Hotel is a small (53 rooms) intimate place in which to enjoy the downtown region in a setting much like a country inn. This property may be small in size, but it has a large number of amenities to offer its guests: an excellent shopping arcade, an outdoor "rum shop," La Fantasie fine dining restaurant, a gallery featuring local artists, and cultural events scheduled every month. Rooms here are simple, and for the most romantic room consider a split level loft.

Trinidad Hilton, (800) HILTONS, (809) 624-3211 ext. 6040; fax (809) 624-4485. $$

- downtown
- fine and casual dining
- shopping arcade
- freshwater pool
- tennis

Conrad Hilton's personal project still exudes an air of comfort and elegance amid a bustling city. This hotel is known as the "upside-down

Hilton" because the lobby and ground level make up the top floor and the guest rooms are located downhill.

Visitors are met by walkways of smooth teak, grown on the island and used in furniture and railings throughout the hotel. Rooms are similar to those found in other traditional business-oriented hotels, but all include a private balcony overlooking Queen's Park Savannah. Carnival is held directly across the street from the hotel, so during that time come prepared to party.

Tobago

Blue Waters Inn, (800) 742-4276, (809) 660-4341;
fax (809) 660-5195. $

• beachfront
• casual dining
• dive shop

Located in Speyside on Batteaux Bay, this casual resort is perfect for lovers who plan to spend time enjoying nature, either on the resort's 46 acres of tropical foliage or in the clear waters best known as the home of giant manta rays. Activity is the name of the game here, and it comes in forms such as scuba diving, snorkeling, windsurfing, glass-bottom boat tours of the reef, deep sea fishing, tennis, and more.

Coco Reef Resort, (800) 221-1294, (809) 639-8571;
fax (809) 639-8574. $$

• beachside
• fine and casual dining
• freshwater pool
• dive operator
• shopping arcade
• spa

Tobago's largest hotel hugs the Caribbean coastline, combining tropical elegance with island casualness for a wonderfully romantic atmosphere. This new property is located just a mile from Crown Point International Airport. Lacking its own natural beach, the resort constructed a sand beach protected by an offshore breaker, so the calm waters are ideal for lazy afternoon floats. Next door lies Store Bay, a very popular beach, and Pigeon Point, another well-known Tobago stretch of sand.

The most romantic room at Coco Reef is, without a doubt, the Sunset Villa. Set apart from the rest of the hotel, this charming villa is constructed in true Caribbean fashion with a red tin roof, gingerbread trim, and its own private lawn which reaches to the sea. Decks lead down from the villa's porch to overlook the water; here the two of you can pull up lounge chairs and watch the sunset from your own private patio in this intimate spot.

Indoors, the villa reveals its true luxury, with two baths sporting gold tone fixtures and marble floors, a full size living room with wet bar, and a sprawling bedroom with its own patio as well. Romance couldn't ask for a better setting.

Le Grand Courlon, (800) INSIGNIA, (809) 639-9667; fax (809) 639-9292. $$

- beachfront
- freshwater pool
- fine and casual dining
- spa

Tobago's most elegant resort features a new spa with a teak floor for aerobics, massage rooms, juice bar, hot and cold Jacuzzis. Based upon the Eastern philosophy that right angles create stress, the spa walls are curved.

Le Grand Courlon also boasts some romantic rooms with Jacuzzi tubs that are filled upon check-in.

Two wedding packages are available including legal fees, marriage license, cake, champagne, and flowers as well as options such as steel-band music, traditional fruit cake, and photos.

Grafton Beach Resort, (800) 223-6510, (809) 639-0191; fax (809) 639-0030. $$

- beachfront
- casual and fine dining
- freshwater pool
- squash
- watersports

From its beach bar and restaurant to its swim up pool bar, Grafton Beach Resort exudes fun. The 114-room property includes some rooms with king-sized beds (saved for honeymooners, so be sure to let reservations know!), and all with TV, minibar, and air conditioning.

Two wedding packages are available starting at US $400. Packages include legal fees, license, cakes, champagne, and flowers.

Manta Lodge, (809) 660-5268; fax (809) 660-5030. $

• dive shop
• swimming pool
• casual restaurant

If the two of you love diving, then check out the Manta Lodge, one of Tobago's best known properties for scuba enthusiasts. This 22-room property attracts divers as well as bird lovers who come to the island enjoy peace and quiet, reflected by the lack of telephones and televisions in the guest rooms.

Plantation Villas, (800) 74-CHARMS, (809) 639-9377; fax (809) 639-0455. $$$

• beachfront
• freshwater pool
• bar

For villa lovers, these two-story homes are a dream come true. They lie just steps from the sea and from both Le Grand Courlon and Grafton Beach Resorts. The villas, with a full kitchen, living and dining room, and three bedrooms, are filled with locally crafted furniture. Each home tempts residents with wide porches across the back of the homes, overlooking a tropical garden.

Housekeeping services are provided daily, and cooking and babysitting are also available.

Rex Turtle Beach, (800) 255-5859, (809) 639-2851; fax (809) 639-1495. $

• beachfront
• casual dining
• watersports
• tennis, golf

Like its name suggests, this hotel is located right on a beach favored by turtles as a nesting site. The atmosphere here is casual and fun, enjoyed by an international array of visitors who come to soak up Tobago's sun. The hotel offers 125 rooms, each with ocean-view. Honeymooners are treated to sparkling wine and a fruit basket, and those who'd like to get married on their honeymoon will find the services of a wedding coordinator on-site to help simplify arrangements.

Dining

Dining is a true pleasure in either Trinidad or Tobago. On both islands you'll find tasty treats like the roti, a burrito-like fast food that traces its roots to India. Look for "buss up shot" at most diners; this is a roti that's torn up like a "busted up shirt" and is eaten with a fork rather than by hand.

Curried dishes are the star of just about every menu. You'll also find an excellent selection of Chinese food, especially in Port of Spain.

Trinidad

Rafters, Port of Spain. $$–$$$

This elegant eatery is the perfect spot for a quiet evening out in bustling Port of Spain. Attentive service, white table linens, and a decor that highlights the brick walls of this former warehouse, make a special night out. Start with Caribbean crabback, chicken scallopini, or smoked seafood paté and then move on to the house specialties: chicken teriyaki, flame-broiled tenderloin served with jumbo shrimp, seafood au gratin, and garlic shrimp. For beef lovers there's porterhouse steak and rib-eye, and seafood fans can select Tobago lobster tail, curried shrimp, or crab and lobster on a bed of spinach and mushrooms.

Monsoon, Port of Spain. $

When you dine at Monsoon, the two of you may well be the only vacationers in the restaurant. Have a look around, though, and you'll see faces from around the globe. This purple and green decored diner is a lunchtime favorite with downtown businesspeople, many of whom have relocated to this island from other lands.

Rotis are the favorite dish here, and you can take your pick from many fillings: chicken, duck, beef, goat, pork, lamb, shrimp, conch, fish, and vegetable. Rotis are served with vegetables including potato, pumpkin, and *bodi*, a curried vegetable much like green beans.

Tobago

Black Rock Cafe, Black Rock. $$–$$$

Open for breakfast, lunch and dinner, this open-air restaurant is casual and fun. Breakfast consists of exotic dishes such as grilled flying fish or black pudding with *buljol* or smoked herring, or traditional American eggs and toast. Lunch entrees including grilled flying fish and cheeseburgers; dinner includes crabback, lobster Creole, Tobago river lobster (crayfish), and shrimp kebab, all served with Creole rice, roasted potatoes, or French fries. Don't miss the Englishman's Bay Sunset, a potent cocktail made of pineapple juice, rum, triple sec, lime juice, and grenadine syrup that's as colorful as a sunset itself.

Blue Crab, Scarborough. $

This charming outdoor eatery offers local cuisine such as kingfish with pumpkin, pigeon peas, breadfruit salad, and oildown, a breadfruit dish that tastes somewhat like potato salad made with callaloo, coconut milk, and herbs. Blue Crab is a favorite with locals for lunch and dinner and a delightful place to sit out the heat of the day and enjoy a refreshing lime punch. Reservations are required; call (809) 639-2737.

Cocrico Inn, Plymouth. $

This simple diner, located in front of a charming guesthouse, serves some of the island's best dishes: Creole stew, Indian style curried chicken, saucy shrimp, and marinated flying fish. Every dish is as fresh as can be, prepared with breadfruit, okra, callaloo, and lettuce from the owner's garden and lobster caught by fishermen at the water's edge. The mood here is friendly and unassuming and as delightful as going to enjoy Sunday dinner at your favorite grandmother's house. Call (809) 639-2961 for directions.

Jemma's, Speyside. $

Located on the island's north tip, this restaurant is perched up in the trees, a full story above ground. It offers a bird's eye view of the sea, although for many diners it's tough to tear their eyes away from the restaurant's offerings including a top-notch callaloo soup.

Kariwak Village, Scarborough. $$

This small inn is a favorite with diners who are looking for all natural ingredients. The Dalai Lama recently dined here and conducted a seminar in the open air restaurant that's perched beneath thatched palapa roofs. On Friday and Saturday nights, stop by for the all-you-can-eat buffet with favorites such as lamb chops, grilled fish, curried plantains, rice, and eggplant casserole, followed up, if you're lucky, by Guinness ice cream.

Lalls Roti Shop, Scarborough. $

There's nothing fancy about this roti shop. Wild chickens run for their lives just outside the door. There's no air conditioning. Orders are taken at the counter. Drinks are kept in a self-serve refrigerator that also serves as a TV stand.

But the product here is the real thing: rotis and buss up shot made by islanders, for islanders. If you're looking for a real taste of Tobago off the tourist trail, here it is.

Rouselle's, Bacolet. $$–$$$

Island cuisine with a chef's touch is the mark of Rouselle's, an elegant restaurant that specializes in lobster, seafood in Creole sauce, pork chops, and grouper. Dining by candlelight on the restaurant's open air porch is a romantic treat for any couple.

Festivals

When it comes to festivals, no island can beat Trinidad at Carnival. This is more than a festival; it's a way of life. Held the Monday and Tuesday prior to Ash Wednesday, this pre-Lenten blowout is preceded by weeks of parties, balls, competitions, and calypso shows. J'ouvert, Carnival Monday, starts at 2 A.M. as Trinidadians take to the streets in costume. Partiers practice Carnival dances: chipping (a slow shuffle down the street), jumping up (you can picture that one), and wining (a pelvic dance that would put Elvis to shame). Soca music pulsates from giant trucks while steel pans deliver traditional calypso sounds.

On Tobago, summer comes to life at the Tobago Heritage Festival, a late July event that recognizes the cultural heritage of this tiny island. One of the top events is the Old Time Wedding, a reenactment of an 1800s wedding in top hats and morning coats at a historic church. Actually a play that changes every year, the vows are interrupted by dramatic events and locals roar with laughter when the ceremony is overshadowed by the groom's pregnant ex-girlfriend. Following the vows, the wedding party and the onlookers process down to the festival grounds. If you missed Carnival, here's your chance to learn chipping and shuffle along as the whole parade gyrates down the street.

Shopping

We wouldn't say this about most destinations, but some of the best shopping on Trinidad is actually found at Piarco International Airport. These duty-free shops tempt those departing with local liquor, electronics, watches, jewelry, and more. There's also a good selection of locally made items ranging from hot sauces to copper jewelry to tiny steel pans.

Port of Spain is also home to several sprawling malls. The newest and most complete is the Grand Bazaar, an open-air extravaganza with fine shops much like you'd find at home offering clothing, jewelry, Indian clothing, the ubiquitous T-shirt, and spices in a large supermarket.

Non-shoppers will love Tobago: it's tough to spend money on this island. The most colorful shopping is found in Scarborough's open-air market, where tropical fruits and vegetables explode in an artist's palate of colors. Sample a few items (watch out for the fiery Scotch Bonnet peppers!) and buy a bottle of homemade hot sauce and packaged curry, some of the island's top buys.

For more traditional shopping, check out the shops at Coco Reef Resort. Here you'll find jewelry, clothing, and small souvenir items.

"Foodies" will find plenty of gifts to bring home on either island. Coffee lovers can take home Hong Wing Coffee; rum drinkers can check out Royal Oak. Curry, saffron, and other spices are excellent buys at the markets.

Romantic Activities

Nature tours definitely rank as a top attraction on Trinidad. The **Asa Wright Nature Centre** is the island's top spot for naturalists and birders, who can enjoyed guided walks on nature trails or go off on their own in search of multicolor hummingbirds and many of the island's other tropical species. Near Port of Spain, **Caroni Swamp** is a sanctuary that is home to the scarlet ibis. In the sunset hours the sky turns scarlet as these birds come in to roost in the mangroves. Boat tours are available for a closer look at these beautiful birds; for information on boat tours call (809) 637-9664 or fax 625-6980.

Although Trinidad is not known for its beaches, **Maracas Bay**, located on the north shore, is a popular spot with both tourists and residents. About an hour from Port of Spain, the drive to this area is a treat in itself, winding through the Northern Range with views of forests where species such as howler and capuchin monkeys, ocelot, Amazon parrots, and wild pigs can be found. Make a stop at the Hot Bamboo Hut for a taste of spicy mango slices in pepper and a beautiful view of the coastline. Nearby, Maracas Bay offers a full day of fun, with complete changing facilities, chair rentals, watersports, and local food such as "shark and bake," a fast food snack made with fresh shark encased in a pancake sandwich.

In Port of Spain, the **Queen's Park Savannah** is a top stop. This central park, encircled by what is termed the world's longest roundabout, is home to cricket fields, botanical gardens, and tall trucks selling green coconuts. Enjoy a walk around the Savannah, which is lined with grand historic homes, and stop for a drink of coconut water.

Cultural events are scheduled every month at The Normandie, with entertainment ranging from poetry readings to small plays to opera performances held beneath the trees.

Nature attractions are also a big draw on Tobago. Of special interest are the **leatherback turtles** who come to nest on the leeward side of the island between March and August. Come out after sunset between 7 P.M. and 5 A.M. for the best chance of viewing these large marine turtles when they come ashore to lay between 80 and 125 eggs in the sand. The tiny offspring make their run for the sea about two months later.

Cruising Tobago's calm waters is a fun way to look at the island's beautiful coast. The Loafer (809-639-7312), a 50-foot catamaran, departs from Buccoo Reef, the most popular beach on the island for all-day cruises as well as sunset sails and full moon dinners. The all-day trip includes a swim at the **Nylon Pool**, a calm, shallow area in the sea formed by a sandbar close to the surface where guests of all swimming levels enjoy a dip.

Divers often head straight to Speyside, located on the northern tip of the island. Here they might have the opportunity to swim with giant manta rays; dolphins, turtles, whale sharks and porpoises are sometimes spotted. This area is especially rich with a profusion of coral growth and marine life because of Venezuela's Orinoco River. The river's nutrients are carried by the Guyana current that brushes Tobago and provides the island with some of the Caribbean's best diving.

Day trips to other islands are a popular activity for travelers who stay on Tobago for a week or longer. Trips to the Grenadines and Venezuela's Angel Falls are two choices.

Nightlife

Nowhere do the differences between Trinidad and Tobago reveal themselves more than in the amount of nighttime activity found on these two isles. Trinidad pulsates with nightlife, especially in the pan yards where steel bands practice and local residents come to enjoy the sounds of Trinidad. Finding a pan yard involves a little work on your part; no publication lists the yards that are open that night. Have no fear, though, because you'll find that the hotel personnel of Trinidad can tell you where to go for music on any given night.

Tobago's nightlife is much more sedate—except when it comes to Sunday evenings. That's the time for "Sunday School," held every Sunday in the community of Buccoo Village. This open-air street party doesn't get cranked up until near midnight, so come prepared to stay up late and enjoy the pulsating sounds of calypso and soca.

OUR IMPRESSIONS OF TRINIDAD

- wonderful international atmosphere
- exciting annual events
- excellent for nature lovers, especially birders

ROMANCE ON TRINIDAD

- share a roti at a lunchtime diner
- take a drive along the scenic north shore
- spend an afternoon at Maracas Bay and kiss in the shade of tall palms

OUR IMPRESSIONS OF TOBAGO

- great for divers, nature lovers
- wonderful for scenic vistas, relaxed island atmosphere
- poor for shopping, nightlife

ROMANCE ON TOBAGO

- kiss in the spray of the Argyle Waterfall
- take a sunset cruise from beautiful Buccoo Reef
- snorkel hand-in-hand in the clear waters near Speyside

$\mathcal{T}$urks and Caicos

Language	English
Currency	US dollar
Population	12,350
Driving	left side
Best romantic features	scuba and snorkeling, seclusion

Ever wonder what it's like to discover a Caribbean hideaway? An island bathed in tropical pastels, where the sound of lapping surf fills the warm air with the promise of a walk on a chalk-white beach or a dive in turquoise waters filled with fish as colorful as a candy store window?

You will feel like the two of you have made a lucky discovery in the Turks and Caicos (*kay-cos*), an archipelago of nearly 40 islands. Here you will find over 200 miles of pristine beaches, a coral reef system spanning over 65 miles, and a group of islands that offers everything from late-night roulette in an elegant casino to Robinson Crusoe–type solitude on uninhabited islands.

The Turks and Caicos islands are located 1½ hours from Miami, tucked halfway between the tip of Florida and Puerto Rico. This British crown colony, ruled by a governor appointed by the Queen, is better known in the world of banking than by travelers. With its tax-free status and with the stability of the British government backing the islands, the Turks and Caicos has offered offshore banking for American corporations for many years.

The same attributes that make these islands so attractive to businesses also make them appealing to travelers. Daily jet service speeds

travel. Once there, transport around the islands is easy, although con-
ducted on the left side of the road.

Vacationers arrive in Providenciales, better known as simply Provo.
This island is home to the largest portion of the Turks and Caicos
population and to most hotel properties—none over three stories tall
by law.

If you take a boat trip to one of the cays, you might be lucky
enough to see the unofficial mascot of the islands: JoJo. This wild
dolphin has been sighted for over a dozen years along Provo's north
shore, the only case ever documented of prolonged interaction between
an individual wild dolphin and humans. Often seen swimming near
boats, JoJo is protected by his governmental status as an official
national treasure.

Although it is rare to spot JoJo, vacationers are certain to view
wildlife on daytrips to nearby Water Cay, located northeast of Provo.
Here numerous iguanas greet boat passengers (and hope for handouts
of a tasty grape or mango).

A Little History

Some scholars of Christopher Columbus say that the Turks and Caicos
island of Grand Turk may have been the island the explorer called
"Guanahani," his first point of landfall in the New World. Although
this early history remains unknown, historians are sure that these islands
had a raucous and rollicking past as pirates' hideouts. Bermudan pirates
settled Grand Turk and lured ships onto the coral reefs just offshore,
plundering the ships even down to their wood timbers. Many of
the historic buildings on Grand Turk were constructed from this
pillaged lumber.

Growing cotton was unsuccessful in these dry islands, but sea
salt remained a major industry until the middle of this century. On
the island of Salt Cay, you will see the ruins of salt mines just as the
workers left them decades ago, with piles of salt still stacked in now-
decaying buildings.

Compass Points

The chain is composed of nearly 40 limestone islands; only 8 are
considered destinations. Providenciales or Provo is home to about

6,000 residents and to most of the tourist industry. The capital of the Turks and Caicos is the island of Grand Turk, a short hop from Provo. This seven-mile-square island has some historic buildings and the national museum, a must-see for history buffs.

Other inhabited islands include North Caicos, the most verdant island in the chain; South Caicos, a fishing center; Middle Caicos, home of several sea caves; and Salt Cay, a tiny island of only 300 residents that was once the world's largest producer of salt.

The Turks and Caicos are home to an extensive national park and nature reserve system. Over 31 national parks dot the islands, including Provo's Princess Alexandra National Park, with 13 miles of protected beaches, the NW Point Marine, with spectacular wall diving, and Chalk Sound, with small boat sailing on the west end of the island. National park rules make it illegal to hunt or fish, remove any animal or coral, moor vessels over 60 feet except on fixed buoys, or drive boats within 100 yards of shore.

You will quickly see that the Turks and Caicos are not at all lush like many Caribbean islands. The vegetation, aside from palms and tropical species planted by the resorts, is sparse. One unusual species is "the love weed" which some claim will predict the chances for love. If a man plants love weed in front of a woman's house and the plant prospers, so will their love. If the love weed dies, well, it's time to move on.

Just the Facts

Getting There

Visitors to the Turks and Caicos arrive on Providenciales. Service from Miami is available from American Airlines daily and Turks and Caicos Airways six days a week.

To island-hop, book a seat aboard an inter-island charter flight with Turks and Caicos Airways, (809) 946-4255; fax 941-5781.

Government-operated ferry service between Grand Turk and Salt Cay is available Monday, Wednesday, and Friday for US $5 per person.

The airport departure tax is US $15 per person.

Getting Around

Rental cars are available, but they can be tough to obtain and expensive—about US $45 a day for a full-size. Gasoline prices are equally expensive: about US $2.50 a gallon. Taxi service is easier. (Check out the neckties hanging from every taxi driver's rearview mirror. They are required attire for drivers picking up a fare at the airport.)

Entry Requirements

U.S. visitors are required to have proof of citizenship such as an official birth certificate or voter registration card and photo identification, or a passport. Visitors must also show a return ticket.

For More Information

Call the Turks and Caicos Tourist Board at (800) 241-0824.

For the Marriage-Minded

Arranging a Turks and Caicos wedding is a simple process requiring a birth certificate or passport, proof of divorce or death of former spouse if applicable, and proof of church membership for church weddings. The fee for a marriage license is US $50, and a two- to three-day waiting period is required. No blood tests are necessary.

Romantic Resorts

Erebus Inn, (800) 645-1179, (809) 946-4240;
fax (809) 946-4704. $

- mountainside
- freshwater pool
- gym
- restaurant

Overlooking Turtle Cove Marina, this modest inn is a charming spot for those on a budget—plus it offers a great view.

Grace Bay Club, (800) 946-5757, (809) 946-5050;
fax (809) 946-5758. $$$$

• beachfront
• tennis
• fine dining
• complimentary watersports, sailing, golf at nearby course

Provo's most exclusive property, this Swiss-owned hotel has 22 suites
and a regard for privacy. We have seen few properties in the Caribbean
with this level of style. Furnished with items from Mexico and India,
the rooms are decorated in subdued beige tones to put the emphasis on
the brilliant color of the sea just beyond the balcony.

Guests can choose from a list of complimentary activities, or
pamper themselves with a facial, body wrap, or even a massage on the
beach. For some time alone, the hotel can arrange to drop the two
of you off on an uninhabited island with a picnic lunch. At the end of
the day, enjoy a cocktail in the palapa bar, dinner at Anacaona, the finest
restaurant on the island, and some dancing to live music under the
stars. This resort isn't for the budget-conscious, but for those who can
afford it, this is luxury itself.

Le Deck, (800) 528-1905, (809) 946-5547; fax (809) 946-5770. $$

• beachfront
• freshwater swimming pool
• casual restaurant and bar

Le Deck has comfortable rooms sporting a recent refurbishment, an
excellent restaurant, and a central location. Nothing fancy, but you
can't beat the Grace Bay location.

Ocean Club, (800) 457-8787, (809) 946-5880;
fax (809) 946-5845. $$

• beachfront
• casual dining and bar
• freshwater pool
• shopping arcade
• tennis
• walk to golf course and club
• watersports, dive shop

The Ocean Club is casual elegance at its best: rooms with cool tile floors, ceiling fans, fully equipped kitchens, and large screened balconies where the two of you can sit and discuss the underwater beauty you beheld that day.

Turquoise Reef Resort and Casino, (800) 992-2015, (809) 946-5555; fax (809) 946-5629. $$

- beachfront
- freshwater pool
- dive shop, watersports
- tennis
- casual and fine dining
- casino

The only casino in the country is found at this beachside hotel. Easy to spot with its turquoise roofs, the full-service hotel has comfortable rooms, an excellent beach, and a relaxed atmosphere that we enjoyed.

Turtle Cove Inn, (800) 887-0477, (809) 946-4203; fax (809) 946-4141. $

- freshwater pool
- casual restaurant and bar
- dive shop

When divers come up for air, many head to this resort where they find an on-site dive center and packages including two-tank morning dives plus honeymoon packages featuring champagne, dinner, a dune buggy rental or day sail, picnic lunch for two, and more. Located directly off the marina, rooms here are simple but include telephone, cable TV, and a private balcony.

Grand Turk

Hotel Kittina, (800) 548-8462, (305) 667-0966; fax (305) 667-2494. $

- some beachfront rooms
- freshwater pool
- restaurant and bar
- dive shop

This 43-room hotel is simple and spartan. All rooms include TV and air-conditioning as well as private patios. The hotel is primarily a rest stop for dedicated divers, who will find three wrecks offshore and many dive sites just 10 minutes away.

Salt Cay

Mount Pleasant Guest House, (800) 821-6670, (809) 946-6927. $

- casual dining
- horseback riding

This simple accommodation with seven guest rooms plus a dorm room with multiple beds is a favorite with scuba divers. All rooms are furnished with antiques.

Although divers may comprise the biggest part of their guest list, the owners of this inn haven't forgotten romantics. Here you will find one of the most romantic offerings in the Caribbean—at no extra cost. You can arrange to stay overnight on a private, uninhabited island. The inn will take you out by boat and provide tents, a gas grill, bedrolls, food, and a bottle of wine. The rest is up to you. As the owner says, "You can reinvent the wheel as a couple" in this truly Robinson Crusoe–type setting.

Windmills Plantation, (800) 822-7715, (809) 946-6962;
fax (809) 946-7715. $$$$

- restaurant
- pool

It's somewhat surprising to find this exclusive eight-room hotel tucked away on tiny Salt Cay. Perhaps that's what makes this inn so special. Add furniture imported from Costa Rica, a library with over a thousand volumes, a restaurant featuring Caribbean food including Salt Cay lobster (reservations required), horseback trails, and nature trails, and you have a romantic getaway for those looking for the ultimate in privacy. Splurge and book a suite with its own plunge pool.

Shopping

Shopping is one attribute that the Turks and Caicos can't boast. There is a new shopping complex in Provo called Ports of Call, designed to resemble an old Caribbean seaside town. Look for restaurants, crafts and art in this new development near Grace Bay.

For Caribbean art, check out the Bamboo Gallery on Provo, an excellent gallery that's been featured in many newspaper and magazine articles. Here you will find Haitian, Jamaican, and even some Turks and Caicos artwork.

Dining

With the high number of both American visitors and expatriates, you will find many cuisines represented on the islands. For a real taste of island food, sample the conch, served as fritters, salad, and sandwiches, as well as grouper, hogfish, soft-shell crab, and spiny lobster.

Alfred's Place, Turtle Cove, Providenciales. $$

Dine indoors or outdoors (our most romantic choice) at this seafood restaurant overlooking Turtle Cove. Grilled lobster, grilled conch, and red snapper are all good choices that we'd vouch for in a minute.

Anacaona, Grace Bay Club, Providenciales. $$$

Save one night for a special dinner at Anacaona, an Indian word that translates as "feather of gold." This open-air restaurant is true gold, a gem of a property that combines European elegance with Caribbean tranquility. The two of you can enjoy an elegant meal beneath a thatched palapa that rests on Roman columns. The menu is complemented with an extensive wine list and Cuban cigars. Reservations recommended.

After dinner at Anacaona one night, we walked back along the beach to our room at Turquoise Reef, carrying our shoes. With the sound of the surf and the light of the moon, we remember this as one of our most romantic walks in the Caribbean, a treat that we could fully enjoy thanks to the low crime rate on this peaceful island. Call (809) 946-5757 for reservations.

Smokey's on the Beach, Providenciales. $

Popular with locals for seafood platters and late-night reggae on Wednesdays, this casual outdoor restaurant offers some good prime rib, cracked conch, pan-fried or broiled grouper. Service is spotty, but the atmosphere is fun.

Tiki Hut, Turtle Cove Inn, Providenciales. $

This casual restaurant starts the day with Gran Marnier croissant French toast, Belgian waffles, tropical pancakes, and it gets better from there. We enjoyed an excellent lunch here and sampled the conch fritters, made from the Conch Farm's own product, fish and chips, and jerk chicken sandwich. Friday through Monday you can also enjoy dinner at this excellent eatery.

Festivals

The biggest event of the year is the Billfish Tournament every June. Other top holidays include the Queen's Official Birthday Celebration in early June, with parades and official representatives of the British government.

It's not a festival, but the annual migration of the whales is definitely a special event here. During January, February, and March, look for humpback whales just offshore in the Turks and Caicos Island Passage, a 22-mile-wide channel.

Romantic Activities

With the number of tourists relatively low, you will find the number of attractions equally sparse. Don't expect the shopping of St. Thomas or the reggae clubs of Jamaica or the submarine rides of Grand Cayman at this destination. For most couples, the real attraction is being able to **do nothing at all**. Days are spent on the beach or in the water that is so clear it's often cited as the world's top scuba destination.

One unique attraction is the **Conch Farm**, the only farm in the world that raises Queen conch, the shellfish that's become a favorite meal throughout much of the Caribbean. On a guided tour, you will see conch in various stages, from the larvae in the hatchery to juveniles about 4 mm in length, to adulthood. In Provo, the product of this unique farm is served at the Anacaona Restaurant and the Tiki Hut.

Provo Golf Club, (809) 946-5991; fax 946-5992, features a target course; only the greens are actually green. The rest of the course consists of rocky, dry terrain which adds to the challenge. The golf club here is new and the Fairways Bar and Grill is a good place for breakfast or lunch. Golf packages are available from most Provo hotels.

Scuba diving and **snorkeling** are the top attractions of these islands. Visibility ranges from 80 to 100 feet or better and water temperatures hover at about 82 degrees in the summer and 75 or so in the winter months. Beneath the calm waves swim colorful marine animals as exotic as hawksbill turtles, nurse sharks, and octopus. With a one-mile vertical coral wall located offshore, Provo is a diver's paradise.

You will find top operators here as well. In Provo, call Dive Provo, (800) 234-7768, or Turtle Inn Divers, (800) 359-DIVE. In Grand Turk, check with Blue Water Divers, (809) 946-2432, Sea Eye Diving, (809) 946-1407, and Aquanaut, (809) 946-2160; in Salt Cay, call Porpoise Divers, (809) 946-6927.

Save a day to cruise over to **Water Cay**, an island inhabited by friendly iguanas and tropical birds.

History buffs will find reason enough to take a day trip to Grand Turk to visit the **Turks and Caicos National Museum**. We think this is one of the most fascinating museums in the entire Caribbean. The main exhibit features the Molasses Reef shipwreck, which occurred in the Turks and Caicos nearly 500 years ago. The Spanish caravel hit the reef and quickly sank in only 20 feet of water where it remained until the 1970s. Once excavated, it was recognized as the oldest European shipwreck in the New World.

The museum, located in a 150-year-old house on the island's main street, features artifacts from the wreck with interactive displays, video presentations, and scientific exhibits.

The name of this wrecked ship was never learned because, like drug-running planes of today, this was a ship with an illegal booty. Kept off the official records of Spain, the ship was carrying slaves probably bound for the plantations of nearby Hispaniola.

Nightlife

Nightlife is somewhat limited in the Turks and Caicos because of the islands' secluded atmosphere and because scuba divers, after a day in the sun and sea, are ready to hit the sack early and prepare for another day underwater. The two of you will find a few good options, though.

Try your luck at the Port Royale Casino at Turquoise Reef Resort in Provo. The nation's only casino has plenty of action, including over 100 slot machines, Caribbean stud poker, roulette, blackjack, craps, and more.

Or visit the hottest dance spot on the island, Erebus Inn, popular with locals and vacationers. The outdoor club blasts live music under the stars late into the night.

Another hotspot is Smokey's on the Beach. Call first to check the nightly entertainment schedule, then head out to hear some excellent live reggae. We also found the restaurant's setting, cooled by the sea breeze and lit by candles, very romantic.

OUR IMPRESSIONS OF TURKS AND CAICOS

- excellent for divers and snorkelers
- excellent to get away from crowds or travel independently
- poor shopping; limited nightlife

ROMANCE ON THE TURKS AND CAICOS

- rent a bicycle built for two and explore the island
- snorkel in some of the Caribbean's clearest waters
- take long walks on beaches unmarked by footprints other than your own

$\mathcal{U}$.S. Virgin Islands

U.S. Virgin Islands

Language	English
Currency	US dollar
Driving	left

(See specific U.S. Virgin Islands for more detailed information on population and best romantic features.)

A trip to the U.S. Virgin Islands (USVI) is truly "no problem" because you never leave American territory. No need to change money. No need to buy foreign postage stamps. You are still at home, but, oh, what a beautiful home it is.

And a uniquely different home. While still a part of the United States, the U.S. Virgin Islands are a special mix of American and Caribbean. English is spoken but with a distinct Caribbean lilt. Driving is on the left side of the road. And restaurant menus feature a few items that you may not recognize (but you must try).

License plates proudly proclaim this "America's Paradise." It's America's own vacationland, a place for lovers to enjoy some of the greatest duty-free shopping, dance to a Caribbean beat, swim in some of the region's clearest waters, or do some "limin'," kicking back and enjoying a taste of paradise.

The USVI offer three distinct vacations for couples. Shoppers and high-energy types will love St. Thomas, where poinciana-covered hills overlook streets filled with some of the Caribbean's finest duty-free shopping, one of the region's busiest cruise ship ports, and some of the most luxurious resorts in the isles. Next door, tiny St. John is custom-made for nature lovers, who can camp and hike in the national park that covers two thirds of this unspoiled island. And, last but largest,

St. Croix enchants travelers with its small-town charm, picturesque Danish architecture, and one of the Caribbean's finest snorkeling trails.

Island hopping is part of life here. St. Thomas and St. John are just a 20-minute ferry ride apart, and it's just another short hop over to the British Virgin Islands, a popular day trip. Forty miles to the south, St. Croix is connected to its sister islands by 25-minute flights or by high-speed catamaran.

Just the Facts

Entry Requirements

U.S. citizens need proof of identity upon airport check-in but do not need to pass through immigration. It's a good idea to bring along your passport, however, in case you pop over to the nearby British Virgin Islands.

Duty-Free Allowance

You will enjoy the largest duty-free allowance in the Caribbean in the USVI, double that found on other Caribbean islands. Each member of your party can spend up to $1,200 without duty, and you may mail up to $100 in gifts daily.

All visitors over 21 years old can return with five fifths of liquor duty-free (six fifths if one is a Virgin Islands product). Tourist items also have no sales tax.

For More Information

Call (800) 372-USVI for brochures on any of the U.S. Virgin Islands.

St. Croix

Language	English
Currency	US dollar
Population	60,000
Driving	left
Best romantic features	country charm, duty-free shopping

St. Croix boasts some of the best of the two other U.S. Virgin Islands: the bustle of St. Thomas and the eco-tourism of St. John. In St. Croix's cities of Christiansted and Frederiksted, duty-free shopping is on a smaller scale than Charlotte Amalie on St. Thomas, but there is enough jewelry, leather goods, perfume, and china to keep even the most dedicated shopper happy. On the island's far reaches, eco-tourists can hike through a sultry rain forest or enjoy an unparalleled snorkeling trail where fish as bright as gumdrops swim among century-old coral.

St. Croix has its own unique ambiance for the couple in love. Much of this charm comes from its residents, friendly locals known as Cruzians or Crucians (because Christopher Columbus first christened this island Santa Cruz). Scattered among 80 square miles, many Cruzians carry on the agricultural heritage that has sustained the most fertile of the Virgin Islands for centuries. In its bucolic fields, cattle graze peacefully amid the picturesque ruins of tall sugar mills, reminders of the island's former number one crop.

Your first look at St. Croix will probably be at the Alexander Hamilton Airport, located on the southwestern end of the island. From here, most travelers head to the communities on the north and south sides of the island.

On the south shore, Frederiksted is the quieter of the island's two cities, a sleepy port that springs to life when a cruise ship pulls into town. In 1995 after Hurricane Marilyn wreaked havoc on St. Thomas, the popularity of this cruise destination soared and several new shops popped up on the city's waterfront streets. In the coming months, both Frederiksted and Christiansted will be adding casinos.

Shopping has always been a major feature of the north shore city of Christiansted, which combines Old World Danish architecture with modern shops and restaurants. Christiansted bustles with visitors on its narrow streets near the waterfront in an atmosphere that's much more laid back than St. Thomas's Charlotte Amalie. (The best way to shop is to stroll the downtown area, but if you are looking for a specific address, pop in a store and ask for directions. Street numbers run down one side of the street to the edge of town, cross the street, then start back in the opposite direction.)

Save time during your shopping to enjoy a look at the historic buildings that make Christiansted picturesque. One-hour guided tours of these cities, listed in the National Register of Historic Places, are available from Take-A-Hike, (809) 778-6997.

A Little History

Adding to St. Croix's unique charm is its rich history. The island is a melange of American and Caribbean elements, with a peppering of other cultures as well. Seven flags have flown here: Spain, Holland, England, France, the Knights of Malta, Denmark, and now the United States. Each culture left its mark on the flavor of the island, but none so much as the Danes, whose legacy stretched from 1733 until 1917.

We didn't realize how powerful this legacy was, both to the island and the citizens of Denmark, until we toured the Cruzan Rum distillery with a group of Danish tourists. The Danes weren't there for the frothy piña coladas that awaited at the end of the tour. "We are here," one sunburned blonde explained, "to see what a mistake our country made."

The Danish influence is best seen in the pastel-tinted brick and mortar architecture in the towns of Frederiksted and Christiansted, named for Danish kings.

In 1989, St. Croix received a brutal blow from Hurricane Hugo, with damage ranging into the billions of dollars. We are happy to say that barely a trace of the storm's wrath remains on the island, which has blossomed and shows a fresh face following post-hurricane renovation at virtually every property.

Compass Points

St. Croix is the most pastoral of the U.S. Virgin Islands, and it owes its agricultural prosperity to the more gently rolling landscape than is found on its two sister islands.

The island is large enough to have several distinct areas. The eastern end, the easternmost point under the United States flag, is a quiet retreat with a limited number of homes and scraggly vegetation. Continuing westward, the hills become steeper, the vegetation more lush, and the population denser. Farther west, the hills become steep inclines (and where one taxi driver burnt out his brakes when taking us on tour). Here the roads snake between increasingly tall trees that eventually give way to hardwoods such as mahogany and tibet in the island's rain forest.

Just the Facts

Getting There

American Airlines (from Miami and New York's JFK) and Delta (from Atlanta with a stop in St. Thomas) have daily service to St. Croix. USAir flies to St. Croix from Baltimore/Washington.

Take a day trip to St. Thomas with a quick hop between islands on the seaplane, which departs from downtown Christiansted and arrives in downtown Charlotte Amalie. Seaborne Seaplane, (809) 777-4491, provides shuttle service between the two islands; rates are about US $50 each way.

Ferry service from St. Croix to St. Thomas is available on the "FastCat" catamaran ferry operated by Gold Coast Yachts, (809) 777-FAST. The trip from downtown Christiansted to downtown Charlotte Amalie takes one hour.

Getting Around

Taxis are easy to obtain on St. Croix. In Christiansted, stop by the taxi stand on King Street near the Little Switzerland shop; in Frederiksted the taxi stand is located at Fort Frederik. Licensed taxi services bear a license plate number that begins with the letters "TP."

Another option is the bus, an inexpensive way to get around the island and feel like a local. Clean and air-conditioned, bus service costs about US $1. For routes and more information, call (809) 773-7746.

Rental cars are readily available; all you will need is a valid U.S. driver's license. Remember that driving is on the left side of the road.

Traveling among the USVI is as easy as moving from city to city. You can hop a ferry or seaplane (between St. Croix and St. Thomas), and there's no need to show documents on arrival.

Entry Requirements

You will need proof of identity upon airport check-in, but incoming travelers do not need to pass through immigration. It's a good idea to bring along your passport, in case you decide to take a day trip to the nearby British Virgin Islands.

For More Information

For brochures on St. Croix and the other U. S. Virgin Islands, call (800) 372-USVI.

For the Marriage-Minded

The USVI has a handy brochure, "Getting Married in the United States Virgin Islands," that you can order by calling (800) 372-USVI.

Begin your wedding plans with an application for marriage license. Send, by courier or express mail, your typewritten and notarized application and a US $50 money order for the license to the Territorial Court of the Virgin Islands, Family Division, P.O. Box 929, Christiansted, St. Croix, USVI 00821. For questions, call (809) 778-9750. Make a copy of your application and bring them with you to St. Croix.

Before the wedding, pick up the marriage license at the Territorial Court. The court is open 8 A.M. to 5 P.M., Monday through Friday, and is closed on holidays (including many local USVI holidays). Saturday pick-up at 10 A.M. can be arranged by special request.

The application must be sent to the court at least eight days in advance, but allow more time for processing.

To simplify paperwork, many resorts and hotels have in-house consultants to help. Contact your resort for assistance. Other help can be obtained from Creative Wedding and Honeymoon Experts, (809) 778-5933, or Pastor Desmond Trim, (809) 778-3313; fax (809) 773-1672.

You will find plenty of beautiful sites for a romantic wedding. For privacy with an unbeatable view, sunrise services performed on Grassy Point down on the south shore are very popular. Or head to Point Udall (you will need a four-wheel drive vehicle for this), and exchange vows at sunrise as you become the first Americans to see the start of the day on this easternmost point of the United States. Or end the day with a romantic ceremony aboard a sunset cruise offered by one of the resorts on the island.

To get married at sea, give a call to Big Beard Adventure Tours, (809) 773-4482, or Mile Mark Watersports, (809) 773-2628 or 773-3434.

Romantic Resorts

The Buccaneer, (800) 255-3881, (809) 773-2100;
fax (809) 778-8215. $$$

- beachfront
- freshwater pools
- golf, tennis
- dive shop, watersports
- fitness center and spa
- shopping arcade
- fine and casual dining
- hosted nature walks

No other hotel in St. Croix, and few in the Caribbean, boasts the impressive history of The Buccaneer, located east of Christiansted. Once owned by Charles Martel, one of the Knights of Malta, the estate had walls three feet thick and was tucked just behind a hill to hide it from view of pirates. Later, the stately manor was the residence of the young Alexander Hamilton.

Today, the original estate is supplemented with modern rooms to complete the 146-room resort but the rich historic atmosphere remains. Every week, guests and staff come together at the manager's cocktail party, hosted in a stone sugar mill that stands as a reminder of the island's early plantation past.

History at the Buccaneer doesn't just end with the facilities— it extends to the resort owners as well. Today the ninth generation of the Armstrong family to reside on St. Croix operates the expansive resort.

The Buccaneer is also well known for its sports facilities, especially tennis and golf. Eight tennis courts are located halfway down the hill from the main house. Golfers can take their best swing at an 18-hole course with views of the sea. Packages with unlimited golf are available.

The on-site wedding coordinator can assist the two of you and customize your special day by helping you select a site and plan your ceremony. Couples can choose from weddings in the historic sugar mill, along three private beaches, or on top of a hill overlooking the sea or even select a "Jump the Broom" Afrocentric wedding ceremony.

Hibiscus Beach Hotel, (800) 442-0121, (809) 773-4042; fax 773-4668. $$

- beachfront
- freshwater pool
- casual restaurant and bar

The 37 guest rooms (each with an ocean view) are pretty stark, almost in the style of a chain motel. It does have a pretty stretch of beach, though, and it is an economical choice for those on a budget. Plus, this property is convenient, 15 minutes from the airport and about 10 minutes from Christiansted. The best feature is its Friday night dance show (see Nightlife).

The Hibiscus offers a package called "Weddings Cruzan Style" that includes the services of an officiating minister, a bridal bouquet and boutonniere, a wedding cake, a photographer for three hours including a roll of 36 prints, proofs, and negatives, a bottle of champagne, dinner for two at the hotel including wine or champagne, for $540, not including accommodations.

Hotel Caravelle, (800) 524-0410, (809) 773-0687; fax (809) 778-7004. $

- downtown
- swimming pool

This modest European-style hotel is especially convenient for those who want to immerse themselves in the shopping of Christiansted. Located downtown right on the waterfront, this 43-room inn is within walking distance of just about everything in Christiansted, from art galleries to the historic fort to fine dining. It is an excellent choice for anyone on a budget, and you can splurge on the penthouse suite with a living room, full kitchen, large bedroom, and two baths for less than the cost of a standard room at many other island properties.

Want to exchange vows on the sea? The Caravelle offers a "St. Croix Married at Sea" package aboard the Renegade, a 42-foot catamaran that is large enough for 38 guests. Vows are conducted by Captain "Big Beard," who has performed over 300 weddings. The package includes a sunset wedding ceremony on the sea, a bottle of champagne, wedding cake, dinner for two at the hotel restaurant, an Island Safari tour, flowers, wine, personalized gift, polo shirts and beach bag, and a room with a king-size bed. The staff of Hotel Caravelle can coordinate all the arrangements (with 10-day notice), and for landlubbers they can arrange for a wedding on the harbor or at the hotel pool.

Hotel on the Cay, (800) 524-2035, (809) 773-2035; fax (809) 773-7046. $$

• beachfront
• casual restaurant
• watersports center

Known to its fans as "Hot C," this charming property is located on a tiny cay with an unbeatable view of Christiansted. Protestant Cay rises from the turquoise waters of the harbor just a one-minute ferry ride (free for guests) from downtown.

Along with 55 guest rooms (each with a kitchenette), Hotel on the Cay offers the only beach in downtown Christiansted. It's enjoyed by guests from many nearby hotels who pay the toll of what must be, considering its length, the priciest ferry ride in the Caribbean: $3 per person for the round-trip haul.

Tamarind Reef Hotel, (800) 619-0014, (809) 773-4455; fax (809) 773-3989. $$

• beachside
• freshwater pool
• watersports, nearby marina
• casual restaurant and bar

This is one of our favorite budget-priced accommodations in the Caribbean, thanks to sparkling clean rooms, an excellent snorkel trail, and the hotel's friendly on-site owners, Dick and Marcy Pelton. St. Croix's newest hotel, the 46-room property is located east of Christiansted just off the reef. All of the rooms include a refrigerator, coffee maker, air conditioning, phones, and many include kitchenettes. The atmosphere here is laid back and comfortable, perfect for couples (and families) to enjoy the tranquil east end of St. Croix and the snorkel trail in the inlet in front of the hotel.

Just a few steps from the hotel, the Green Cay Marina is home to boats that offer daily tours to Buck Island as well as deep-sea fishing excursions and scuba diving trips.

Westin Carambola Beach Resort, (800) 228-3000, (809) 778-3800;
fax (809) 778-1682. $$$

- beachfront
- casual and fine dining
- freshwater pool
- golf, tennis
- watersports, dive shop

Overlooking Davis Bay, the Westin Carambola Beach Resort is the most
lavish resort on the island. We loved this hotel from the moment our
transport began descending the steep hill on the island's western side
and we caught sight of the hotel's trademark red roofs. Scattered
throughout the lush grounds, the guest rooms are housed in two-story
villas, each with louvered windows and private, screened porches. Dur-
ing our stay here, we began every morning with room service breakfast
on the screened porch, listening to the sea. Most of our evenings ended
there as well, watching the palms sway in the moonlight. This ranks
as one of our most romantic trips to the Caribbean. (Second-floor
rooms are the most romantic. Ceilings soar to a West Indian peak, and
porches are above the view of pedestrian beachcombers.)

No matter where you stay, you are only steps away from the beach
along walkways that wind through grounds filled with hibiscus,
bougainvillea, oleander, elephant's ear, philodendrons, banana trees,
and towering palms.

Carambola was once part of the Rockresort chain, a handful of
exclusive resorts developed by Laurance Rockefeller in the 1960s and
'70s. Rockefeller himself had a vacation home at Carambola, the
200-year-old Davis Bay Suite that once was a sugar mill. Damaged in
Hurricane Marilyn, the suite has been restored to its original splendor
and is now one of many popular wedding sites on this lavish property.
The suite features two bedrooms and two bathrooms as well as a
living room and verandah. A wedding planner at the Westin Carambola
can help lovers select plenty of other beautiful sites, from seaside to
quiet shaded areas tucked beneath towering banana trees.

Shopping

Shopping on St. Croix means a trip to Christiansted or Frederiksted.
Until recently, most shopping took place in Christiansted, the larger

of the two communities, but as the cruise ship business has grown, Frederiksted is offering more duty-free shops aimed at those who have only a few hours to shop.

One of our favorite Christiansted shops is the American West India Company (Strand Street), which also has branches in Key West and on Sint Maarten. This shop offers items from throughout the Caribbean: amber jewelry from the Dominican Republic, art from Haiti, sauces from Jamaica. Caribophiles should save time for a look around this interesting shop.

Jewelry is a popular purchase here and one of the most unique items is the "St. Croix Hook," developed by Sonya's Lts. (Number 1 Company Street). While we were selecting a bracelet, the clerk at Sonya's told us that "the Hook" is very popular among divers of both sexes. The bracelet features a simple hook clasp that gives a clue to the wearer's romantic status: if the hook is pointed down, it signifies the wearer is single, pointed up and turned toward the heart it symbolizes attachment.

You will find batik wraps at Java Wraps (Company and King Cross Streets), fine perfumes at the St. Croix Perfume Center (corner of King and Queen Cross Streets), and high-dollar goods at duty-free shops such as Colombian Emeralds (Queen Cross Street) and Little Switzerland (Hamilton House, King Street), known for its Rolexes, crystal, and jewelry.

Larimar, the light blue semi-precious stone known as "the gemstone of the Caribbean," is sold at many shops on St. Croix. The largest collection is at Larimar Mines in both Frederiksted (on the waterfront) and Christiansted (on the Boardwalk behind King's Alley).

A unique memento of your St. Croix visit is a *mocko* (rhymes with cocoa) *jumbie*, seen at Carnival and other special celebrations. The mocko jumbie sways high above the crowd on tall stilts covered with bright pants and wears elaborate headgear. A remembrance of an African tradition, the mocko jumbie is a Virgin Islands cultural icon. You can buy brightly colored statues of the mocko jumbie at Silver and Tings (Pan Am Pavilion on Strand St.), Many Hands (Pan Am Pavilion), and Folk Art Traders, or gold and silver pendant interpretations at Sonya's.

For those looking to bring back a taste of St. Croix, Cruzan Rum is sold throughout the island, as is Chococo, a chocolate and coconut liqueur made in St. Croix.

The newest shopping center in Christiansted is King's Alley Walk. This development boasts over 20 retail shops as well as restaurants and bars and hotel suites, all located just steps from the seaplane dock.

In Frederiksted, at a small crafts market just west of the cruise pier, the two of you can shop for homemade hot sauces, T-shirts, and inexpensive jewelry, usually entertained by a live band. There is a fair amount of additional shopping down the street in waterfront shops such as the new Colombian Emeralds (gemstones) and the Royal English Shop (china and crystal). For local art, stop by the Frederiksted Gallery, which offers paintings, sculpture, and pottery with an island touch.

Dining

St. Croix has a wide variety of dining options, from gourmet restaurants to fast food chains. You will find many cuisines represented here, including Caribbean, Italian, French, and, yes, Danish. Don't miss the conch here, it's an island specialty. The shellfish is often served with a side dish called fungi (*foon-gee*), a tasty accompaniment that's somewhat like cornbread dressing. The most popular beer here is Heineken.

Christiansted

Alley Galley, 1100 Strand Street. $

Stop by this downtown deli for an economical (and tasty) meal: a breakfast ham and cheese nestled in a freshly baked croissant or a sandwich of turkey or ham on fresh bread. You can wash it down with beer, wine, or even piña coladas on tap.

Brass Parrot, Buccaneer Hotel. $$$

This is one of our favorite restaurants, both for its unsurpassed cuisine and for its unbeatable nighttime view of the lights of Christiansted twinkling in the distance. The glass-walled restaurant features a Northern Italian menu.

Comanche Club, Strand Street. $$

Located on the second floor in what is known as the Comanche Restaurant Bridge, this open-air restaurant is a romantic yet casual spot for a seafood dinner by candlelight. Start with an appetizer of conch in mushroom caps, escargot, or conch fritters, then move on to prawns stuffed with shellfish, fried scallops, lobster, or, our favorite, tender conch Creole with fungi.

Top Hat, 52 Company Street. $$$

This elegant restaurant features Continental cuisine as well as Danish dishes. Reservations are recommended; call (809) 773-2346.

Tutto Bene, 2 Company Street. $$$

This Italian restaurant is popular with locals and visitors alike. Lunch is served weekdays and dinner daily in this cafe that has been praised by both *Gourmet* and *Bon Appetit* magazines. Favorites include beef or cheese ravioli, spinach lasagna, spaghetti carbonara, and veal marsala.

Other Areas

Le St. Tropez, Frederiksted, (809) 772-3000. $$

Just a block from the cruise pier, this French bistro offers plenty of Gallic delights: soupe de poissons, escargots Provençal, coq au vin Bourguigon, and more. Open for lunch on weekdays and romantic candlelight dinners daily except Sunday.

Westin Carambola. $$$

If there is any doubt that this west end hotel serves the best Sunday brunch on the island, then have a look around at the diners: many are local residents stopping by after church services. The buffet is impressive by any standards. We dined on shrimp and shark, wandered over to the carving station, sampled the pasta, and then indulged in island desserts. A steel pan band entertains diners during the buffet.

Festivals

St. Croix celebrates year-round, reaching a crescendo with the Crucian Christmas Festival in early January. The island follows all the traditional U.S. holidays and adds a few of their own, including Organic Act Day on June 19 to celebrate the establishment of the USVI self-government for local matters, Emancipation Day on July 3, Hurricane Supplication Day in late July, Hurricane Thanksgiving Day on October 16, and Virgin Island Liberty Day on November 7.

The island enjoys a party atmosphere during the Mumm's Cup Regatta in early October at the St. Croix Yacht Club, when over 75 yachts vie for honors presented by the G.H. Mumm and Co. of France. Racing between Buck Island and Teague Bay, the vessels compete for a silver cup and the winning captain's weight in champagne.

The island rocks out during the St. Croix Jazz and Caribbean Music and Art Festival in late October, when both nationally and locally known performers fill the air with music.

Romantic Activities

The best way to see what St. Croix has to offer you and your mate is to get an overview aboard a **guided island tour**. St. Croix Safari Tours, (809) 773-6700 or 773-9561 evenings, offer excellent tours in open-air safari vehicles with bench seats. Tours last about 5½ hours and include visits to both island cities, as well as all the major attractions.

In Christiansted, save time to admire the **Danish architecture** such as the Old Scalehouse. This seaside building, looking like carved lemon sherbet, was constructed in 1856 to weigh sugar, the product of over 100 stone mills scattered across the island in the late 19th century. After weighing, the sugar was loaded on ships that arrived in St. Croix with a ballast of brick, which in turn was used to construct many of the homes and businesses. Near the Old Scalehouse, **Fort Christiansvaern** is now operated by the U.S. Park Department. Sneak a kiss as you view the city from the yellow fortress, now open for self-guided tours.

Traveling west from Christiansted, the island becomes progressively more lush. This natural abundance is best seen at the **St. George Botanical Gardens**, a 16-acre park where 800 species of Caribbean plants thrive among the ruins of a sugar plantation. Bougainvillea as colorful as crepe paper lines the walkways that lead visitors on a self-guided tour of an orchid house, a rain forest, and even a cactus garden. With a year-round backdrop of tropical splendor, this is one of the most popular wedding sites on the island.

The lavish lifestyle enjoyed by plantation owners during the 19th century is preserved at the **Whim Greathouse**. Here we toured an elegant home that combined English gentility with Caribbean practicality, filled with fine imported furniture as well as floor-to-ceiling shuttered windows and cool plank floors. If you're lucky, you will be able to sample some freshly made johnnycakes, baked in the plantation's detached cookhouse. (And don't miss the gift shop filled with Caribbean cookbooks, perfumes, and crafts.)

St. Croix's southern city, **Frederiksted**, lies just a few miles from the former plantation house. A stop for many cruise ships (a new dock was constructed here in 1994 to replace damage done by Hurricane Hugo), the town is a smaller version of Christiansted with a red, rather than yellow, fortress guarding the waterfront. Shopping includes duty-free boutiques featuring china and crystal to a vendor's market for inexpensive T-shirts and jewelry.

St. Croix's best treasures, however, are not the man-made ones but the natural areas found at opposite ends of the island. From Frederiksted, take Rt. 76 or the Mahogany Road north for a trip to the **rain forest**. The small rain forest has thick vegetation where sunlight is filtered through mahogany, yellow cedar, and tibet trees. This forest is home of LEAP, the Life and Environmental Arts Project, where skilled artisans craft everything from sculptures to spoons from the hardwoods found in the rain forest. Another romantic way to enjoy the rainforest is on horseback. Paul and Jill's Equestrian Stables, (809) 772-2880 or 772-2627, offer rides through this lush area.

Just off the coast of the far northeast side of the island lies St. Croix's other natural treasure: **Buck Island**. Several outfitters take snorkelers on half- and full-day trips to this island to swim along the Buck Island Reef National Monument. Here, in about 12 feet of water, snorkelers follow a marked trail for a self-guided tour of this undersea world. Several companies offer tours to this site, including Big Beard's Adventure Tours, (809) 773-4482, Capt. Heinz's Teroro II, (809) 773-3161, and Mile Mark Watersports, (809) 773-2628, a very friendly group of operators who have a store in downtown Christiansted near the Old Scalehouse.

If the two of you are ready to head below the water's surface, there are plenty of dive operators to take you to coral formations and offshore wrecks in the St. Croix vicinity. In Christiansted, call Mile Mark Charters, (809) 773-2628, VI Divers Ltd., (809) 773-6045, or Cane Bay Dive Shop, (800) 338-3843 or (809) 773-9913; in Frederiksted, try Cruzan Divers, (809) 772-3701.

Nightlife

Nightlife is pretty quiet on St. Croix, but you will find some entertainment at the hotels. The Westin Carambola has a Friday night pirate's buffet followed by Caribbean acts such as a Mocko Jumbie and a fire-eater. The Buccaneer has a steel band; call for weekly schedule.

Every Friday, the Hibiscus Beach Hotel, (809) 773-4042, offers an unbeatable show that pulses with the fervor of island dancing and music. Authentic local steps are performed by the Caribbean Dance Company. The show is available with dinner or a show only. Reservations are required for this popular presentation.

OUR IMPRESSIONS OF ST. CROIX

- a romantic getaway with quiet atmosphere of smaller islands and some of the excitement of larger ones
- good duty-free shopping
- limited nightlife
- good range of moderate and high-priced hotels
- excellent for independent travelers

ROMANCE ON ST. CROIX

- stroll hand-in-hand through the historic streets of Christiansted
- sample beaches on the calm north shore
- take an afternoon cruise to Buck Island

St. John

Language	English
Currency	US dollar
Population	3,000
Driving	left
Best romantic features	eco-tourism, camping, hiking

Nature lovers, set your sights for tiny St. John. This is the eco-tourism capital of the Caribbean, an island where the two of you, from the luxury of a beautiful resort or a posh villa or the inexpensive accommodations of a tent or cabin, can hike, snorkel, and tour an island where two thirds of the land is preserved as a national park.

The stewardship of the island's natural beauty began with Laurance Rockefeller. Developer of Caneel Bay Resort, the multimillionaire donated much of the island to the National Park Service in the 1950s. Today, preservation of this island's resources lies in the hands of the park service and a developer named Stanley Selengut, a leader in the world of eco-tourism who operates several eco-friendly properties on the island. St. John leads the world in sustainable tourism resorts where guests make a minimal impact on nature.

Most travelers arrive in St. John by ferry from St. Thomas. The ferry docks in the town of Cruz Bay, a funky community filled with artisans, boaters, and campers looking for provisions. Like the rest of the island, Cruz Bay has a laid-back casual atmosphere where shorts and T-shirts are the uniform both day and night. This is the most relaxed of the U.S. Virgin Islands and a far cry from the frenzied atmosphere of St. Thomas.

A Little History

St. John's history goes back as far as 870 B.C., when ancient native peoples may have carved petroglyphs in Reef Bay Valley. Over seven centuries later, Columbus claimed the Virgin Islands for Spain.

In 1694, the Danish West India Company claimed St. John for itself and early in the next century the first Danes arrived in Coral Bay to begin European settlement. The next century brought a proliferation of plantations, and the island's population soared to 2,000 slaves and a handful of overseers. Before emancipation in 1848, the slaves rebelled and overtook the island for a six-month period.

Following emancipation, the land gradually returned to its natural state. In 1956, Laurance Rockefeller donated 5,000 acres to the national park service, followed six years later by the addition of 5,600 offshore acres to the park.

Compass Points

St. John is mountainous, with plenty of twisting roads, steep drop-offs, and beautiful vistas. It is the smallest of the USVI, only 28 square miles, but driving around the island can be a slow undertaking because of the winding roads. Roadblocks in the form of wild burros are often found in the undeveloped reaches of the island.

Somewhat dry, St. John has plenty of natural, although not incredibly lush, vegetation. Don't miss the love bush, an indigenous species with slightly frayed leaves. Legend has it that lovers should pick a leaf and carve their initials into it. After planting, if the leaf takes root and grows, so will their love.

Just the Facts

Getting There

St. John does not have an airport, so you will arrive by boat. Most visitors arrive via ferry service from St. Thomas. From Red Hook, it's a 20-minute, US $3 one-way cruise; from Charlotte Amalie the journey costs US $7 and takes 25 minutes. For a schedule call (809) 776-6282. A private water taxi from Red Hook is a wonderful luxury; call Per Dohm's Water Taxi at (809) 775-6501.

Getting Around

There is plentiful taxi service in St. John, especially from Cruz Bay. Typically, visitors at the hotels and north shore campgrounds don't rent cars but rely on taxi service and shuttles. However, villa guests and visitors to Estate Concordia on the south shore often rent cars because of the distance. Most rentals on the island are small jeeps. Note to young lovers: you must be at least 25 years old to rent a vehicle on St. John.

Entry Requirements

You will need proof of identity upon airport check-in, but incoming travelers do not need to pass through immigration when they reach St. Thomas. It's a good idea to bring along your passport, however, in case you decide to take a day trip to the nearby British Virgin Islands.

For More Information

For questions on the U.S. Virgin Islands, call (800) 372-USVI.

For the Marriage-Minded

The USVI has a handy brochure, "Getting Married in the United States Virgin Islands," that you can order by calling (800) 372-USVI.

Begin your wedding plans with an application for marriage license. Send, by courier or express mail, your typewritten and notarized application and a US $50 money order for the license and application fee to Attention: Administrator/Clerk of the Court, Territorial Court of the Virgin Islands, P.O. Box 70, Charlotte Amalie, St. Thomas USVI 00804. For questions, call (809) 774-6680. Make a copy of your application and bring it with you to St. Thomas.

Before the wedding, pick up the marriage license at the Territorial Court office in Charlotte Amalie. The court is open 8 A.M. to 5 P.M., Monday through Friday, and is closed on holidays (including many local USVI holidays). Saturday pick-up at 10 A.M. can be arranged by special request.

The application must be sent to the court at least eight days in advance, but allow more time for processing. If you will be married by a judge, there is an extra US $200 fee.

Romantic Resorts

Caneel Bay, (800) 928-8889, (809) 776-6111;
fax (809) 693-8280. $$$

- beachfront
- watersports, scuba diving
- freshwater pool
- tennis
- fine and casual dining
- tour desk

Caneel has the air of old-world Caribbean elegance that tells you, without a word, that this resort was a Laurance Rockefeller development. Tucked within the Virgin Islands National Park, Caneel boasts seven beaches and natural beauty that is surpassed only by the resort's high-quality service. Spread out across the lush property, 171 cottages combine "casual elegance" with "St. John camping" to come up with a property where you can feel like you are camping while enjoying plenty of pampering. Cooled by trade winds and a ceiling fan, each cottage has furnishings from the Philippines, screened walls that are open to a pristine view, and cool terrazzo floors as well as an ice chest for daily ice delivery.

Guests check in when they arrive at the airport in St. Thomas and board private ferry service to the resort. (The ferry service is available several times daily so guests can hop to St. Thomas for a little shopping.) Private ferry service is also available three times a week to the resort's sister property, Little Dix Bay, on Virgin Gorda. (Bring along your passport or proof of citizenship to take this jaunt to the British Virgin Islands.)

Along with plenty of complimentary diversions (including the Peter Burwash International tennis program), introductory scuba diving clinic, windsurfing, Sunfish and kayaks, and movie presentations, other activities are available at additional charge: half- and full-day sails, beach barbecue, sunset cocktail cruise, guided snorkel trips, fishing charters, massages, and boat charters.

The focal point of Caneel Bay is its beaches: seven pristine stretches of sand. Guests can hop aboard the resort shuttle for quick drop-off at any of these beaches; don't forget to request a picnic lunch to take along!

Overlooking one of those beaches, Turtle Bay Point is especially popular for weddings and vow renewals. Other couples opt for private Honeymoon Beach or Paradise Beach, or for the hotel grounds. An on-site wedding planner makes arrangements simple.

Like the island's other luxury resort, Caneel Bay remained closed at press time due to Hurricane Marilyn. Rooms are being completely refurbished but will still convey the casual elegance of the resort when it reopens this fall.

Cinnamon Bay Campgrounds, (800) 539-9998, (809) 776-6330 or 693-5654; fax (809) 776-6458. $

- beachfront
- campsites, tents, cabins
- general store
- snack bar, restaurant
- watersports center

Campers keep the bare sites, tents, and screened shelters of this popular campground full year-round. Managed by Caneel Bay, this campground is located on the grounds of the national park and features accommodations near beautiful Cinnamon Bay Beach, St. John's longest stretch of sand.

Tents (which measure 10 × 14 feet) are outfitted with four cots with bedding, a solid floor, an ice chest, water container, and cooking and eating utensils. Outdoors, a propane stove and lantern, charcoal grill, and picnic table are available.

Cottages (15 × 15 feet) are actually screened shelters with the same features as well as electricity. All accommodations share bathhouses with cool water showers.

The atmosphere is very relaxed, as campers enjoy the Caribbean at their campsite, on the beach, and on daily ranger-led tours of the national park. Don't be surprised to see a family of wild burros roaming the grounds.

The most romantic cottages are units 10 A through D, a seashell's throw from the water. Tent site 21 is the closest to the water, and bare site 24 is best for beach buffs. We hear that you practically have to inherit a reservation to secure these most-popular sites, but give it a try anyway.

Estate Concordia, (800) 392-9004; fax (212) 861-6210. $

• mountainside

"Eco-tents" are the latest creation of eco-tourism by the same developer as Maho, Harmony, and Estate Concordia. These canvas tent cottages are specifically designed to be light on the land, to rely on high-tech advancements such as ultra light reflective materials, and to provide facilities such as compost toilets, while at the same time being ecologically friendly.

Each of these unique resorts was founded by Stanley Selengut, a man who has been referred to as the father of eco-tourism. Selengut works to show resort owners and guests new technologies and a way of living that they can apply to their everyday lives. Guests learn that with solar power they can enjoy many of the same conveniences as back home, although perhaps not on demand. Feel free to bring along your electric hairdryer to this resort, but just don't expect to blow dry your hair before the sun rises.

The resident managers of this natural complex, a husband-wife team, came to St. John as honeymooners themselves at Maho Bay.

Today they recognize how romantic camping can be for couples looking to experience the Caribbean in a slightly nontraditional way.

Harmony, (800) 392-9004; fax (212) 861-6210. $$

• mountainside
• casual restaurant

As its name suggests, this was designed to be a resort in tune with
nature. Solar power, recycled materials, low-flush toilets, and a com-
plete awareness of the environment makes this an eco-sensitive resort,
but with a higher number of creature comforts than are found at its
sister property, Maho. These units include energy-efficient refrigera-
tors, a computer to track energy use, comfortable furnishings (either
two twin beds in the bedroom studio units or two queen beds in the
living room studios), private baths, a deck with furniture, and kitchen.

Maho Bay Camps, (800) 392-9004, (809) 776-6240 or 776-6226;
fax (809) 776-6504. $

• mountainside
• casual restaurant

From the minute you arrive at Maho, you will know that this is no
ordinary campground. From the help-yourself center where guests
leave unused food, toiletries, books, and other items for other guests to
use, to the network of raised boardwalks that connect the tent
cabins and protect hillside vegetation, this resort's focus is on environ-
mental camping.

Every 16 × 16 feet unit has screened sides with roll-down privacy
shades, a sleeping area with mattress-covered beds and bedding, a
futon sofa that pulls down into a sleeper, a cooking and dining area
with cooler, propane stove, and fan, and an outdoor balcony. Barbe-
cue grills and bath houses are scattered throughout the property.

The campgrounds enjoy a beautiful open-air restaurant perched
high above the sea. Breakfast offerings include (in addition to the
obligatory granola) items such as bacon and cheese omelets and
amaretto French toast. (Breakfast prices are under US $5.) Dinner
entrees are also inexpensive and range from jerk chicken to BBQ spare
ribs to vegetarian walnut loaf.

Hyatt Regency St. John, (809) 693-8000; fax (809) 693-8888. $$$

At press time, Hyatt St. John remained closed as construction workers put the finishing touches on changes necessitated by Hurricane Marilyn. The future of this property remains up in the air and a reopening date has not been set. For information on this resort, contact the hotel directly.

Villas

St. John boasts a number of exquisite private villas for the ultimate in privacy. For brochures of these homes, many with private pools, contact a villa broker such as Catered To . . . Ltd., (800) 424-6641, Vacation Vistas, (809) 776-6462, Windspree, (809) 693-5423, McLaughlin Anderson Vacations, Ltd., (800) 537-6246 or (800) 666-6246, Caribbean Villas, (800) 338-0987, Destination St. John, (800) 562-1901, and Villa Portfolio, (800) 858-7989.

Shopping

St. John offers a very different shopping experience than nearby St. Thomas. Duty-free shopping is available, but by far the emphasis here is on hand-made items: clothing, pottery, jewelry, and artwork.

The most concentrated shopping is found at Mongoose Junction in Cruz Bay across from the National Park dock. Here, look for batik fabrics at the Fabric Mill, beautiful ceramics at the Donald Schneel Studio, and gold and silver jewelry (including representations of the petroglyph used as a symbol for Caneel Bay) at R & I Patton Goldsmithing.

Dining

For the most part, dining on St. John is a casual affair, with restaurants featuring a continental mix to satisfy mainlander appetites.

Ellington's, Gallows Point. $$

This sunset favorite features lobster, fresh fish, steaks and pasta, accompanied by a fine selection of wine. Caribbean music is featured nightly. Reservations are requested; call (809) 693-8490.

Equator, Caneel Bay. $$$

Featuring cuisine from countries around the equator, this popular restaurant sets a global tone and is far more interesting than traditional hotel eateries. Designed with large beams that radiate across the circular, open-air dining room like longitudinal lines, the restaurant offers a great sunset view across the sea to St. Thomas. Highlights of the menu include pepper-cured Tandoori lamb on Egyptian couscous with mango pickles, wok-fried whole catfish with Polynesian ponzu and fried rice, and Brazilian T-bone steak with churrasco sauce.

Reservations are recommended; call (809) 776-6111, ext. 223.

The Fishtrap, Raintree Inn, Cruz Bay. $$

This casual, open-air restaurant specializes in, you guessed it, fish. Start with shrimp cocktail, conch fritters, or Fish Trap chowder, then get serious with rock lobster tail, sea scallops, shrimp scampi, or surf and turf. Burgers and pasta dishes including fettucine alfredo with shrimp or scallops round out the menu.

Mongoose Restaurant, Mongoose Junction, Cruz Bay. $$

Take a break from your shopping at this casual eatery that features pork loin, chicken parmesan, and Cajun grilled mahi mahi.

Paradiso, Mongoose Junction. $$

It seems that Italian food remains universally in demand, so if it's pasta that you're craving, head up to the second level of Mongoose Junction for linguine al pesto e broccoli or linguini con fruitti di mare.

Festivals

Any visit to St. John is celebration enough, but several times a year the island parties with a purpose. In the summer months, the St. John Festival and Cultural Celebration recognizes the heritage of the island. In June and July, Carnival rocks the entire island with pulsating parades, and live music. In November, St. John's boating enthusiasts come out for the Thanksgiving Regatta.

Romantic Activities

The biggest attraction of St. John is the national park. Start with a visit to the **Virgin Islands National Park Visitors Center**, located on the waterfront in Cruz Bay. Here you will find information on hiking, camping, snorkeling, and guided programs.

After you have your bearings, head out to the park by taxi or rental jeep. Hike on one of the many marked trails, snorkel the guided underwater trail at **Trunk Bay**, stroll along the self-guided Cinnamon Bay Nature Trail, or visit ruins of **Annaberg Sugar Plantation**.

St. John is the only island in the Caribbean that offers **snuba**, a unique blend of scuba and snorkeling that allows would-be divers to descend to 20 feet below the surface. Snuba St. John, (809) 693-8063, hooks guests up to a floating air tank so "C" cards are not required.

Nightlife

As you might expect on an island that emphasizes camping and enjoying nature, nightlife can be a little quiet on St. John. One popular exception is Fred's, a hip hopping joint in Cruz Bay that's a favorite with locals and visitors alike. Located just across from the Lemon Tree Mall, this nightspot charges cover on Wednesday and Friday, but has music nightly, usually until midnight.

OUR IMPRESSIONS OF ST. JOHN

- beautiful beaches and parks
- funky atmosphere that's more American than Caribbean
- best camping in the Caribbean
- best for those looking for natural beauty and content with limited nightlife and shopping

ROMANCE ON ST. JOHN

- take an early morning hike
- enjoy a swim in beautiful Trunk Bay

St. Thomas

Language	English
Currency	US dollar
Population	48,000
Driving	left
Best romantic features	beaches, duty-free shopping

St. Thomas is one island that vacationers seem to either love or hate. Ask any Caribbean traveler about the largest of the U.S. Virgin Islands and you will be sure to receive an opinion—either good or bad.

Those strong feelings emanate from the island's omnipresent bustling atmosphere. With cruise ships that discharge hundreds of frenzied shoppers on its streets every day, this island is not the ultimate place for peace and quiet.

It is, however, the spot to go if the two of you enjoy shopping, fine dining, or lavish resorts. Charlotte Amalie (*a-mal-yah*) has a busy cosmopolitan atmosphere where the laid-back West Indian ambiance is juxtaposed with traffic jams, congestion, and a frenzy brought on by cruise ship passengers trying to pack in all they want to see (and buy) into one short, glorious visit.

But beyond Charlotte Amalie's boundaries, the island enjoys a slower pace. Here, on overlooks high above the city's lights, couples can share some of the Caribbean's most glorious sunsets. On the island's fringe of powdered sugar beaches, the two of you can catch up on your limin'—lazing the days away beneath towering palms.

St. Thomas received a brutal blow from Hurricane Marilyn in September, 1995. Today the island shows a fresh face, with practically every resort sporting a renovation. At press time, the tourism business continued to rise, and airlift to the island was on the increase. Blue tarp roofs, the evidence of U.S. Federal Emergency Management Agency (FEMA) efforts, still dot the landscape, especially in residential areas. As far as tourists go, however, it's business as usual across the island.

A Little History

First inhabited by the Arawaks and Caribs, the modern history of St. Thomas begins in 1493 when Columbus named this hilly isle

San Tomas. The fertile land here was first used for tobacco, then became known for its sugar crop. The island changed hands among the Danish, the French, and the British several times, but in 1917 the United States purchased the Danish West Indies for $25 million in gold.

Compass Points

The population of St. Thomas is clustered around the port city of Charlotte Amalie and, to a much lesser degree, the waterfront town of Red Hook.

St. Thomas is a hilly island, with lush tropical foliage and twisting, winding roads that provide beautiful vistas but make travel slow-going.

Just the Facts

Getting There

American Airlines offers flights from JFK/New York, Miami, and Washington/Dulles via San Juan. Direct service from Baltimore/ Washington is available aboard USAir, and service from Atlanta is available on Delta. Direct flights from Miami are also available on Prestige Airways, (800) 299-8784.

Getting Around

You will never have to look far for a taxi cab; in fact, they'll often come looking for you. However, if the two of you need a ride from Charlotte Amalie between about 3 P.M. and 5 P.M., you may have to check with several taxi drivers. During this time, they start picking up cruise passengers to return to the ship and won't take less than a full car or van load. Check for licensed taxi services by looking for license plates that begin with the letters "TP."

The two major towns—Charlotte Amalie and Red Hook—are connected both by road and ferry.

Charlotte Amalie is a very much a pedestrian city, and you will be able to shop and dine all day without need of a taxi. After dark, however, use common sense precautions when striking out. Like other cities its size, Charlotte Amalie has its share of crime.

Entry Requirements

You will need proof of identity upon airport check-in, but incoming U.S. citizens do not need to pass through immigration when they reach St. Thomas. You can also travel to nearby St. John and St. Croix from St. Thomas without proof of citizenship. It's a good idea to bring along your passport, however, in case you decide to take a day trip to the nearby British Virgin Islands.

For More Information

Call the U.S. Virgin Island Tourist office at (800) 372-USVI.

For the Marriage-Minded

The USVI has a handy brochure, "Getting Married in the United States Virgin Islands," that you can order by calling (800) 372-USVI.

Begin your wedding plans with an application for marriage license. Send, by courier or express mail, your typewritten and notarized application and a US $50 money order for the license to Attention: Administrator/Clerk of the Court, Territorial Court of the Virgin Islands, P.O. Box 70, Charlotte Amalie, St. Thomas USVI 00804. For questions, call (809) 774-6680. Make a copy of your application and bring it with you to St. Thomas.

Before the wedding, pick up the marriage license at the Territorial Court office in Charlotte Amalie. The court is open 8 A.M. to 5 P.M., Monday through Friday, and is closed on holidays (including many local USVI holidays). Saturday pick-up at 10 A.M. can be arranged by special request. The application must be sent to the court at least 8 days in advance, but allow more time for processing.

Secret Harbour Beach Resort, (800) 524-2250 or (800) 742-4276, offers wedding packages for guests and non-guests which include a one-bedroom suite to prepare for the ceremony, the wedding ceremony, champagne, taxi pickup at the cruise ship terminal for passengers, flowers, and T-shirts. Additional services can include photography, video, cake, music, dinner, or a sunset sail.

Similarly, Sapphire Beach Resort and Marina, (800) 524-2090, also offers wedding packages for cruise ship passengers in port for the day and for guests. Four wedding packages are available, everything from a wedding official to flowers to champagne and cake (in the least expensive package) to live music, sunset cruise, videotaping, and candlelight dinner for more generous budgets.

If you won't be working through a resort, several wedding consultants on St. Thomas can handle everything from the application to the ceremony. Weddings by IPS, (809) 774-4598, Fantasia, (800) FANTASA, and Weddings the Island Way, (800) 582-7484, offer many packages for various budgets.

Romantic Resorts

Blackbeard's Castle, (800) 344-5771, (809) 776-1234; fax (809) 776-4321. $

- fine dining
- hillside
- freshwater pool

High above Charlotte Amalie perched on Government Hill, Blackbeard's Castle has stood as a symbol of St. Thomas since 1679. Built to protect Fort Christian, the structure was said to have been used from 1716 to 1718 by the pirate Blackbeard, famed for his long, black beard braided and strung with colored ribbons.

Whether Blackbeard ever eyed the harbor from this tower is uncertain, but one thing is well known: the site is now a romantic hotel. The small property, formerly used as a plantation and as a private residence, now has 24 quiet rooms.

Elysian Beach Resort, (800)-74-CHARMS, (809) 775-1000; fax (809) 776-0910. $$

- beachfront
- fine and casual dining
- freshwater pool
- tennis
- watersports

Everything about Elysian spells comfort and casual elegance. The two-story suites, where you will ascend a spiral staircase to a king-sized sleigh bed. The private balconies with a view of pools and palms giving way to a turquoise sea. The open-air dining areas where the two of you can enjoy Caribbean specialties over a glass of wine or a tropical drink.

Elysian has a wedding consultant on-site to help plan a ceremony for just the two of you or for your families to enjoy. For wedding information, call the consultant at (800) 753-2554.

Marriott's Frenchman's Reef Beach Resort, (800) 524-2000, (809) 776-8500; fax (809) 776-3054. $$

This hotel-style property is popular with conventions and meetings, but it's also a good place for those looking to get married on the island. The "Weddings in Paradise" package offers a ceremony in a gazebo that overlooks the Caribbean sea, and an on-site wedding director with full-time staff. Four packages assist couples on any budget, from a simple tropical wedding to a royal wedding with Dom Perignon, sunset cruise, video, and a full-day Caribbean sailing excursion.

Wedding renewals are offered to guests who stay at the resort for a minimum of three nights, with one fee covering minister's fee, bouquet and boutonniere, cake, photos, champagne, and service by the sea. For more information on wedding packages, call the wedding director at (800) FOR-LOVE.

Ritz-Carlton St. Thomas, (809) 775-3333; fax (809) 775-5635. $$$$

- beachfront
- casual and fine dining
- freshwater pool
- watersports
- tennis

Formerly the Grand Palazzo, this is one of the most elegant hotels in the Caribbean, an ultra-luxurious resort designed to make its visitors feel like royalty. From the moment you enter the marble entry of this resort styled to replicate a Venetian palace, you will know that this is a step above even the luxurious resorts for which the island is known. Maintaining a one-to-one guest-to-staff ratio, the resort is for those vacationers who are ready for privacy and pampering.

The hotel's hibiscus-colored roofs dot the shoreline of Great Bay. Here, amid stark white buildings punctuated with bougainvillea and other tropical splendors, await some of the island's most luxurious guest rooms. Marble baths, seersucker robes, and French doors leading out to private balconies greet guests. Away from their rooms, visitors continue to enjoy the finest in amenities, including sailing, snorkeling, and a private yacht.

Dining is an equally elegant affair. In the hotel's continental restaurant filled with towering palm trees overlooking Great Bay, long trousers and collared shirts are requested in the evenings. Similarly, long trousers or dress shorts are requested at the informal terrace restaurant with grilled items and pasta.

At press time, the resort was completing finishing touches on changes wrought by Hurricane Marilyn, but planned to reopen as a member of the Ritz-Carlton family once the grounds are returned to their previous splendor.

Sapphire Beach Resort and Marina, (800) 524-2090, (809) 775-6100; fax (809) 775-4024. $$$

- beachfront
- casual dining
- watersports, dive shop
- daily shuttle to Charlotte Amalie and Red Hook

Sapphire Beach Resort and Marina is perched on one of the island's most beautiful stretches of sand and offers excellent snorkeling in calm, shallow waters just offshore. Located about half an hour from the airport, this resort includes beachfront and yacht harbor view suites and villas, each with fully equipped kitchens, television, and daily maid service.

If you are traveling with children, you can still enjoy a romantic getaway thanks to the complimentary KidsKlub, a day-long program for children ages 3 to 12. Children stay and eat free. A NiteKlub and Teen Scene program is also available to guests.

A special package is available for lovers, including a sunset sail for two, champagne, airport transfers, T-shirts, and more. Weddings are popular at Sapphire. During our stay, we watched a beautiful beach wedding, with the bride and groom in traditional dress against the backdrop of the sea whose color could genuinely be described as sapphire.

Secret Harbour Beach Resort, (800) 524-2250, (809) 775-6550; fax (809) 775-1501. $$$

- beachfront
- casual restaurant
- freshwater pool, hot tub
- tennis
- watersports, dive shop

They call themselves "the most romantic little beach resort in the Caribbean." Judge for yourself. Perched on a beautiful swath of sand, this resort offers beach-front studios or one- and two-bedroom suites, each with fully equipped kitchens, cable TV, air conditioning, ceiling fans, and beachfront balconies or patios, all looking right out to sea and, in the evenings, to the setting sun.

With a seven-night package, weddings are free and include a one-bedroom beachfront suite, the wedding ceremony, imported champagne, a US $50 gift certificate (to reimburse the cost of the wedding license), flowers, and T-shirts.

Secret Harbour also offers a second honeymoon package with a vow renewal ceremony.

Even if you are not getting married, you will find that Secret Harbour is an excellent romantic destination, combining comfort with economy, since units offer guests the ability to prepare their own meals.

Chartered Yachts

If love means nights being rocked to sleep by gentle waves and days spent exploring various anchorages, then consider a vacation aboard a chartered yacht. These luxurious vessels boast the niceties of a fine hotel room, including private bath, gourmet meals, and television and VCR, and come crewed with a captain and cook. Call Regency Yacht Vacations, (800) 524-7676, for information on these unique excursions, where the itinerary is selected based on your needs. A few vessels are small enough for two-person charters, but most accommodate between four and twelve persons. Prices are all-inclusive.

Villa Rentals

Like St. John, St. Thomas has a large number of villa homes available. For brochures of these homes, many with private pools, contact a villa broker such as Catered To . . . Ltd., (800) 424-6641, Vacation Vistas, (809) 776-6462, Windspree, (809) 693-5423, McLaughlin Anderson Vacations, Ltd., (800) 537-6246 or (800) 666-6246, Caribbean Villas, (800) 338-0987, and Villa Portfolio, (800) 858-7989.

Shopping

Ah, a travel writer could do an entire book on the shopping in St. Thomas. This is where serious duty-free shoppers come to seek out bargains from around the globe on jewelry, perfumes, leather goods, and gemstones.

The Waterfront Highway (Kyst Vejen), Main Street (Dronningens Gade) and Back Street (Vimmelskaft Gade) run parallel to the waterfront of Charlotte Amalie. These streets, and the alleys that connect Waterfront Highway and Main Street, are filled with non-stop shops. Start near the Vendor's Plaza (good for crafts purchases and inexpensive T-shirts), then begin your walk down crowded Main Street, where the sidewalks are always packed with shoppers and the street is continually lined with taxis and jitneys.

Our favorite shops are tucked in the alleys, refuges from the crowds where you can shop, dine, or drink in a little peace. Here the walls are brick, recalling the area's history. In the 19th century, this was the Danish warehouse district.

These picturesque alleys are also home to several excellent malls. The A.H. Riise Gift and Liquor Mall, located between Post Office Alley and Hibiscus Alley off Main Street, includes shops such as Colombian Emeralds, Calypso Boutique, Mapes Monde Caribbean Print Gallery, and Gucci.

Dining

Dining on St. Thomas can be as elegant or as casual as you wish. Just as its shops offer merchandise from around the globe, look for cuisine from the many cultures represented here as well. Don't miss the local offerings: fungi *(foon-gee)*, a side dish much like a cornbread stuffing, and conch *(konk)*, the shellfish that's prepared as an entree or appetizer.

Caesar's, Marriott's Morningstar. $

This open-air eatery is a good stop for lunch. Start with Caesar or pesto bread and follow up with grilled chicken or clams chioggia, linguine with baby clams.

Gladys' Cafe, Royal Dane Mall West, Charlotte Amalie. $$

Popular with locals and visitors, this restaurant specializes in local fare. If you like conch, here's the place. Conch fritters, conch chowder, conch salad platter, conch in lemon butter sauce, you name it. Also look for sauté shrimp in lemon and garlic sauce. Don't miss the fungi.

Festivals

The biggest party of the year is Carnival, the April celebration that brings the island alive with colorful parades, calypso, mocko jumbies, and dancing in the streets. It's a time when vacationers can party with islanders and celebrate during a whole month of activity.

Other top events include the Rolex Cup Regatta, departing from the St. Thomas Yacht Club in April and French Heritage Week in July with arts and crafts and activities in Charlotte Amalie's Frenchtown.

Romantic Activities

The most romantic attractions on St. Thomas are undoubtedly its **beaches**. The number one stretch of sand is **Magens Bay**, a picture postcard–perfect beach where you will find everything you need, from beach chairs to a beach bar, to allow you to luxuriate all day here.

To have a look at the undersea life, take a 50-minute cruise aboard the **Atlantis Submarine**, (800) 253-0493 or (809) 776-5650. The dives depart from Havensight Mall and carry up to 46 passengers to a depth of 90 feet below the surface. Here's a chance for non-divers to enjoy a look at sponges, coral, and an array of colorful tropical fish. The trip is safe and comfortable. Bring along your camera, but because of the portholes you won't be able to use the flash. (Buy some fast film— 400 ASA or faster—to capture these memories.)

For the best view of St. Thomas from above, ride the **Paradise Point Tramway**, which also departs near Havensight Mall. Aboard ski-lift gondolas, you will rise to one point that never sees snow: the top of Flag Hill. From here you will see the Charlotte Amalie harbor dotted with cruise ships. Gondolas ascend to the point from 9 A.M. to 4:30 P.M. every day, or you can take a taxi (on a very crooked and bumpy road) to the point. Once on top, enjoy a frozen Bushwacker or a mango margarita at "The Bar." Stick around for the best sunset in the islands and watch the lights of Charlotte Amalie come out.

Another excellent view of Charlotte Amalie is from the lookout on **Skyline Drive**. Here all the guided tours stop for a quick photo and the chance to buy a T-shirt from a conveniently located vendor. Your jitney tour will undoubtedly stop at **Mountain Top**, the peak of St. Peter Mountain. A more touristy version of Paradise Point, this lookout is home to a mega-gift shopping complex, mucho tourists, US $5.50 banana daiquiris (they claim to be the home of the original banana daiquiri), and, we must admit, a beautiful view. From the lookout, you will have a great view of Tortola, Jost Van Dyke, and Magens Bay.

Nightlife

Much of the nightlife on the island centers around the resort hotels. Limetree and Sapphire Beach each feature popular local bands on a regular basis. Gladys' Restaurant in Charlotte Amalie has a jazz band every Friday night.

OUR IMPRESSIONS OF ST. THOMAS

- excellent for shoppers
- poor for couples who want to be away from crowds
- good variety of resorts and attractions

ROMANCE ON ST. THOMAS

- shop in downtown Charlotte Amalie
- enjoy a Bushwacker at The Bar atop Flag Hill while the sun sets over Charlotte Amalie

$\mathcal{C}$aribbean Tourist Boards

Antigua and Barbuda Tourist Office
610 Fifth Avenue, Suite 311
New York, NY 10020
(212) 541-4117

Aruba Tourism Authority
1000 Harbor Boulevard
Weehawken, NJ 07087
(800) TO-ARUBA

Bahamas Tourism Centre
150 East 52nd Street
New York, NY 10022
(800) 4-Bahamas

Barbados Tourism Authority
800 2nd Avenue, 2nd floor
New York, NY 10017
(800) 221-9831

British Virgin Islands Tourist Board
370 Lexington Avenue, Suite 313
New York, NY 10017
(800) 835-8530

Cayman Islands Department of
Tourism
420 Lexington Avenue, Suite 2733
New York, NY 10170
(212) 682-5582

Curaçao Tourist Board
475 Park Avenue South, Suite 2000
New York, NY 10016
(800) 3CURAÇAO

Jamaica Tourist Board
801 2nd Avenue, 20th floor
New York, NY 10017
(800) 233-4JTB

Puerto Rico Tourism Company
575 5th Avenue, 23rd floor
New York, NY 10017
(800) 223-6530

St. Kitts and Nevis Tourism Office
414 East 75th Street
New York, NY 10021
(800) 582-6208

St. Lucia Tourist Board
820 Second Avenue, 9th floor
New York, NY 10017
(800) 456-3984

St. Martin
French Government Tourist Office
610 5th Avenue
New York, NY 10020
(900) 990-0040

St. Maarten Tourist Office
675 Third Avenue, Suite 1806
New York, NY 10017
(800) 786-2278

Trinidad and Tobago
Sales, Marketing, and Reservations
Tourism Services
7000 Boulevard East
Guttenberg, NJ 07093
(800) 595-1TNT

Turks and Caicos Tourist Board
P.O. Box 128, Pond Street
Grand Turk, Turks and Caicos Islands
(800) 241-0824

U.S. Virgin Islands Division of
Tourism
1270 Avenue of the Americas, Room
2108
New York, NY 10020
(800) 372-USVI

$\mathcal{R}$omantic Adventures

There is no shortage of activity in the Caribbean: take a stroll down the beach, a swim in crystal-clear waters, or a walk around the towns with their fascinating tropical colors and exotic atmosphere. All are excursions worth an afternoon outing. Here are suggestions if you are looking for a little more adventure:

- race aboard St. Maarten's Stars and Stripes yacht
- stand on Aruba's Natural Bridge and feel the salt spray in your face
- shop in Curaçao's Floating Market among Venezuelan boats
- see amber specimens used in *Jurassic Park* at the Dominican Republic's Amber Museum
- swim between the boulders to the shady grottos of the Baths on Virgin Gorda in the British Virgin Islands
- listen to Foxy make up a calypso tune about you at Foxy's Tamarind Bar on Jost Van Dyke in the British Virgin Islands
- bare it all on Hawksbill's remote nude beach in Antigua
- party until the hour your wake-up alarm usually goes off at Hedonism II in Negril, Jamaica
- enjoy afternoon tea on Barbados
- watch a cricket game on Barbados or Jamaica
- join the human daisy chain that snakes its way up Dunn's River Falls in Ocho Rios, Jamaica
- kiss in the dark recesses of Rio Camuy caves in Puerto Rico
- order a Flaming Bob Marley in Jamaica—and see if you can drink it before the straw melts
- watch for the Green Flash at sunset—that rare moment when the sun disappears into the sea and creates the illusion of a vermilion flash of light

- swim with stingrays on Grand Cayman
- take a moonlit walk and look for tiny tree frogs
- enjoy his and her massages—on the beach
- play a game of dominoes at a neighborhood rum shop on Barbados
- jump off the cliffs at Rick's in Negril, Jamaica
- scuba dive with manta rays near Speyside, Tobago

APPENDIX C

$\mathcal{B}$est of the Caribbean

Best Bird Life: Rocklands Bird Sanctuary, Anchovy, Jamaica; Asa Wright Nature Centre, Trinidad

Best Botanical Garden: Diamond Waterfall and Gardens, St. Lucia

Best Casino: Atlantis Resort, Paradise Island, Bahamas

Best Disco: Hedonism II, Negril, Jamaica

Best Duty-Free Shopping: Charlotte Amalie, St. Thomas, USVI

Best Historic Attraction: Brimstone Hill Fortress, St. Kitts

Best Jerk: Pork Pit, Montego Bay, Jamaica

Best Merengue: Dominican Republic

Best Music: anywhere in Jamaica

Best Nude Beach: Orient Beach, St. Martin

Best Place to View Sunset: Rick's, Negril, Jamaica; Paradise Point, Charlotte Amalie, St. Thomas, USVI

Best Pool Landscaping: Sonesta Beach Hotel, Curaçao

Best Room with a View: 7F, Anse Chastanet, St. Lucia

Best Rum Punch: Rawlins Plantation, St. Kitts

Best Shopping: Charlotte Amalie, St. Thomas

Best Snorkeling: Turks and Caicos; Buck Island, USVI; Anse Chastanet, St. Lucia

Best Underwater Fun: Atlantis Submarine; Stingray City, Grand Cayman

Best Water Attraction: Atlantis Hotel, Paradise Island, Bahamas

$\mathcal{I}$ndex

Walt Disney World for Lovers
Rick and Gayle Perlmutter

U.S. $14.95 Can. $19.95

Not just for kids anymore, Walt Disney World is also paradise for adults! Luxurious resorts. Live jazz bands. World-class dining. Dancing under the stars. Golf, tennis, hot tubs, hiking, swimming, biking, and horseback riding. Glorious Florida sunshine. Whether you're planning a romantic getaway or the ultimate fantasy wedding, let *Walt Disney World for Lovers* be your guide to America's most popular honeymoon destination.

How to Romance the Man You Love— The Way *He* Wants You To!
Lucy Sanna

Hardcover: U.S. $14.95 Can. $19.95
Paperback: U.S. $12.00 Can. $16.95

The language of love may be universal, but Lucy Sanna knows that when it comes to romance, men and women are worlds apart. Bridge the communication gap. Learn the truth about what he'll find utterly irresistible. In this book, men from all over America reveal their wildest fantasies, secret soft spots, and all the little things that make them melt.

How to Romance the Woman You Love— The Way *She* Wants You To!
Lucy Sanna with Kathy Miller

Hardcover: U.S. $14.95 Can. $21.95
Paperback: U.S. $12.00 Can. $16.95

For women, the right kind of romance is an aphrodisiac. Do you know how to flirt with your partner, court her, write a playful love letter? Do you know what surprises will delight her, what gifts she will cherish? Could you use some tips for creating a romantic getaway? Perhaps a few new techniques for keeping children, pets, and relatives at bay while you romance the special woman in your life? Discover all this and more inside *How to Romance the Woman You Love—The Way She Wants You To!*

Hawai'i, The Big Island, 5th Edition
John Penisten

U.S. $15.00 Can. $19.95

This is the must-have guide to the islands for every family traveling to Hawai'i. In this, the fifth edition of *Hawai'i, The Big Island*, author John Penisten highlights the best hotels and restaurants for families as well as the best beaches and day-trip destinations. Fully updated with the most current information by one of the best-known and most respected travel writers in the business, this is the book to make your trip to Hawai'i truly a trip to paradise.

Maui and Lana'i, 7th Edition
Dona Early and Christie Stilson

U.S. $15.00 Can. $19.95

In the seventh edition of this comprehensive guide to the islands of Maui and Lana'i, authors Christie Stilson and Dona Early give families the information they need to make the most of their next Hawaiian vacation. As long-time visitors and part-time residents of the island, Stilson and Early offer readers up-to-date listings of restaurants children will love, hotels that let kids stay free, and other tips to help families make the most of their travel dollars.

Kaua'i, 4th Edition
Dona Early and Christie Stilson

U.S. $14.95 Can. $21.95

Here is the complete traveler's reference and guide to the tropical paradise of Kaua'i, completely revised and updated to reflect changes in accommodations, scenery, roads, and more. With an emphasis on family travel (and an eye on the family budget!), this book provides travelers with all they need to know about this sun-drenched getaway—including more than 125 restaurants and recommendations, Hawaiian language and history, accommodations for all budgets, and recreational opportunities.